AFTER EMPIRE:
The Emerging Geopolitics of Central Asia

AFTER EMPIRE:

The Emerging Geopolitics of Central Asia

Edited by
JED C. SNYDER

NATIONAL DEFENSE UNIVERSITY PRESS
Ft. McNair, Washington, DC

BGL 8185-5/1

GIFT
4/5/96

After empire

DK
859.5
.A36
1995

National Defense University Press Publications

To increase general knowledge and inform discussion, the Institute for National Strategic Studies, through its publication arm the NDU Press, publishes *Strategic Forums*; McNair Papers; proceedings of University- and Institute-sponsored symposia; books relating to U.S. national security, especially to issues of joint, combined, or coalition warfare, peacekeeping operations, and national strategy; and a variety of other works designed to circulate contemporary comment and offer alternatives to current policy. The Press occasionally publishes out-of-print defense classics, historical works, and other especially timely or distinguished writing on national security.

Opinions, conclusions, and recommendations expressed or implied within are solely those of the authors, and do not necessarily represent the views of the National Defense University, the Department of Defense, or any other U.S. Government agency. Cleared for public release; distribution unlimited.

Portions of this book may be quoted or reprinted without permission, provided that a standard source credit line is included. NDU Press would appreciate a courtesy copy of reprints or reviews.

NDU Press publications are sold by the U.S. Government Printing Office. For ordering information, call (202) 512-1800 or write to the Superintendent of Documents, U.S. Government Printing Office, Washington, DC 20402.

Library of Congress Cataloging-in-Publication Data

After empire : the emerging geopolitics of Central Asia / edited by Jed C. Snyder.
     p.   cm.
    Includes bibliographical references.
    1. Asia, Central—Politics and government—1991-   2. Asia, Central—Foreign relations.   3. Asia, Central—Ethnic relations. 4. National security—Asia, Central. 5. Islamic fundamentalism—Asia, Central. I. Snyder, Jed C.
DK859.5.A36   1995
327.58—dc20   95-42840
                                                CIP

First Printing, October 1995

For sale by the U.S. Government Printing Office
Superintendent of Documents, Mail Stop: SSOP, Washington, DC 20402-9328
ISBN 0-16-051682-X

RECEIVED

APR 1 1 1996

KENNEDY SCHOOL
LIBRARY

CONTENTS

FOREWORD

When the Soviet Union collapsed, fifteen sovereign states suddenly appeared on the geopolitical landscape. None were less prepared for independence than the five republics of Central Asia. The peoples of Kazakhstan, Kyrgyzstan, Uzbekistan, Turkmenistan, and Tajikistan had existed for seven decades in a semifeudal state of suspension. The region, so dependent upon Soviet largesse that its rich cultural heritage was nearly smothered, had been the object of imperial competition for centuries—Soviet domination being merely the latest.

The Institute for National Strategic Studies is engaged in a multiyear project to examine the evolution of the new states comprising Central Asia and the Transcaucasus. This book, which completes the first phase of this project, incorporates research papers and discussions originally presented at a conference of leading scholars from the United States, Russia, Europe, and the Middle East who gathered to examine the region's political, economic, social, and security evolution since 1989. As the papers illustrate, the West's image of Central Asia as a homogeneous belt of Islamic countries with uniform views of the region's future orientation is false. The papers also illustrate that hyperbolic prognoses of an "Islamic implosion" threatening to embroil the region in violent insurrections, possibly spreading throughout the former Soviet Union and the Middle East, are false as well. They have simply not materialized. Islam, in fact, has yet to emerge as a potent political force in Central Asia.

This region is now lifting itself from economic obscurity and political isolation. Although distinct national identities are only in formative stages today, each of the five Central Asian states is likely to move in an individual direction, motivated by distinct national interests. The key issue is the extent of Russia's influence in Central Asia and its long-term implications for the region's security. *After Empire* makes an important contribution to the better understanding of this very complex, indeed mysterious, region.

ERVIN J. ROKKE
Lieutenant General, USAF
President, National Defense University

ACKNOWLEDGMENTS

This volume represents nearly 2 years of effort, from organization of the initial conference through final editing of the manuscript. During this process, the INSS support staff worked diligently to ensure the successful completion of this project. Conference administration was very ably overseen by Joyce Alston. Debbie Jefferson, Linda Semple, and Carol Stiner ensured that the infinite number of logistical details were attended to in a timely and professional manner. The two conference rapporteurs, Todd Perry and Michael Lebrun, prepared an excellent summary of the conference proceedings. Delonnie Henry was responsible for initial preparation of the manuscript, which was superbly edited by Mary Sommerville of the NDU Press.

INTRODUCTION

Jed C. Snyder

The fall of the Soviet empire encouraged Western scholars and observers alike to anticipate a period of political chaos, civil unrest and a series of ethno-religious explosions among the former Soviet republics of Central Asia.[1] The general expectation was that the removal of a repressive Soviet control structure would unleash the subliminal forces of political radicalism and religious extremism which along with all forms of non-Soviet political expression had been suppressed in the 15 former republics of the USSR for seven decades.

UNEXPECTED CALM

The newly independent nations of Kazakhstan, Kyrgyzstan, Uzbekistan, Turkmenistan, and Tajikistan have not followed the path which many had predicted. The nightmarish scenarios of regional upheaval have not materialized largely for three reasons: (1) the prevalent Western assumption that these new nations would each be prepared for and eager to pursue their independence was dramatically wrong; (2) the penetration of Soviet influence in Central Asia was much deeper than realized and therefore administrative and political structures had been more thoroughly transformed and "Russified" than was appreciated, and (3) largely as a result of the first two factors, those who were elected to lead the new nations of Central Asia did not represent a new generation of leaders. Indeed, with one exception (Kyrgyzstan) they were drawn from the senior ranks of the Communist apparat. Finally, following the end of Soviet rule, where conflicts have occurred along the southern periphery, in both the Caucasus and in Central Asia, (most notably the violence in Tajikistan, Abkhazia, and Nagorno-Karabakh) Russian manipulation may be as much to blame as intrinsic ethnic hatreds.

DIVERSITY AND IDENTITY

As the events of the last five years have illustrated, Central Asia should not be regarded as a homogeneous belt of Muslim nations. While there are important religious and cultural threads running throughout the fabric of the region, recognizing the diversity of the southern states and the lack of a unified view among them on most issues, is fundamentally important to understanding the region's complexity. The notion that a Central Asian "bloc" would emerge from the rubble of the Soviet Union has been shown to be false, in virtually every aspect of state relations—politics, economics, religion, and military and foreign affairs.

Among the most distinct differences which characterize Central Asia is the Turkic/Persian cultural and linguistic divide. The region is dominated by the Turkic-speaking populations which reside in four of the five former republics. The Persians of Tajikistan who speak an Eastern dialect of Farsi, also inhabit the Persian centers of Bukhara and Samarkand, which lie in present-day Uzbekistan. The region's population is a mix of indigenous and migratory groups, due largely to several centuries of imperial conquest, nomadic movement and periodic migration, either voluntary or by force, as during the Stalin period.

Until the 20th century, the region could also be divided between two lifestyles, nomadic and sedentary. The nomadic peoples occupied the northern steppe of present-day Kazakhstan and Krygyzstan, as well as the extreme south in Turkmenistan, while the settled communities generally remained in Uzbekistan and Tajikistan. Generally, the northern populations were less orthodox in their interpretation and practice of Islam, while the people of the more settled areas were more faithful in adherence to Islamic traditions.[2]

Soviet rule came to Central Asia in the early 1920's, and with it an attempt to break down any sense of national identity that had emerged over several hundred years. These efforts, directed by the central authorities in Moscow, were collectively known as the National Delimitation. Under this program, new boundaries which tended to cut across the region's most important defining parameters —clan and tribe— were established, which resulted in the somewhat artificial national structures that exist today. With the introduction of collectivization and mass education, Central Asia was assimilated into the Soviet state.

With the notable exception of the rebellion in Tajikistan, there has been relative calm in Central Asia since independence. The five new nations lying between the Caspian Sea and China have evolved neither politically nor economically to the point where their natural resource and other economic potential have yet emerged. The rich but largely untapped oil and gas fields of the two former Central Asian republics, Kazakhstan and Turkmenistan, have enormous strategic value, but the feudal state of the regional economies and the (exaggerated) expectation of an impending Islamic explosion have so far combined to discourage large investment. The deeply entrenched tradition of Russian-dominated administration and control in this region gave Moscow time to adjust its relations with this newly independent region. Unlike in the Baltic states, Moldova or Ukraine, where Moscow faced revolutionary nationalist rebellions, Central Asia was content to take Moscow's direction until that direction disappeared. To be sure, nationalist movements sprang up in Central Asia, including *Birlik* (unity) in Uzbekistan, and there was scattered violence in the Fergana Valley, but the level of revolutionary fervor was comparatively muted.

While the region never rejoiced in Moscow's efforts at integrating the south into the Russian heartland, the smothering of Central Asian nationalism had long-ago dampened any revolutionary zeal. Whereas Mikhail Gorbachev's policies of *glasnost* and *perestroika* ignited upheaval in virtually every other region of the former Soviet empire, Central Asia (with the exception of Tajikistan where the 201st Russian division in Dushanbe was to play a key role in restoring a pro-Russian government) was quiescent.

Finally, roughly 40,000 Russian troops remain deployed throughout Central Asia where they function as the only border security force for which the five new governments are grateful since after nearly four years after independence, they still lack national militaries (or in some cases even organized constabularies) of their own. Put simply, post-Soviet Central Asia continues to look very much like Soviet Central Asia and the Russian influence is generally tolerated if not welcome. This is in stark contrast to other regions, notably the Caucasus, where the Russian military presence has been a key factor in fomenting instability and upheaval.

THE SHOCK OF INDEPENDENCE

Central Asia did not leave the Union of Soviet Socialist Republics, it was pulled out from under them. In a referendum held on March 17, 1991 (nine months before the USSR ceased to exist) the Central Asians overwhelmingly voted to remain within the Union. During the August 1991 coup against Mikhail Gorbachev, popular opinion in Central Asia favored the plotters with the Central Asian leaderships publicly voicing their support—Uzbekistan, Turkmenistan, and Tajikistan immediately, Kazakhstan and Kyrgyzstan soon thereafter. In the months that followed the failed coup, the former party chiefs of four of the Central Asian states (Kyrgyzstan was the exception) unilaterally, without popular referendum or by parliamentary vote, declared the independence of their republics. This was probably meant more as a political gesture, and not intended to sever completely their ties from the center upon whom the Soviet system had made them economically dependent.

There was no Soviet Union from which to secede following the sudden announcement on December 8 ,1991 that the Presidents of Belarus, Ukraine, and Russia had formed a commonwealth. Two weeks later a meeting of all the republican leaders in Alma Ata voted to enlarge the Commonwealth of Independent States (CIS) by eight more members, to include all five of the Central Asian republics. Thus, the CIS was not to be an all-Slavic union as some of its Russian architects had originally envisioned. The broadening of CIS membership had immediate repercussions for Moscow's relations with the former republics of Central Asia.

The issue of how and whether a collective security system linking the CIS members would be successfully erected was a prominent question, still unresolved as this book goes to press in September 1995. The course of collective security has not been smooth. At the Tashkent CIS summit in May 1992, Turkmenistan refused to sign the Collective Security Treaty, in which aggression against any one member would be regarded as aggression against all. The six signatories (Russia, Uzbekistan, Kyrgyzstan, Tajikistan, Kazakhstan, and Armenia) promised not to join any alliance directed against other participating states and to seek peaceful resolution of inter-state disputes. When the formal signing of the CIS Charter took place in January 1993, however, only four Central Asian republics participated; Turkmenistan still refused to sign any collective security arrangement, preferring bilateral agreements and a more independent stance from Russia.

As the leaders of the newly independent states quickly discovered, nation-building in Central Asia is frustrated by the unique cultural, linguistic, religious, and poetic history of this region. While the vast majority of Central Asia's 50 million people are of Turkic origin, the diversity of the region's population and its cultural heterogeneity can only impress the visitor or observer, particularly when one considers the conditions under which such diversity was suppressed under a series of imperial masters. What was once the crossroads of transcontinental trade routes and the heart of the ancient "Silk Road" is today a neglected and decayed portion of the former Soviet empire.

A NEW "GREAT GAME?"

There is a remnant of the struggles waged by the ancient Khanates and Persia and of the efforts by the British, Russian and Ottoman empires to secure their hold in this region—that is, the expectation that "The Great Game" of the early 19th century, which found Tsarist Russia competing with imperial Great Britain, will be replayed in Central Asia, albeit under very different circumstances. While it may be difficult to foresee such competition emerging today, students of the earlier period of imperial intrigue and competition are prepared to speculate. Peter Hopkirk, among the best of the Central Asian chroniclers, reminds his readers that distant threats tend to be underestimated in this region. Discussing British concerns in the early nineteenth century over Russian designs on India, Hopkirk writes:

> The Russian threat to India seemed real enough at the time, whatever historians may say with hindsight today. The evidence, after all, was there for anyone who chose to look at the map. For four centuries the Russian Empire had been steadily expanding at the rate of some 55 square miles a day, or around 20,000 square miles a year. At the beginning of the nineteenth century, more than 2,000 miles separated the British and Russian empires in Asia. By the end of it this had shrunk to a few hundred, and in parts of the Pamir region to less than twenty. No wonder many feared that the Cossacks would only rein in their horses when India too was theirs.[3]

The heart of Eurasia could still explode into a series of inter-state wars, fueling rivalries between states whose leaders have not yet determined who their allies and adversaries are. The climate of instability could encourage neighboring powers to become involved in a new cycle of competition for regional political influence and access to unexploited, but potentially handsome, resource riches.

Predicting the foreign and security policy directions of the Central Asian nations remains difficult, as the nations' civilian and military leaders grapple with the politico-economic implications of independence from Moscow. Internal stability and economic survival is the paramount concern. Yet, as the Central leaders recognized early, Russia's inability to continue subsidizing the region's economy would force them to explore relations with neighboring and distant powers, on a more urgent basis than was originally anticipated. It is within this evolving geopolitical landscape that potential competition for strategic influence and economic benefit among Russia, Iran, Turkey, Pakistan, India, and China, will evolve.

THE SOVIET LEGACY AND RUSSIAN INTERESTS IN CENTRAL ASIA

As post-independence, nationalist pressures in Central Asia grew, so did concern for the viability and safety of the Russian communities in the newly independent states. This issue, however, was more politically charged than substantive. Concern for the safety of the Russian diaspora became an important political rallying point in Russian President Boris Yeltsin's continuing struggle to appease an increasingly nationalist-rightist alliance which opposed many of his domestic and foreign policies, and resented Russia's diminished post-Cold War status. Much of the worry regarding the future of these Russian communities is focused on the cumulative political effects of discriminatory practices against ethnic Russians. In many cases, the titular native nationalities actively discourage continued dependence, for example, on the Russian language in the conduct of state business. Anti-Russian demographic pressures are most serious in Kazakhstan where the Russian population approaches 45 percent of the total. This is in stark contrast to the significantly smaller Russian communities in Tajikistan (10 percent), Uzbekistan (11 percent) Turkmenistan (13 percent) and Kyrgyzstan (22 percent).

The first reaction to Central Asian independence, of many Russians living in Central Asia, was to leave and return to the Russian Federation. The wave of Russian emigration robs the region of already scarce technical expertise, and therefore threatens the ability of these fledgling states to build new institutions and infrastructures necessary to administer struggling nations. Russian flight has also begun to drain Central Asia of its political and governing elite, in many cases in the absence of programs to train indigenous managers. By the end of 1994, well over three million Russians had fled the region.

As Russians left Central Asia, Moscow and the new regional leaders debated the extent to which Russia would cede control over the struggling economies in the south. Under the extreme centralization of the Soviet system, there had been no real power in the republics. All economic planning was done in Moscow and the planning directives handed down without debate. The breakup of the Soviet Union left all of the new republics without independent economies; they were all still tied to and therefore dependent upon Moscow. Similarly, all political appointments came from Moscow. Local leaders (with some exceptions) were not permitted to remain in any one region long enough to develop a local power base, until the last years of the Brezhnev stagnation, when national party leaders were permitted to develop fiefdoms within their republican party systems. These were the men in power when independence occurred.

In four of the Central Asian states (Kyrgyzstan being the exception), the Presidents are all former first secretaries of the Soviet Communist party in their respective countries. With the collapse of the Party, the leaders of the Central Asian communist organizations (many of whom can be described as 'born-again nationalists') were forced to dissolve their party structures or face an immediate problem of legitimacy and credibility with the already confused and disillusioned public. The only leader who refused to dissolve the party structure was Khakar Makhamov in Tajikistan. This error forced him from power shortly after the failed August 1991 coup against Mikhail Gorbachev.

If the regional leaders and populations were unprepared for this transition, so was Moscow. During the first eighteen months of independence, Russian authorities refused to articulate a policy toward Central Asia. The immediate priority for Moscow was to reinforce ties to the West, which held the only prospect for economic assistance.

Russian concern for the region's evolution was sparked belatedly by rumblings among the politically active in the region, including the nascent, but more radical Islamic movements which openly called for Islamic confederations between the Central Asian states and neighboring Islamic governments of Afghanistan, Pakistan, and Iran. This was construed by some Russian leaders as a threat to the integrity (and perhaps survival) of the Russian communities in the 'Near Abroad' countries which number perhaps 10 million. The fate of the Russian diaspora in the 'Near Abroad' nations was for a time a paramount Russian concern, with many arguing that the ethnic Russian communities are subordinate only to Moscow and should have the right of "self defense."

This debate among Russia's foreign policy elite was further complicated by a building internal struggle over how Russian foreign policy should be anchored. Two competing schools of thought quickly emerged - the "Atlanticists" and the "Eurasianists." The Atlanticist school, heavily influenced by the emerging economic realities of Russia's stagnating position, argued for closer ties with the West and a jettisoning of any residual imperial pretensions toward the former Soviet republics. The Eurasianists, among whom are many xenophobic nationalist patriots, foresaw potential challenges from China and an Islamic explosion on Russia's southern frontiers, which could only be deterred or addressed by maintaining a strong diplomatic and military posture toward Central Asia and the Caucasus. In addition, many Eurasianist sympathizers were unprepared to accept reform-minded approaches to economic growth, stubbornly adhering to Soviet models of command economy orthodoxy.

Increasingly (but not exclusively), the Atlanticists were centered in the Ministry of Foreign Affairs, and the Eurasianists were concentrated in the Parliament, where concerns like protection of the Russian diaspora dominated the political debate.

These two competing policy approaches reflect a deep division among Russian policymakers over whether the `Near Abroad' regions can be neatly compartmentalized as either assets or liabilities. From this perspective, Central Asia will be assessed quite differently from other regions of the former Soviet Union (FSU).

INDEPENDENCE, REFORM AND POLITICAL REALITY

Several of the region's post-Soviet leaders have encouraged the development of personality cults, broadening their mandate for personal political power and reinforcing their nationalist credentials, but also raising serious doubts as to the future of political pluralism and democratic practice in the region. They are not without their local detractors and rivals. With the resurrection of Islam, many observers believe that regional Islamic leaders will (and perhaps already have) provoked radically orthodox Islamic clerics to establish the foundation for future fundamentalist regimes. Thus, there is a growing expectation of many that an Islamic revival may yet sweep through Central Asia, centered in the Fergana Valley and more particularly in Uzbekistan, where the strongest Islamic roots have survived. The appearance of personality cults among the newly nationalist (i.e.,former party figures) leaders may serve to fuel a variety of radical movements, including the Islamic variants.

The immediate challenges for the new states in Central Asia are simply, stability and governance. The small indigenous elites in the region were unprepared for the responsibilities which they inherited from a well-organized and highly educated Soviet bureaucracy. With the exception of Kazakhstan (whose relationship with Moscow was uniquely close) only a tiny percentage of the indigenous regional elites were given the benefit of professional training in Moscow. This reinforced the dependence of local governments on Russia's economic and financial largesse and acted to smother efforts by more politically aggressive figures to build competing structures of local authority.

From the perspective of the Central Asian nations, the costs of independence were high, particularly in the economic sphere. Central Asia had been the least economically developed of the Soviet regions. The area is predominantly agricultural; the population is 60 percent rural with comparatively little industrialization, except in Kazakhstan. By the mid-1970s, only 16 percent of the population of Central Asia was employed in industry as compared to more than 36 percent in the slavic republics of Russia, Belarus and Ukraine. The region's rich natural resources were the primary source of raw materials for the Slavic republics, and were generally not used to develop local industry.

The Central Asian nations have attempted to form confederal associations in order to pool their resources, address the problem of non-common currencies and to increase their political weight with Moscow. Moscow's initial hope that all of the Central Asian nations would remain within the ruble zone dissolved as the value of the ruble plummeted and the regional leaders realized that their fledgling economies could actually be in the losing position of subsidizing Russian economic decline. While four of the five nations have established their own currencies and three have formed a regional economic grouping, the diversity of these economies and societies, and the deep suspicion of the leaders regarding each other's motives and goals, have severely constrained any collective approaches.

In the immediate political glow of independence from Moscow, Central Asian leaders talked openly of five autonomous and prosperous nations which could effectively compete with Russia for the world's financial attention and trade. When the euphoria of this new independence faded, the economic reality of Central Asia's isolation became apparent. Kazakhstan's president, Nursultan Nazerbayev, recognized this danger and thus became an early booster for a successor union of republics, designed to perpetuate a degree of republican economic interdependence with Russia. Nazerbayev led the effort by Central Asia to preserve the CIS as the most viable economic link to Moscow. As a result, his credibility with the other Central Asian leaders as a voice for independence and autonomy has declined. Kazakhstan's relationship with Russia is unique among the Central Asian nations. Its border with Russia, its large Russian population and (until recently) its unique regional status as a nuclear power, are all determining factors in Alma Ata's delicate foreign policy balancing act.

THE TAJIKISTAN VIRUS AND INSTABILITY IN AFGHANISTAN

The civil war in Tajikistan fundamentally reordered Central Asian perceptions of regional foreign policy concerns and forced Dushanbe's neighbors to reconsider whether they could regard external security as merely a second-order priority. Three of the Central Asian states (Turkmenistan is again the exception) reluctantly contributed forces to a CIS peacekeeping contingent in Tajikistan, but the forces were small and politically insignificant if compared to the Russian contribution, the reinforced 201st Motorized Rifle Division in Dushanbe. Nevertheless, this collective action suggests the potential to bring these states together in a foreign policy crisis, at least for a time.

The key Central Asian leader in the Tajikistan civil war is the Uzbekistan President, Islam Karimov, who, more vociferously than the other regional leaders, sounded the alarm over `Islamic fundamentalism' as the real threat in Tajikistan. Karimov sought to describe the struggle in Tajikistan as one between the forces of secularism and stability, led by pro-Moscow President Rahman Nabiyev (deposed in September 1992) and the rebellious elements in the country who supported Islamic fundamentalism. This distorted picture ignored the complexity of emergent regional politics (including the coalescing of moderate Islamic opposition groups and discounted (deliberately) the depth of anti-Russian feeling among much of the Tajik population. Karimov's real concern was focused more on the threat to his own position - a simmering Islamist opposition developing in Uzbekistan, which he believed would be emboldened by the Tajik civil war,

The political wildcard in the emerging geopolitical map of Central Asia is Afghanistan. The government in Kabul is a fragile and fractious coalition of *Mujahedeen*, caught in a state of competing warlordism, a remnant of the patchwork alliance that repelled the Soviet invasion of 1979. The Afghan war deepened the country's ethnic and tribal divisions. Those living north of the Hindu Kush are distinctly separated from the Pushtun-dominated areas of the south, both of which compete with the central government in Kabul. The disintegration of Afghanistan could encourage more aggressive Central Asian governments, particularly Uzbekistan, to take advantage of an opportunity to extend influence and territorial control. In addition, Afghanistan's territorial integrity is of great concern to a regional U.S. ally, Pakistan. Afghanistan is a vital land bridge connecting Central Asia and South Asia, and thus opportunities for Islamabad to assume a larger profile in Central Asia are limited by Afghani instability.

Afghans have much closer ethnic ties to the people of Central Asia than any of the other neighboring states; they are closely related to the Uzbeks, Tajiks, and Turkmen. Nearly twice as many Tajiks inhabit Afghanistan than currently live in Tajikistan, a fact which explains continued Afghan assistance to the rebels fighting the Russian puppet government in Dushanbe. Large, politically-active Uzbek communities dominate parts of northern Afghanistan, further adding to the complexity of the regional political equation.

CENTRAL ASIA'S NEW GEOPOLITICS

Just as independence spurred exaggerated expectations of economic windfalls, so did it fuel expectations of the region's geopolitical resurrection. Encouraged largely by Western (principally U.S.) suggestions that the absence of Soviet authority in the region would create a political vacuum, the state with perhaps the greatest expectation of fraternal ties to the region, Turkey, moved quickly to probe the limits of relations with its "Turkic brothers." Ankara's leaders saw an opportunity to act as the Western emissary to a largely mysterious and closed world. Turkey also understood that U.S. support for a large Turkish footprint in the region was motivated largely by fears of Iranian hegemonic ambitions in the region. Images of crusading Shi'a mullahs spreading the Ayatollah Khomeini's revolution alarmed Washington policymakers. The United States hoped that Turkey's status as a secular Muslim state, firmly anchored in the Western community, would persuade Central Asia's new leaders to adopt a Turkish model of governance and reform. Yet this cold war approach was not to be successful, at least not initially.

The Turks were quickly disappointed and disillusioned with the tepid welcome offered by their Turkic cousins. Turkey found that its linguistic affinity with the Central Asian states was more distant than expected. Regional dialects had developed over the last century, which presented serious barriers to communication. In addition, Central Asians understood that Turkey had experienced its own difficulties with its NATO partners, some of whom (particularly in Western Europe) failed to recognize Turkey's value as a bridge to the Middle East and Asia. As a senior Kazakh official noted to the author during a 1993 trip to the region, Turkey would first have to convince its own allies of its importance before expecting a warm welcome outside of Europe. Finally, Turkey's growing internal difficulties have severely constrained Ankara's opportunities in Central Asia. The mounting costs of the Kurdish insurgency, the current weakened state of its Prime Minister, and economic stagnation all inhibit Turkey's role as investor in or adviser to Central Asia.

Despite obstacles to an aggressive Turkish policy toward Central Asia, evolving competition for Caspian Sea oil and gas is likely to compel Ankara to be persistent in its efforts to court the region's leaders. As Western investment in the oil and gas fields of Kazakhstan, Turkmenistan, and Azerbaijan inevitably grows, Turkey will insert itself into the emerging geostrategic equation. Increasingly, Turkey will find itself competing with Russia and Iran for access to Caspian oil and the political clout that would accrue to Ankara with leverage on the energy issue. The Turkish Straits may become a key conduit to transport oil from the region to Western markets. But, Turkey's preferred transit plan will compete with an existing Russian pipeline network and competing Iranian transport schemes. While the context for regional competition may have changed, the "Great Game" in Central Asia continues.

Among Central Asia's neighbors, none is more suited to a decisive role in the region's economic development and political direction than China, overshadowing both Iran and Russia. While China has chosen so far to play only a minor role in the "New Great Game"; its strategic concerns regarding the region's evolution (particularly the eastern portion of Central Asia, which it borders) may be greater than Russia's, considering the cultural affinity of the population in Chinese Turkestan (Xinjiang province). Chinese authorities are alarmed by increasing signs of Turkic-Moslem separatism, which has surfaced among the estimated 7 million Kazakhs, Uighurs, and Uzbeks living in Xinjiang. The region, which is roughly divided between Han Chinese and Turkic peoples may hold enormous mineral and petroleum deposits, and is home to the Chinese nuclear test site at Lop Nor.

China's investment strategy in Central Asia has been cautious, although in the last 2 years it has become a major trading partner for Kazakhstan and Kyrgyzstan. Beijing would like a stake in recovering and transporting Kazakhstan's oil, but this would require building expensive pipeline networks, because unlike other potential investors in the region, China has no sea lines of communications linking it directly to Central Asia.

U.S. INTERESTS

It is difficult to identify U.S. interests in Central Asia as "vital." While states adjacent to this region (Russia, China, Iran, Turkey, Pakistan), are important to U.S. strategic objectives, there is less contact between Washington and the Central Asian capitals than with other regions of the former Soviet Union. From a strictly military and security perspective, Kazakhstan's relationship with Russia elevates Central Asia to a higher strategic level for the United States, although with the removal of all Soviet-era nuclear warheads from Kazakhstan in April 1995, the immediate U.S. concern over a nuclear-generated crisis between Moscow and Alma-Ata has diminished significantly.

The United States has an interest in promoting democracy in the region, but at the moment, authoritarian rule seems to be the preferred model for the majority of Central Asia's leaders. With the exception of Kyrgyzstan (and even here the regime's commitment to genuine democratic pluralism is questionable), none of the region's governments have enthusiastically embraced Western concepts of free and open political expression and are more frightened of free enterprise than they are attracted to it. The region is rich is mineral resources and hydrocarbon deposits, but extraction and transport of this wealth remains very problematic, chiefly for political reasons.

There is some good news for Western interests, however. As noted earlier in this introduction and throughout this volume, radical Islam has not yet taken root in a way which could threaten stability. In addition, Russia seems sufficiently content with the region's political direction, to avoid taking actions which could precipitate further upheaval.

Finally, Washington is not inclined to make a commitment to Central Asian economic development, particularly when the potential for crises in other regions of the former Soviet Union are likely to more directly impact U.S. interests (e.g. Ukraine-Russian relations, additional Chechnya-like secessionist insurrections).

In sum, U.S. influence in and leverage upon the governments in the region are limited and to a certain extent hostage to the actions of key neighboring states. Unless the region experiences unanticipated shocks, Washington's direct involvement in Central Asian affairs will likely remain marginal.

The issues outlined in this introduction are all addressed in greater detail and with greater authority by a group of scholars and regional policy specialists who came together at the National Defense University for a major international conference in 1993. The first section of this volume features papers by seven noted experts originally presented at this conference and subsequently revised for publication. The papers are organized in four sections: national identity and domestic stability; the role of Islam; relations with Russia and regional security concerns, and competition for influence by neighboring states.

In the first section, Shirin Akiner provides a comprehensive look at Central Asia's social and political roots and analyzes the complex historical factors that are influencing contemporary efforts by Central Asians to define and develop a new identity. In the second section, Mehmet Saray provides a Turkish view of Islam's origin in Central Asia and briefly discusses the Soviet attitude toward Islam as a religious force in the region.

The third grouping of papers begins with an analysis by Eugene Rumer who traces Central Asia's position and importance to Russia, in the context of Moscow's post-Soviet objectives on foreign and security policy. He also analyzes the policy debate in Russia among officials and the policy elite, involving competing schools of thought regarding the future of Russia's external policy, and Central Asia's relative importance in that debate. Bess Brown then assesses the security interests of the Central Asian states, from the perspectives of each of the five national leaderships and elites in the region, and includes an analysis of Central Asian views regarding the CIS. This section of the volume concludes with an essay by Maxim Shashenkov who takes a detailed look at the evolution of military and strategic concerns in Central Asia. He focuses on military planning and the debate over the political difficulties in erecting multilateral defense structures. Shashenkov also illuminates these policy issues in the context of relations with

Russia and the varying approaches of each of the regional nations toward the CIS.

The final two chapters focus on key neighbors. Ross Munro, an Asian specialist, addresses an issue which has received relatively little attention by Western analysts—China's policy toward and interest in Central Asia's post-Soviet evolution. Particular attention is paid to economic and ethnic issues. Munro also addresses India's strategic interest in this region, which he regards as minimal at the moment. Finally, Patrick Clawson addresses the trade, investment and overall economic, political, and security impact of those states neighboring Central Asia and the Caucasus regions, on the former Soviet South. Particular attention is paid to Iran, Turkey, and Pakistan.

Following these analyses, there is an encapsulated summary of the conference discussions, which highlight the papers and present commentaries by noted experts.

The editor is grateful to the Institute for National Strategic Studies at the National Defense University for its support of the project which has resulted in this volume. He assumes all responsibility for the content.

NOTES

1. Portions of this introduction are drawn from the author's chapter, "Central Asia and the New World Disorder," in Jasjit Singh (ed) *The Road Ahead: Indo-US Strategic Dialogue* (New Delhi: Lancer International, 1994).

2. For an analysis of Central Asia's origins, See Shirin Akiner, "Post-Soviet Central Asia: Past is Prologue," in Peter Ferdinand (ed.) *The New States of Central Asia and Their Neighbors* (New York: Council on Foreign Relations Press, 1994), 4-35. Also see the Akiner chapter in this volume.

3. Peter Hopkirk, *The Great Game: The Struggle for Empire in Central Asia,* (New York: Kodansha International, 1990,), 5.

AFTER EMPIRE:
The Emerging Geopolitics
of Central Asia

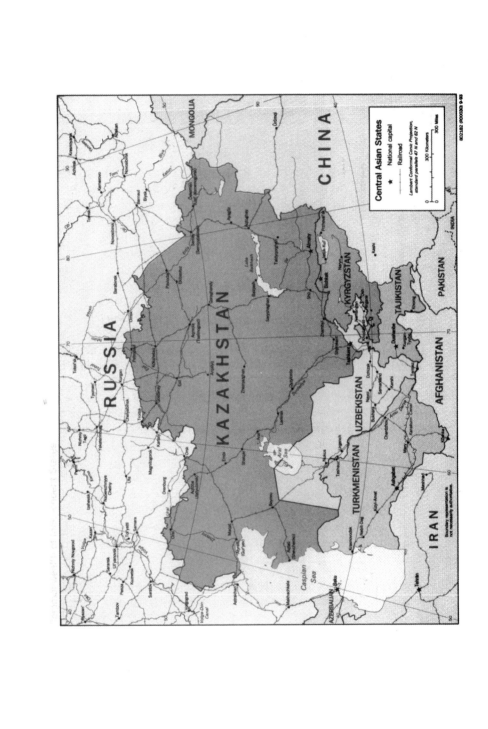

Central Asian States

★ National capital

Railroad

Lambert Conformal Conic Projection,
standard parallels 47 N and 62 N

0   300 Kilometers

0   300 Miles

RUSSIA

MONGOLIA

CHINA

KAZAKHSTAN

KYRGYZSTAN

TAJIKISTAN

UZBEKISTAN

TURKMENISTAN

AFGHANISTAN

PAKISTAN

INDIA

IRAN

AZERBAIJAN

Caspian
Sea

Aral
Sea

Boundary representation is
not necessarily authoritative.

802218C (R00330) 9-93

1. The STRUGGLE for IDENTITY

Shirin Akiner

As used here, "Central Asia" refers to the territory divided among the republics of Kazakhstan, Kyrgyzstan, Tajikistan, Turkmenistan and Uzbekistan.[1] It covers an area of some 4 million sq. km., an area considerably larger than India and slightly smaller than the combined territories of Algeria and Libya. The largest republic is Kazakhstan, which dominates the northern tier. The largest population, however, is found in Uzbekistan (1989: 19.8 million), which is also the most centrally located, sharing common borders with all four of the other Central Asian republics.

Central Asia is a region of great physical contrasts: high mountain ranges in the east and south-east bordering China and Afghanistan; steppe lands in the northern belt (Kazakhstan); semi-desert and desert regions in the center (southern Kazakhstan, Uzbekistan and Turkmenistan); and river valleys and oases in the south (particularly the broad belt of the Ferghana Valley that stretches from the foothills of Kyrgyzstan and Tajikistan through southern Uzbekistan). The highest concentrations of populations have traditionally been in the fertile valleys of the south; the lowest have been in the desert regions of the center and the barren mountains of the southeast. This remains the pattern today, although industrialization has increased population densities in the central and northern provinces of Kazakhstan and, to a lesser

Dr. Shirin Akiner, Director of the Central Asia Research Forum at the School of Oriental and African Studies, University of London, is currently directing four British Government funded training projects with Kazakhstan and Uzbekistan. Her publications include *Islamic Peoples of the Soviet Union* (1986), *Cultural Change and Tradition in Central Asia* (1991) and "Post-Soviet Islam," in the *Harvard International Review* (1993).

extent, in selected areas of the other republics. The combined population of all five republics numbers approximately 50 million.

The region is rich in hydrocarbons and minerals. However, the harsh climatic conditions and the scarcity of water and land suitable for sustaining human life have meant that these resources have always required careful husbanding. During the Soviet period, the introduction of large-scale, intensive agriculture, supported by massive irrigation schemes and a dangerously heavy reliance on chemicals, destroyed the delicate ecological balance and resulted in serious environmental damage. The desiccation of the Aral Sea, once the fourth largest inland sea in the world, is a powerful illustration of the consequences of inappropriate development policies.[2] Urban and industrial pollution and contamination caused by the prolonged exposure to radiation (as in Kazakhstan in the vicinity of the Semipalatinsk nuclear testing site) are not yet widely acknowledged problems, but in the affected areas they pose as great, if not indeed greater, threats to the quality of life.[3]

THE PEOPLE

The earliest sedentary inhabitants of Central Asia were probably of eastern Iranian origin. Their descendants, numbering some 200,000 today, survive in the Badakhshan region of Tajikistan. Subsequently, western Iranian settlers, forebears of the modern Tadzhiks, moved into the oasis belt; later still, from the sixth century a.d. onward, successive waves of Turkic nomads spread across the plains, in time becoming the dominant ethnic element in Central Asia. Some in the south adopted a sedentary way of life and intermingled with the Iranian population (forebears of the modern Uzbeks); others remained nomadic (Kazakhs, Kyrgyz and Turkmen) until they were forcibly settled in the 1930s as part of the Soviet program of collectivization. Many other peoples have settled in Central Asia at various times. These include such ancient groups as the Bukharan Jews, as well as more recent Slavic immigrants. There are also significant numbers of "punished peoples," those who were deported to Central Asia (primarily to Kazakhstan and Uzbekistan) on the eve of and during World War II. They include Koreans, Germans, Greeks and Crimean Tatars.[4] Today, in each of these five republics, some 100 different "nationalities" (in the Soviet sense of the term) are represented. The percentage share of the main indigenous peoples in the

4

overall population of the republics varies from approximately 40 percent of the Kazakhs in Kazakhstan to approximately 70 percent of the Uzbeks in Uzbekistan and the Turkmen in Turkmenistan.

Islam was first introduced into the southern belt of Central Asia by the Arabs in the second half of the seventh century. It soon attracted converts amongst the settled peoples, but took centuries longer to gain ground amongst the nomads, some of whom were only finally Islamicized in the 19th century under Russian rule. The cities of the south became renowned centers of Muslim learning, but the distant fringes of the nomadic world had little more than a superficial acquaintance with Islam. Lying at the heart of the Eurasian landmass, Central Asia was the crossroads of the transcontinental trade routes for centuries, the so-called "Silk Roads." A meeting place and melting pot, the region fostered cultures of immense variety and vitality. During the 16th century, however, primarily as a result of the shift from land to sea routes, Central Asia suffered economic decline and lost something of its earlier preeminence in the arts and sciences, although short-haul trade with eastern Turkestan, India, and Iran continued to flourish. The burgeoning state of Muscovy came into prominence during this period, which was to prove to be of great significance in the future. Diplomatic and commercial links between Central Asia and this new power in the West gradually increased to the point that the absorption of Central Asia into the Russian empire became virtually inevitable.

PRE-SOVIET IDENTITIES

For centuries, the chief cultural division in Central Asia was between the nomads of the steppe and the desert and the settled populations of the oases and river valleys. It was not an ethnically or religiously based divide since the overwhelming majority of the indigenous population, whether settled or nomadic, was Turkic by origin and, with minor exceptions, Sunni Muslim by religion. However, neither ethnic nor religious bonds were strong enough to bridge the gulf between these two very different societies. Delicate alliances and balances of power were constructed at the margins of their coexistence, but no matter how close the collaboration, each group retained its own separate identity and an innate hostility toward the other group. Echoes of this are still to be found today.

Within these two broad divisions of nomads and settled peoples, there were further subdivisions based on clan, tribal and regional affiliations. Among both nomads and settled peoples, the primary socio-political structure was a pyramid. At every level, from the nuclear family unit upwards, there was a clearly defined hierarchy of power with its concomitant implications of allegiance and responsibility. Clusters of families formed clans (or sub-tribes), clusters of clans constituted tribes;[5] at the apex was the khan, who wielded supreme authority. Such "state" formations were essentially tribal confederations, although among the settled peoples, the administrative structures were considerably more formalized and bureaucratic than amongst the nomads. The dominant powers were: in the south, the Khanates of Bukhara, Khiva and Kokand; in the north, the three Kazakh Hordes (the Big, the Little, and the Middle).[6]

If there was little sense of nationhood in the modern, Western sense in pre-Soviet Central Asia, the clan/tribal structures nevertheless provided a framework of self-definition that amounted to proto-national identities. These group identities were underpinned in a variety of ways. Amongst the nomads, there was a highly developed sense of genealogy—every Kazakh, for example, was required to know by heart his lineage for seven generations back in order not to violate kinship taboos (this tradition is still very much alive today). Blood lines were important because, like the written deeds of title of settled, literate communities, they established inheritance rights in such matters as access to water and grazing grounds. For the settled peoples, genealogical ties did not have quite the same significance (although they were nevertheless important), but there was a stronger sense of regional identity that was linked most commonly to a town or some other geographical feature. Shared cultural traditions also played a powerful role in creating communal identities. These included visual symbols such as the exclusive use of certain designs or color combinations in their textiles and oral epics that recounted the historic triumphs and defeats of the group. The societies with the strongest and most broadly based sense of tribal identity were the Kazakhs and the Turkmen. On the eve of the Soviet era, partly owing to pan-Turkic influences and partly to Russian liberal thought, the Kazakh intelligentsia were beginning to transmute this tribal awareness into a sense of political identity.[7] The same was true of the intelligentsia in the

Bukharan Khanate, although by virtue of the complex nature of the urban population, it was a more diverse, multi-ethnic culture.

Religion was not a strong marker of identity before the advent of the Russians; since the great majority of the population was Islamic, religion was an integral part of the fabric of society as a whole. Nevertheless, there were differences the Muslims perceived amongst themselves. Skirmishes were not uncommon between the Shia and Sunni communities in Bukhara and Samarkand (the former were absorbed by the Sunnis during the Soviet period); moreover, the Sunni Turkmen tribesmen considered the Shia traders from Iran fair game for capture and sale in the slave markets, on the grounds that they were not "true" Muslims. There were also tensions between the Bukharan Jews and the Muslims. However, after the Russian presence had been firmly established in Central Asia in the latter half of the 19th century, Islam did become an important factor in the self-definition among and between the Central Asians and the newcomers. It was not that the Russian invasion provoked fanatical religious opposition (there was in fact very little serious resistance compared with that most other colonial powers encountered elsewhere), nor that it prompted a wave of solidarity amongst the indigenous peoples, but it did arouse a general sense of "otherness," encapsulated in the term "Muslim," which came to be interpreted as being synonymous with "local." In this loose sense, the term was to have wide currency, especially at the popular level (in rural areas, traces of this usage are still to be found today).

FORMATION OF SOVIET IDENTITIES

National Delimitation of Central Asia

In 1924, after the establishment of Soviet power in Central Asia, the National Delimitation was enacted, creating five administrative units. Two of these, Turkmenistan and Uzbekistan, were immediately granted the status of full Union republics; Tajikistan (originally included within Uzbekistan) acquired Union status in 1929, Kazakhstan and Kyrgyzstan in 1936.[8] These republics were entirely new state formations with no basis in historic nation states. They were created not in response to popular demand, but at Moscow's behest.

It has been argued by some that the motives for the National Delimitation were purely those of a "divide and rule" policy. Such considerations may have played their part, but there were also strong ideological reasons for creating these nation states. First, it was a symbolic gesture of decolonization, marking a watershed between the repressive Tsarist regime and the supposedly liberating force of Marxism-Leninism. Second, the Soviet Union, in theory at least, purported to be a free association of sovereign states. In Central Asia, such states did not exist; therefore it was necessary to create them so that these new formations could then "choose" to become members of the Soviet polity. Third, there was a belief amongst Soviet theoreticians that economic and social development could best be achieved in "national" states, where it would be possible to provide better (i.e., more specifically orientated) cultural and educational facilities for the larger ethnic groups. The creation of the national republics, far from being a fail-safe mechanism for control, was potentially a high-risk strategy that might easily have led to the consolidation of national movements inimical to the Soviet state. These ambiguities—on the one hand, genuine attempts to foster national identity; on the other, a cynical exercise in sham "political correctness"—were never resolved and in some ways counterbalanced each other, providing just enough substance to flesh out the theory of national self-determination, but not enough to constitute a threat.[9]

The dividing lines between the new states were not drawn in an arbitrary fashion, but closely followed ethno-linguistic boundaries. Decades of research by Tsarist philologists, geographers and ethnographers had produced a body of scholarly work on the dialectal and tribal groupings of the region, and it was this that helped to establish the basis for the division.[10] The reliance on ethno-linguistics stemmed from a belief in the correlation between language and "nation," a theory which had its roots in German Romanticism.[11] It had found particular resonance in Central and Eastern Europe, where it gave a shape and focus to nascent political aspirations. Thus, from the Russian point of view, it was a natural enough approach to take when creating these new states. What made it inappropriate in this context, or at least curious, was the fact that language had not previously been a significant marker of identity in Central Asia. The majority of the population, particularly in the settled regions of the south, was multi-lingual, moving with ease between *Turki, Farsi* and a range of different dialects. Nevertheless, since there was a high degree of congruence between language/dialect groupings and clan/tribal/regional identities, the lines of partition did not greatly violate traditional socio-cultural formations. Rather, they emphasized divisions that had formerly been implicit, but not articulated as such. Within its own terms of reference, the Delimitation was largely successful because it succeeded in encompassing within the borders of its own eponymous republic, without any shifting of populations, some 90% of each of the main ethno-linguistic groups (Uzbek, Turkmen, Kyrgyz and Kazakh). The exceptions were the Tadzhiks, whose history had for so long been intermingled with that of the Uzbeks that it was impossible to make an equitable territorial division between the two groups. The Tadzhiks, the smaller and less influential group, were the losers: not only did approximately a third of their number remain within the boundaries of Uzbekistan, but they were dispossessed of the very core of their culture, the historic centers of Bukhara and Samarkand—something that has never ceased to cause resentment and anger. There were other cases of the territory of one group being awarded to a neighboring republic, though none was quite as emotionally charged as Bukhara and Samarkand.[12] At the time, no open protest was possible. Seventy years later, however, some of these old grievances have re-emerged, giving rise to new tensions.

Sovietization of Society
The creation of the new republics was the first step in a truly massive feat of social engineering. State-manipulated social transformations have been attempted elsewhere (e.g., in Iran and Turkey), but never on such a large scale. Every public and many private areas of human activity were affected, ranging from education to entertainment, language to dress, patterns of employment to patterns of marriage. The architectural environment was likewise transformed, particularly in the capitals of the republics, where broad avenues, high-rise concrete apartment blocks and gleaming government offices replaced the intimate jumble of narrow streets and crumbling mud-brick structures of the older world, signaling the advent of a new era. Selected historical monuments were preserved as museum exhibits, but otherwise the onslaught on the relics of the past was ferocious and relentless, a vivid metaphor of the changes that were taking place in society as a whole.[13]

The avowed goal of this campaign was to raise the socioeconomic level of the region to the same standard as that of other parts of the Soviet Union and, in so doing, to bring about full political, economic and social integration.[14] Given the low starting point, this was an extremely ambitious program, and seven decades later it was still far from being accomplished. However, if in this might be deemed a "failed transformation," there was nevertheless significant progress in a number of areas. Major strides were made in such fields as health care and education. Literacy rates, for example, were raised from an average of 5 percent in 1926 to 99 percent by 1970. While it is true that "99 percent" is probably an overestimation or that the definition of literacy used in the relevant census surveys was very basic, literacy is undoubtedly widespread and levels are impressive, far superior to those in comparable countries such as Iran, Pakistan, Egypt and Turkey.[15] Similarly, infant mortality, though higher than in Russia, is nevertheless far lower than in most Middle Eastern countries.[16]

These and other achievements were not simply steps toward a better standard of living, but weapons in the struggle to deconstruct traditional society in order to replace it with a new social architecture. Education was saturated with ideological content, whose chief purpose was to inculcate a sense of the inherently superior nature of the Soviet regime. It was a message that was ceaselessly propagated by the mass media (radio, television, newspapers, street slogans, posters, etc.) and all forms of public entertainment, including new Western- and Soviet-style art forms such as the theater, opera, ballet, and cinema.[17] The emancipation of women (abandoning of the veil, compulsory education, employment outside the home, equal legal status with men) was an attempt not only to improve the lot of women, but also to alter the very nature of the most intimate family relationships.[18] The changes of the script from the Arabic to the Latin (c. 1930) and then to the Cyrillic (1940) were likewise introduced in the name of progress, but they had the additional function of deepening the gulf between the old order and the new. Inevitably, in a climate such as this, the fiercest campaign of repression was reserved for Islam, a religion that offers both a belief system and an alternative social blueprint. Not only were individual believers persecuted, but the institutional framework of the religion, including its schools, colleges and law courts, was destroyed within the first decade of Soviet rule. Other potential sources of dissent, whether political or purely intellectual, were eradicated during the purges of the 1930s. This systematic elimination of everything that did not conform to the norms of the new world vision greatly facilitated the introduction of Soviet institutions and ideas. The urban communities were more deeply influenced by these developments than were those in rural areas (who constituted the great majority of the indigenous population), yet the changes were so radical and far-reaching that within two to three decades a profound metastasis had taken place within Central Asian society as a whole.[19]

Change and Continuity in Central Asian Identities: The Coopting of Tradition

The ideological and institutional Sovietization of society was accompanied by efforts to transform traditional identities into "modern" identities that conformed to the Soviet theory of ethnically-based nationalities. In the case of the larger groups, such identities were specifically linked to the historical development of the eponymous republics. Thus, embryonic state nationalisms were nurtured, yet at the same time defused because their sphere of influence was tightly controlled and always subordinated to the over-arching Soviet identity. This two-tiered hierarchy was made explicit in such symbols of state sovereignty as national flags, emblems, anthems and constitutions; also it was reflected in the republican branches of such all-Union institutions as the Communist Party, Young Communist League (Komsomol), and trade/professional unions. The "national" element in such manifestations was almost entirely cosmetic, of virtually no structural significance. As political rhetoric, however, it was a useful device because it provided a verisimilitude of independence.

Local sensibilities were flattered and manipulated by the construction of anachronistic national histories which were entirely focussed on manufacturing myths that reinforced the notion of separate nationalities on the one hand, and the rightness and inevitability of membership of the Soviet community on the other. The fashioning of new literary languages (in some places to replace existing forms, in others to introduce writing for the first time), replete with grammars, dictionaries and literatures, emphasized the "modern" and progressive nature of the new order and at the same time helped to consolidate the new identities.[20]

11

The most important factor in the successful enforcement of Soviet rule was the coopting of local elites. There were certainly Slav commissars whose brief was to ensure that the Central Asians remained loyal to the "center," but had the system been imposed and administered solely by outsiders, it surely would not have become as firmly ensconced as it did. From the very beginning, the new regime was successful in creating vested interests, not only for loyal political activists, but also for the intelligentsia and other respected members of society.[21] Those who were prepared to serve the system were rewarded with privileges of every description; those who could not be so suborned were either forced to flee abroad or to risk "repression" (death or imprisonment). It is hardly surprising that many chose the former course. This had implications that went far beyond the fate of individuals: in a society that was still largely illiterate, where great respect and trust were traditionally accorded to the oqsoqollar ("white beards"), the fact that senior figures were prepared to give their support to the new regime bestowed upon it an automatic legitimacy.

The former power structures remained virtually unchanged; the client-patron networks that had flourished in pre-Soviet society proved to be as effective—and necessary—in the Soviet period. For the most part, they continued to be based on traditional clan/tribal/regional loyalties. Scarcely perceptible to the outsider, they formed parallel networks of influence and support.[22] Those in positions of authority were still able to provide protection and advancement for their dependents, who in return gave absolute allegiance. On the positive side, this offered a degree of protection against the encroachments of the state; on the negative side, it facilitated the spread of organized criminal fraternities, the so-called "mafia." Thus, while the Central Asians appeared to be wholly subservient to the formal organs of power, in reality they practiced a high degree of covert autonomy. Change was forced upon them, but the tensions that might otherwise have been created were mitigated by this inner core of stability and continuity. An effective mechanism for compartmentalizing public and private spheres, it enabled the great majority of Central Asians to accommodate with apparent ease a variety of seemingly contradictory and even mutually exclusive identities and loyalties.[23]

Intimations of a National Awakening

Many Western observers expected the Soviet invasion of Afghanistan to trigger a wave of disaffection among the Central Asians, but this did not happen. On the contrary, existing conditions in Afghanistan, far from evoking envy and admiration, reinforced confidence in the superiority of the Soviet system. However, other forces were already stirring which would, in the course of the next few years, bring about a change in attitudes towards Moscow. The first was a consequence of the anticorruption campaigns of the mid-1980s. Corruption was rife throughout the Soviet Union, but the Central Asians were singled out for particular punishment. It is true that in Central Asia, especially in Uzbekistan, fraud and embezzlement were carried to extremes more spectacular than elsewhere in the USSR. Nevertheless, by their own standards, the Central Asians had played the game fairly, and senior officials in Moscow also benefited from their operations. What the Central Asians bitterly resented was the humiliation and ridicule that was heaped upon them by the all-Union press. Moreover, the criminal investigations soon took on the aspect of a political purge, reminiscent of those of the 1930s. In Uzbekistan, thousands of innocent people were arrested; the First Party Secretary, Sharaf Rashidov, died in 1983 and is generally believed to have committed suicide. In Kazakhstan, the long-standing First Party Secretary, Dinmukhammad Kunayev, was removed from office in December 1986; Kazakh students held a protest meeting, but this was brutally dispersed. There were few other obvious signs of discontent, but it became clear that the Central Asians would not accept such heavy-handed treatment from Moscow for much longer. Their easy-going tolerance had given way to barely concealed resentment.[24]

Another important development that occurred in the 1980s was the renewal of interest in Islam. Constant religious persecution had by this time undermined the position of Islam to such an extent that it was little more than a cultural affiliation for most Central Asians. They knew nothing of Islamic precepts and lacked the most elementary knowledge of prayer postures and rituals. (The role of Sufi movements in keeping alive the faith appears to have been negligible). However, in the mid-1980s a grassroots Islamic revival movement took shape in the Ferghana Valley. Reminiscent of the revivalist movements that were appearing elsewhere in the Soviet Union, it seems to have been a spontaneous reaction to the spiritual vacuum created by Soviet materialism. It had no more than a few thousand adherents, but symbolically it was a turning point because it marked the beginning of a return to traditional values. A few years later, the state itself began to adopt a more conciliatory attitude towards Islam. More new mosques were opened in 1989 alone than in the whole of the previous decade. Again, this was part of a general change of attitude towards religion in the Soviet Union, but in Central Asia it had the added affect of giving new emphasis to the indigenous, non-European culture.

At the very end of the 1980s, the first informal sociopolitical movements began to appear. They were primarily concerned with environmental and cultural issues. Independence was definitely not on their agenda. The most active group was *Birlik* ("Unity"), founded in Uzbekistan in late 1988. By 1989, however, it was already falling apart. A splinter group, *Erk* ("Freedom"), was founded shortly after (despite its challenging name, *Erk* was in many ways more conservative and pro-official policy than *Birlik).* After an initial burst of enthusiasm, neither party was able to retain much popular support. In 1992 the respective leaders of the two parties were each still claiming to have a membership of 40,000 to 50,000. In reality, however, there was little evidence of this, and official harassment, coupled with public indifference, had virtually destroyed both parties by the autumn of 1993.

The fourth element of chance that emerged at the end of the 1980's was the sudden outbreak of interethnic violence. The first incidents, in June 1989, involved Meskhetian Turks and Uzbeks; later, there were similar clashes between Uzbeks and Kyrgyz and, on a smaller scale, between Turkmen and Azerbaijanis. There had been no history of such conflicts. The fact that they occurred at all was as shocking as the actual atrocities.[25] The incidents revealed a malaise far deeper than had hitherto been suspected. They also provided a sudden illumination of the extent to which the power of the "center" had declined. Previously, the fear of Moscow had been sufficient to prevent such clashes; now, sensing an opportunity to extend their own power, local groups were becoming more aggressive.

Despite the stirrings of disaffection and hostility toward Moscow that had surfaced at the end of the 1980s, in the referendum held on 17 March 1991 on the future of the Soviet

14

Union, over 90 percent of the Central Asians (98 percent in Turkmenistan) voted to remain within the Union.[26] Not even the most radical activists had as yet begun to think seriously about the possibility of independence. The leader of *Birlik*, Abdurahim Pulatov, was adamant that the premature severing of links with the Western republics would seriously jeopardize the development of democracy in Central Asia. He feared—with sad prescience—that independence would put the political clock back at least a century.[27]

Perturbed by the way in which Moscow seemed to be losing its power to control and to provide stability, most Central Asians welcomed the August 1991 coup attempt against Gorbachev. The Presidents of Uzbekistan, Turkmenistan, and Tajikistan gave signs of support for the plotters; the Presidents of Kazakhstan and Kyrgyzstan, after a slight hesitation, spoke out against them. After the coup had been defeated, however, the President of Uzbekistan initiated steps to secede from the Union. Tajikistan, Kyrgyzstan, and Turkmenistan followed suit within the next couple of months. In each case, these moves were made on the sole authority of the President of the republic in question. There was no discussion of the matter; even members of the respective parliaments had no forewarning of the impending declarations of independence. The chief motivation appeared to be a face-saving device to extricate the presidents from the humiliation of having had to depend on a telephone call to decide their fates. The reaction of the general public was not one of jubilation, but rather of bewilderment and anxiety.[28]

Independence

The formal demise of the Soviet Union occurred on 8 December 1991, when without prior consultation or warning, the Presidents of Russia, Belarus and Ukraine announced the creation of a Slav Commonwealth. By implication, the Soviet Union ceased to exist, and all its constituent republics were now free and independent entities. It was thus, unexpectedly, without a struggle of liberation or any other rite of passage, that decolonization was thrust upon the region. At a summit meeting of the heads of the former Soviet republics held in Alma Ata 20-21 December, it was decided that the original concept of the Commonwealth of Independent States (CIS) be enlarged to include eight other states, amongst them all five of the Central Asian republics. There was little enthusiasm for the new grouping, but it was generally accepted that it was necessary, at least initially, to provide a framework within which new inter-republican relationships could be formulated.

The question that was most frequently asked by foreign observers at that time was: are these newly emergent states viable? Given the high level of dependence on the center, the degree of integration into all-Union structures and the total lack of preparation for independence, the nervousness about the future of the Central Asian republics was hardly surprising. Two years later, however, the prognoses were more optimistic. Great strides had been made toward creating independent institutions (e.g. in the banking sector), improving international communications and transport networks, developing diplomatic and commercial links with the outside world (by 1993 each republic had direct links with over 100 foreign countries) and securing membership in international organizations. Intensive training programs were initiated in such fields as banking, financial management, accountancy, law and diplomacy; some were held abroad, some in the republics themselves. These measures will not have much immediate effect, but they are of vital importance for the transition to a market economy because in time they will raise the general level of indigenous technical and administrative expertise. The Central Asian republics undoubtedly have the potential to achieve a high level of prosperity. In order for this to become a reality, however, it is imperative that they maintain domestic stability. This may not be easy.

THREATS TO DOMESTIC STABILITY

Economic and Social Disruption
Currently, the chief threat to the stability of the Central Asian republics comes from mounting economic and social pressures. Since independence, soaring inflation, the sudden increases in fuel and energy prices, the disruption of the supplying of industrial materials, spare parts, foodstuffs, pharmaceutical and other essential items, the disbanding of Union-owned enterprises, and the collapse of the rouble zone have all caused serious hardship.[29] The situation is aggravated by the high rate of growth of the population. The ever-growing demand for new employment opportunities was becoming difficult to satisfy while the Central

16

Asian republics still formed part of the Soviet Union; today, in the harsh economic climate of the post-independence era, it will be virtually impossible to generate the necessary increase in jobs.[30] Unemployment levels cannot but rise, a matter for grave concern in a region where the ratio of potential wage-earners to dependents is low. There has already been a sharp deterioration in living standards, a trend that is unlikely to be reversed in the near future. This has caused a marked heightening of social tensions, especially in the poorer, rural areas. Frustration and disillusionment are widespread, furnishing a ready breeding ground for extremism and violence.

As elsewhere in the CIS, there has been an explosion of crime in Central Asia. The "mafia networks" that previously were constrained by fear of the "center" (Moscow) have now become a dominant force in society. Black-marketeering, bribery, extortion and robbery with violence have mushroomed. Cross-border smuggling of every conceivable commodity, from icons to uranium and from weapons to luxury goods, is now rife. The most serious development, however, is the proliferation of drug-related crimes; huge quantities of opium and other narcotics are being cultivated in all five republics, some for domestic consumption (users as young as 10 years of age have been apprehended), some for dispatch to the CIS and possibly thence via the Baltic States to Western Europe.[31] The law enforcement agencies struggle to combat these and other criminal activities, but they are massively outnumbered. The "mafia networks" have infiltrated society to such an extent that they have in effect become the king makers—very little is decided without their involvement. The criminalization of society makes the process of reform doubly arduous. It is also a powerful disincentive to foreign commercial involvement, the very thing that is most needed to aid in the recovery of these economies.

Post-Soviet Identities

A second threat to domestic stability lies in the possibility of ethnic clashes. Relations between the various ethnic groups are inevitably tense in this period of the redefinition of post-Soviet identities and the renegotiation of power in the republics. The collapse of the Union removed in a single stroke the rationale for existence of the Soviet "nationalities." One response espoused by some intellectuals has been to reject the "new" national identities

17

and seek a return to larger, older groupings. Amongst the Turkic peoples, especially the Uzbeks, this has led to a certain enthusiasm for the idea of a Turkestani, or more broadly, a pan-Turkic identity. Similarly, some Tadzhiks are attracted by the idea of a greater Iran. The great majority of Central Asians, however, are giving new emphasis to the smaller, older allegiances of clan, tribe and region. These never ceased to exist but were largely invisible during the Soviet period. Today, they are reemerging into the open, more often than not as factors in the struggle to fill the power vacuum left by Moscow. Events in Tajikistan have provided a frightening example of the hostility that can still exist between clans that have shared a common "nationality" for some 70 years. The dangers of clan/tribal fragmentation are less acute in the other republics but should not be discounted entirely. There are indications of renewed rivalry between the Kazakh Hordes, particularly members of the Big (in power for most of the Soviet period) and the Middle (severely repressed during the 1930's); in Turkmenistan, there are persistent hints of the revival of old antagonisms between the various tribes and subtribes, especially those of Merv (Mary), Ashkhabad and Chardzhou. In Kyrgyzstan, the division is between the northern and southern regions; in Uzbekistan, between the traditional power bases of Ferghana, Samarkand and Tashkent. It is unlikely that there will be prolonged conflicts among these different groups, but sporadic outbursts of violence are more than probable. Matters are complicated by the fact that these regional/clan groupings frequently form the basis of government (regional and central) as well as "mafia networks," thus there are power struggles in progress at various levels and in various spheres.

Although older identities are now re-asserting their influence, the national identities that were so assiduously cultivated over the past 70 years have also acquired an emotional force that provides its own legitimation. They are an integral part of contemporary Central Asian culture. However, a certain re-definition of these identities is inevitable. While the internal strains and divisive tendencies make it premature, perhaps, to speak of the rise of nationalism, a stronger, more aggressive sense of group identity is undoubtedly emerging. Confrontation with other ethnic groups through economic competition (for jobs, housing, social benefits, etc.) and disputes over land and water rights is serving as a catalyst in the mobilization of chauvinistic xenophobia. The most

18

acute, and potentially most dangerous, tensions are between neighboring ethnic/national groups—traditional enemies with long-standing, long-buried grievances against each other (e.g. Kyrgyz vs. Uzbeks, Turkmen vs. Uzbeks). It is not unlikely that this will one day lead to the re-drawing of state boundaries. The official position of all the governments is that they are opposed to such measures. However, justifications for possible future action (e.g. the annexation of the Khodzhent region of Tajikistan by Uzbekistan) are already being rehearsed in more militant circles.

The general deterioration of economic and social conditions has aroused fears for the safety of the nonindigenous ethnic minorities (particularly Russians, but also other Slavs, Koreans, Germans, Greeks, etc.). To date, there has been little physical aggression toward them, and it is unlikely that this would ever occur except in conditions of a total break-down of law and order. They are not perceived to be a threat in the way that neighboring indigenous groups are, partly because they are relatively few in number, partly because by their very nature they represent a less permanent menace. (It is noteworthy that Muslim immigrants from related ethnic groups, e.g., Meskhetian Turks and Azerbaijanis, are seen as more serious rivals and treated accordingly.) However, there is growing discrimination against them in other, indirect, ways. The language laws (making the main indigenous language the official state language) were seen as symptomatic of the general move to exclude the minorities from public life. The harassment, though not formally sanctioned, is all-pervasive and causes the "outsiders" to feel as if they are second-class citizens.

This phenomenon is largely the consequence of Soviet nationality policies. The republics were supposedly created to facilitate the development of the main indigenous groups. However, although these states have now acquired independence and are therefore required by generally accepted international standards to provide full and equal rights for all their citizens, nevertheless, the eponymous groups still expect to maintain, even enhance, their special status. This presents the current governments with a dilemma. Almost exclusively composed of erstwhile Communists who are still struggling to re-invent themselves as nationalist heroes, they need to win popular support, but at the same time, they cannot risk ethnic unrest since this will ultimately constitute a threat to their own positions. The public rhetoric, therefore, is full of ambiguities—on the one hand, the concept of nationality as defined by citizenship (i.e., nonethnically based) is promoted, but the strong emphasis on the culture of the main indigenous group is in fact favoring the emergence of an ethnocracy. The new "state ideologies" (as they are termed) are intended to provide a new national focus for society to replace the "internationalism" of the Soviet period. This has certainly pleased the main eponymous groups, but it has caused some alarm among the minorities.

The civil war has triggered a sizable exodus of Russians from Tajikistan, reducing the Slav population by about a half. A more limited out-migration is also in progress from Uzbekistan, Turkmenistan, and Kyrgyzstan. Some degree of population movement would have occurred even if the Union had not disintegrated because by the mid-1980s the rapid rate of increase of the indigenous peoples was already creating severe economic strains.

The current upheavals have accelerated the process, however, since many fear that nationalism (and fundamentalism) will eventually make their continued presence in these republics untenable. If the political situation is stabilized and confidence restored, the rate of emigration will undoubtedly decrease; at present, the question is still open, and the majority of the nonindigenous peoples are waiting nervously to see what the future will bring.

The situation in Kazakhstan is markedly different from that in the other four republics: here the Slavs (mostly Russians) and Kazakhs are equally balanced at approximately 42 percent each. The Slavs are located in compact settlements in the rich, industrialized north, abutting the border with Russia, and they are well organized, with experienced political action groups (the miners) and paramilitary formations (the Cossacks). They regard this region as their birthright and are determined neither to leave it nor to accept the status of second-class citizens. Militants amongst them have long been demanding secession in order either to form an autonomous Slav state or to seek unification with Russia. At present, the majority of Russians in Kazakhstan are prepared to accept the *status quo* since they are in a relatively strong position, having a significant degree of administrative autonomy within their own regions. Significantly, the President requires Slav support in order to safeguard his own position, which is increasingly under pressure from Kazakh extremists. The latter believe that more positive government action should be taken to improve conditions in the deprived rural areas, where the majority of Kazakhs are located. They also want a greater degree of "Kazakhification" of all aspects of public life. The President is trapped between Scylla and Charybdis: whichever path he chooses has inherent dangers.

The level of tension between the two communities fluctuates constantly, influenced by both domestic conditions and by external factors, primarily, of course, by the situation in Russia. The general mood is of deep uneasiness. Even the most sober Kazakhs are not excluding the outbreak of armed conflict, possibly within the next 5 years.[32] If this were to happen, it would most probably lead to the dismemberment of Kazakhstan. The Kazakhs have little with which they could defend themselves effectively—they do have nuclear missiles on their territory, but, apart from the fact that these would be of little use in such a conflict, they are guarded by Russian troops who also have operational control over them. The republic is in the process of establishing its own army, but this will be a long and expensive exercise; it is not likely to have a truly effective national military force for many years.[33] Moreover, there would inevitably be questions concerning the loyalties of a republican (i.e. multi-ethnic) army in conditions of a civil war of this nature. Equally, the Kazakhs could probably not count on much support from any of their CIS neighbors; on the contrary, some would undoubtedly be far from displeased to see Kazakh power diminished. Thus, if the Kazakhs wish to preserve their territorial integrity, they must act with extreme caution. Despite its enormous potential wealth, the future of this republic is possibly the most precarious.

Islam

The third perceived threat to domestic stability is the growing influence of Islam. Since the disintegration of the Soviet Union, Islam has come to play an increasingly prominent role in Central Asia. At the most basic level, it has come to signify, as it did in Tsarist times, a yardstick for differentiation between "them" and "us." Many Central Asians feel deeply betrayed by the way in which the Slav republics have treated them. They are determined now to stress the gulf that separates them, where previously they had preferred to emphasize their common Soviet culture. There is also a pride and excitement at rediscovering an important part of their heritage in Islam. To a considerable extent, this serves to fill the vacuum created by the evaporation of the Soviet ideological framework. Knowledge of the religion is still extremely low, but attendance at the Friday prayers and other such outward manifestations of Islamic piety became more prevalent during 1993-1994.[34]

At another level, Islam has become a political tool that those in power are seeking to appropriate in order to boost their nationalist credentials. Senior government figures are eager to display their respect for Islamic conventions. Thus, for example, the President of Uzbekistan has prohibited the inclusion of portraits on the national banknotes on the grounds that it is not fitting for a Muslim state to violate the Islamic prohibition against the depiction of the human form. The President of Kyrgyzstan has gone so far as to state that his republic should become "Islamic," which he apparently defines as showing greater respect for Islamic values. Islam has become so much a part of contemporary political discourse that even members of secular civil rights movements have resorted to justifying their positions in terms of "religious correctness." However, this has had unfortunate repercussions since it has enabled officialdom to claim that such groups are "fundamentalist" and should therefore be prevented from corrupting the public; as under Soviet rule, the present governments seek to establish a monopoly over Islam. This tendency is most pronounced in Uzbekistan, but similar situations are to be found in the other republics.

National and subnational rivalries have caused a further fragmentation of Islam. The unified Islamic administration that was created after World War II to serve the training and organizational needs of the five Central Asian republics has been almost completely dismantled. Each republic now has a national administration headed by a member of the main indigenous group. As under Soviet rule, but now replicated at the republican level, the official religious hierarchies are independent in name alone: in reality, they are government marionettes. This serves to discredit them in the eyes of some believers. It provides ample pretext for unofficial religious leaders to establish opposition camps. There is one formal Islamic party, the Islamic Revival Party, which was officially registered for a period in Tajikistan but not elsewhere. Apart from a few pockets of support, however, in the Ferghana Valley and Tajikistan, it does not have a wide following.

Muslim missionaries from countries such as Saudi Arabia, Libya, Pakistan, Bangladesh, Iran and Turkey are adding to the diversity and internal rivalries of contemporary Central Asian Islam.

The areas in which the Islamic revival is strongest are those in which economic deprivation is worst—the countryside and the poorer suburbs of the city. Here, unemployment is high, poverty endemic. The Soviet system held out the dream of a better future, but the dream was shattered before the promise was fulfilled. This has left a legacy of bitterness, anger, and an incipient anti-Western movement. Democracy is rejected as but another Western/imperialistic device to ensnare the unwary. Islam, by contrast, it is argued, offers genuine salvation. Such sentiments are strongest in the south in areas that were traditionally more orthodox. However, they are also beginning to appear in the north in Kazakhstan and Kyrgyzstan. Islam attracts them, not so much as a body of doctrine and precepts but as the voice of protest, and also of hope. Whether or not this trend continues will depend very much on how successfully the new governments are able to solve the economic problems of the region and to re-integrate these alienated sections of the population into a civil society.

CONCLUSION

The social and cultural changes that have taken place in Central Asia over the past 70 years are too deeply rooted to be undone. A high degree of modernization, Westernization, and secularization has been achieved in urban areas; although rural areas have been less affected, here, too, conditions have been raised to a level that compares favorably with that of most developing countries. However, beneath the surface, Central Asia has retained much of its societal conservatism. Traditional networks are still in place, power structures largely unaltered. Those in senior positions are treated with a deference so deep that it stifles free discussion and makes the implementation of new ideas and new working practices an exceptionally slow and difficult process. Would-be opposition parties find little popular support since criticism of established authority is regarded as *lese-majesty.*

The governments in all five republics are heavily dominated by former Communists. The Presidents of Uzbekistan, Kazakhstan, Turkmenistan, and Kyrgyzstan came to power under Soviet rule and are typical products of that system—shrewd pragmatists, jealous of their own power, skilled at survival.[35] In Tajikistan, the leading figures are newcomers as a result of the upheavals of 1992, but there has been little qualitative change there, too. The style of government throughout the region has become markedly more autocratic since the collapse of the Soviet Union. Potential political rivals are rapidly eliminated, mostly by bureaucratic measures, though occasionally there are rumors of untoward "accidents." Unless there are serious civil disturbances, the current leaders are likely to remain in power for some time to come. Even if individuals were to be displaced, however, there would probably be little change in the nature of government since there are as yet no organized opposition groups. Rivalries are of a personal rather than an ideological nature.

In the immediate future, the chief threat to stability is likely to arise out of deteriorating social, economic and environmental conditions. These create heightened tensions within the society which are readily translated into interethnic clashes. It is quite possible that over the coming years there will be sporadic outbreaks of violence. Some of these, especially where territorial disputes are involved, may well turn into ongoing, but relatively low intensity, local conflicts. Most probably, the incumbent governments will be able to contain such threats and thus prevent them from spreading. In such uncertain conditions, however, when weapons, drugs and dollars from a variety of sources are flooding into the region, there is always a possibility that what begins as a minor incident could well have far-reaching repercussions.

Of more serious long-term significance is the growing alienation and frustration becoming entrenched in the densely populated regions of the south, particularly in the Ferghana Valley. Here, deprivation, disillusionment, and anger, combined with the crudest forms of Islamic extremism, are creating a groundswell of opposition that in time could spread throughout the region. This would be a more difficult threat to combat. However, the experience of such countries as Algeria and Egypt have shown that it is by no means easy to dislodge an incumbent state government. An uneasy coexistence between the various factions is the most likely outcome in the foreseeable future.

This paper has tended to refer to "Central Asia" as though it were a unified bloc. This is a convenient generalization, but it should be treated with caution. Historically, there have always been marked differences among the various regions and ethnic groupings. Soviet rule had a superficially homogenizing effect, and today there are many points of similarity among these new states. They share the same flawed legacy and face common problems of re-adjustment and restructuring. From this point onwards, however, the inherent differences will undoubtedly come into sharper focus. Some of these will be the result of culturally determined factors, others, the result of their different locations, resources and regional infrastructures. Relations with expatriate communities abroad (e.g., with Uzbeks in Saudi Arabia), as well as the revival of cross-border ethnic links (e.g., with Turkmen in Iran, Tadzhiks in Afghanistan), will also have an effect on domestic affairs. Since independence, the idea of closer regional cooperation in Central Asia has not materialized. However, little of substance has yet emerged. Relations among these republics are still in the process of evolution. They have little experience as yet of working together since in the past most links were with Moscow, not with neighboring republics. Today, there are many areas in which regional collaboration is essential (e.g., water management). However, old rivalries are re-emerging, especially between the formerly nomadic peoples and the traditionally settled peoples (most notably, between Kazakhs and Uzbeks), and this is creating severe obstacles to closer cooperation. As of now, hopes for Central Asian unity appear to have slightly less chance of success than pan-Arab unity.

The outlook for the Central Asian republics is fraught with uncertainties; on balance, however, it is not wholly unpromising. These republics face severe problems, but they also have the advantage of rich human and material resources. The key to future prosperity undoubtedly lies in domestic stability; if this can be maintained, it will be possible to carry out the economic restructuring that is so urgently needed. It will also encourage foreign industrialists to invest in the region and assist in its development. There are undoubtedly several potential threats to the stability of the region, but it is probable that the state governments will succeed in containing them. There is little chance that these republics will opt for Western-style democracy, but, equally, it is not very probable that they will turn to Islamic fundamentalism. Strong, authoritarian rule is the most likely course, and, although it may not be very pleasant to live under, it will probably ensure the stability that could eventually lead to prosperity.

CODA

The purpose of this paper has been to explore the politics of national identities as they have evolved in the course of this century and the current implications for domestic stability. Today, Central Asia is in a state of flux; existing identities are being redefined, new aspirations being fashioned. Within the region itself, there are so many variables that it is difficult to predict with any degree of certainty the likely course of events. The situation is complicated still further, however, by the active involvement of a number of foreign powers. A discussion of these issues lies outside the present brief, but it must be borne in mind that no assessment of domestic stability in the region can be complete without a detailed analysis of what effect these external influences (which in themselves are not static) are likely to have.

A brief *tour de horizon* reveals that the chief player in the foreseeable future, as it has been for some four centuries past, will undoubtedly be Russia. The economies and the infrastructures of the former "center" and the republics on the periphery are still so tightly linked that it is unlikely that there will be any significant uncoupling in the near future. There are fears in Central Asia that Russia will try to re-assert direct control over the region. This at present does not seem to be very likely, but it is quite probable that Russia will influence Central Asian affairs from the sidelines or in limited peacemaking/peacekeeping operations. The question of the Russian minorities in Central Asia (numbering some 10 million) is a matter of serious concern to the government in Moscow, as it is also to Russian public opinion. If these minorities were felt to be under threat, it would almost certainly prompt the Russian government to take punitive action against the offending states. If and when the fate of these minorities is secured, however, it is likely that Russia's interest in the more remote reaches of Central Asia will be reduced. It is not inconceivable that Kyrgyzstan and Tajikistan could be abandoned eventually. Turkmenistan is already steering a more independent course and will probably continue to keep its distance from Moscow. Uzbekistan and Kazakhstan, on the other hand, are vital to Russia's strategic interests. The missile bases (which, while no longer housing Russian nuclear wepaons, could someday house a

Kazakh nuclear capability) in the latter make Russia's relations with Kazakhstan a matter of special concern. Close relations between Moscow and these two republics are likely to be maintained the longest.

Of the other regional powers, China is certainly the most powerful and the one that is likely to have the greatest influence on Kazakhstan and Kyrgyzstan. In the case of Kazakhstan, an alliance with China could be crucial as a protection against Russian aspirations for secession.[36] As for other near neighbors, India is seeking to develop low-profile but solid commercial and technical links with the republics. It is also keen to counter Pakistan's hopes of establishing a foothold in the region, and, moreover, it must keep a watchful eye on China's developing relationship with the new states. Pakistan, Iran, and Turkey all feel that they have historic and emotional links with Central Asia and that this will enable them to form a "special relationship." However, they are hampered by the fact that their economies are not strong enough to enable them to provide the republics with the level of assistance required (and expected). Afghanistan will undoubtedly continue to be a source of regional instability for many years to come. It could have a destabilizing effect on Tajikistan and possibly Uzbekistan as well, although to date its influence has been limited. If, on the contrary, peace is restored, Afghanistan could well be an important economic partner for these republics, particularly with respect to transport routes. Of the Middle Eastern countries, Saudi Arabia, with its considerable financial resources, and Israel, with its highly developed technological expertise, are likely to be most influential—illustrating very nicely the Central Asians' determination not to be drawn into any single ideological camp.

APPENDIX 1: Ethnic Composition of Republics
(1989 CENSUS)

Country	Numbers	Percentage of Total
Kazakhstan		
Total	16,464,464	100.0
Kazakhs	6,534,616	39.7
Russians	6,227,549	37.8
Germans	957,518	5.8
Ukrainians	896,240	5.4
Tatars	327,982	2.0
Uighurs	185,301	1.1
Koreans	103,315	0.6
Kyrgyzstan		
Total	4,257,755	100.0
Kyrgyz	2,229,663	52.4
Russians	916,558	21.5
Uzbeks	550,096	12.9
Tajikistan		
Total	5,092,603	100.0
Tadzhiks	3,172,420	62.3
Uzbeks	1,197,841	23.5
Russians	388,481	7.6
Turkmenistan		
Total	3,522,717	100.0
Turkmen	2,536,606	72.0

Russians	333,892	9.5
Uzbeks	317,333	9.0
Uzbekistan		
Total	19,810,077	100.0
Uzbeks	14,142,475	71.4
Russians	1,653,478	8.3
Tadzhiks	933,560	4.7
Kazakhs	808,227	4.1
Koreans	183,140	0.9

Source: *Vestnik statistiki:* Kazakhstan - no. 12, 1990, 70-73; Kyrgyzstan - no. 4, 1991, 76-78; Tajikistan - no. 5, 1991, 74-77; Turkmenistan - no. 6, 1991, 72-78; Uzbekistan - no. 11, 1990, 77-80.

APPENDIX 2: Main Central Asian Nationalities

a) Size of Population in USSR/CIS

	1970	1979	1989	% Growth
Kazakhstan	5,298,818	6,556,442	8,135,818	24.1
Kyrgyzstan	1,452,222	1,906,271	2,528,946	32.7
Tajikistan	2,135,883	2,897,697	4,215,372	45.5
Turkmenistan	1,525,284	2,027,913	2,728,965	34.6
Uzbekistan	9,195,093	12,455,978	16,697,825	34.1

Source: Census returns as recorded in *Itogi vsesoiuznaia perepisi naseleniia 1970 goda; Vestnik statistiki,* 1981; *Vestnik statistiki,* 1990.

b) Percentage of Nationality in Own Republic

	1926	1959	1989
Kazakhstan	93.6	77.0	80.3
Kyrgyzstan	86.7	86.4	88.2
Tajikistan	63.1	75.2	75.6
Turkmenistan	94.2	92.2	93.0
Uzbekistan	84.5	83.8	84.7

Source: *Vsesoiuznaia perepis'naselenia 17 dekabriia 1926 goda,* Moscow, 1929; and as above.

APPENDIX 3: Russian Population in Central Asia

	1926	1959	1979	1989	Increase/ Decline 1979-88
Kazakhstan	1,279,979	3,972,042	5,991,205	6,227,549	+ 236,344
% of total pop.	19.7	42.7	40.8	37.8	
Kyrgyzstan	116,436	623,562	911,703	916,558	+ 4,855
% of total pop.	11.8	30.2	25.9	21.5	
Tajikistan	5,638	262,611	395,089	388,481	- 6,608
% of total pop.	0.7	13.3	10.4	7.6	
Turkmenistan	75,357	262,701	349,170	333,892	-15,278
% of total pop.	7.7	17.3	12.6	9.5	
Uzbekistan	246,521	1,092,468	1,665,658	1,653,478	-12,180
% of total pop.	4.7	13.5	10.8	8.3	

Source: Census returns for 1926, 1959, 1979, and 1989.

NOTES

1.   In Russian usage, this area used to be referred to as *Srednyaya Aziya* ("Middle Asia"), which included Kyrgyzstan, Tajikistan, Turkmenistan and Uzbekistan; Kazakhstan was counted as a separate unit. In 1993, however, the Presidents of the five republics agreed to use the term *Tsentral' naya Aziya* ("Central Asia") for the whole region; formerly, this term had been used for the eastern-most areas of "Inner Asia," i.e., the territory which falls within Mongolia and China. The new usage appears to have been officially sanctioned at the meeting of the five Presidents in Tashkent in January 1993; see report in *Pravda*, 4 January 1993. For a historical survey of the term "Central Asia" and its geographic (and strategic implications) in English, see M. Yapp, "Tradition and Change in Central Asia," *Political and Economic Trends in Central Asia*, ed. S. Akiner, London, 1993, 1-10.

2.   There is already an extensive literature on this subject, most of it repetitive and uncritical. The best survey in English is by B. Z. Rumer, *Soviet Central Asia: "A Tragic Experiment,"* Boston, 1989.

3.   The newspaper of the Kazakh nationalist movement Azat has followed this issue in some detail. See, for example, the long and informative article "Dala taghdyry" ("Fate of the Steppes and Desert") by Rysbek Ibraev in *Azat*, no. 16 (42), 1992.

4.   The best study of this period (though by no means complete) is A. Nekrich, *The Punished Peoples: The Deportation and Tragic Fate of Soviet Minorities at the End of the Second World War* (New York, 1978).

5.   The term "tribe" is used here in a loose sense to refer to the cultural/social groupings of traditional society. These groupings were far from static and extended beyond purely genealogical ties.

6.   The Kazakhs were the first to come under Russian rule (1731-1824 for the Little and Middle Hordes, by 1846 for most of the Big Horde; the remainder of the Big Horde came under Ching rule). The conquest of the Khanates began with the fall of Tashkent in 1865; Bukhara and Khiva became protectorates in 1868 and 1873 respectively; Kokand was fully integrated into the Russian Empire in 1876. For an informed early account in English of the Russians' conquest of Central Asia, see M. Popowski, *The Rival Powers in Central Asia*, London, 1893, 32-50; for a more modern account, especially of the conquest of the Khanates, see D. MacKenzie, *The Lion of Tashkent: The Career of General M. G. Cherniaev*, University of Georgia, 1974, 34-66.

7.   See M. Brill Olcott, *The Kazakhs*, Stanford University Press, 1987, 104-118.

8.   The Karakalpak Autonomous Province was originally subordinated to the Kyrghyz/Kazakh ASSR, but elevated to the status of an ASSR and transferred to Uzbekistan in 1936; Gorno-Badakhshan Autonomous Province formed part of the Tadzhik ASSR/SSR.

9.   There is extensive literature on this subject. For a review of "Self-determination as Stratagem," see Walker Connor, *The National Question in Marxist-Leninist-Theory and Strategy*, 1984, especially 45-66; also G. Gleason, "Leninist Nationality Policy: Its Source and Style," in *Soviet Nationalities Policies*, ed. Henry R. Huttenbach, London, 1990, 7-23.

10.   See further, "Uzbekistan: Republic of Many Tongues," S. Akiner, in *Language Planning in the Soviet Union*, ed. M. Kirkwood, London, 1989, especially 100-103.

11. Fichte, Herder and Schlegel were particularly influential in formulating the theory that language defines the nation. On the emergence of linguistic nationalism in the 19th century, see E. J. Hobsbawm, *Nations and Nationalism since 1780: Program, Myth, Reality*, Cambridge, 1990, 102-111.

12. For example, part of the Hungry Steppe was transferred from the Kazakh SSR to the Uzbek SSR in 1963; many Kazakhs still regard this (and indeed, Tashkent itself) as part of their historic territory.

13. Bosworth Goldman, who travelled through Central Asia in the early 1930's, gave a vivid picture of the physical transformation that was then taking place in Tashkent: "The ugliness of the Russian invasion of the East wore me down as I walked through the tram-ridden streets until I became hypnotized by the myriad telegraph wires. Though the invasion dates from the last half of the nineteenth century, the public buildings are mainly in the style of a French provincial town. The Czarist rule cut deeply into the secretive lives of the native inhabitants, who hid behind the thick mud walls of the old town. The bolsheviks have widened the cut into a crater by razing the houses, which lays bare the sordidness hidden in the cool dark of the low rooms. Streets are driven through the heart of dwellings, destroying the winding charm of the old town. Communal flats rise sheer and stark from the dust; even the good proportions of modern building were unpleasant beside the reserved detachment they were displacing." *(Red Road Through Asia*, London, 1934, 176-177.) An excellent survey of the process of urban development in Uzbekistan is given by V. A. Nil'sen, *Sovremennago gradostroitel'stva Uzbekistane: XIX-nachalo XX vekov*, Tashkent, Gafur Gulyam, 1988. There are comparatively few historic cities in the other Central Asian republics, hence there the urban expansion of the Soviet period did not entail such a dramatic destruction of the built environment of the past.

14. On the contradictory nature of Soviet policies and assertions on this question, see W. Connor, *op. cit.*, 309-311.

15. Estimates for illiteracy among populations aged 15 years and above: Turkey 19.3 percent Egypt 37.1; Iran 46.0; Pakistan 65.2 *(Unesco Statistical Yearbook*, Paris, 1991).

16. Infant mortality rates (IMR) in the first year of life per 1,000 in 1989: Uzbekistan 37.6; Kazakhstan 25.8; Kyrgyzstan 32.2; Tajikistan 43.2; Turkmenistan 54.6 (*Vestnik statistiki*, no. 7, Moscow 1991). These are, of course, average rates; in some parts of a particular republic (e.g., in the vicinity of the Aral Sea), the rates are significantly higher. However, they are still lower than in many parts of the developing world. Cf IMR in: Turkey 74.0; Iran 61.0; Pakistan 108.0 *(The Economist Book of Vital World Statistics*, ed. M. Smith-Morris, London, 1990). It should be noted that there is a slight difference between Soviet and international definitions of IMR and that these statistics are therefore not wholly congruent. Nevertheless, even when allowances are made for a more favorable bias in Soviet statistics, the overall health picture in Central Asia is reasonably good, when compared with other countries with similar social and physical conditions.

17. The first plays in Uzbek and Kazakh, products of the reformist Dzhadid movement, appeared before the October Revolution; it was during the Soviet period, however, that the full-range of Western-style arts was introduced to the region. Practitioners and teachers from the European republics (predominantly Russian) established centers for training and performing these new art forms (orchestras, ballet companies, music, dance and art schools etc.) in the first couple of decades of Soviet rule. There was a similar drive to develop

Western-style sports. Within a generation or two, the Central Asian republics themselves were producing highly skilled artists and performers, some of international caliber. This highly proactive program of cultural assimilation was a very effective force for social integration.

18. G. Massell, *The Surrogate Proletariat*, Princeton, 1975, examines the politics of female emancipation in Central Asia.

19. Derek Scott, *Russian Political Institutions*, New York, 1961 (second ed.), presents a useful summary of the various aspects of "The Web of Management" that enveloped society (191-232).

20. To a greater or lesser extent, the "ideologization of identity" through the standardization of language and the creation of politically acceptable literatures and histories takes place in all developing societies. As Crawford Young points out, these brokers of culture, or "cultural entrepreneurs," are almost always associated with the rise of the middle class and the intelligentsia *(The Politics of Cultural Pluralism*, Wisconsin-London, 1976, p. 45). However, external bodies can also play a role, e.g., missionaries (cf *op. cit.,* 183-184, 228). What appears to be unique in Central Asia during the period of Sovietization is the scale of the operation.

21. Bodies such as the Academies of Sciences and the Unions of Composers, of Artists, of Writers, of Film-makers etc. possessed enormous powers of patronage. Special apartment blocks and numerous other facilities of a standard far superior to that which was available to the average citizen were set aside for their exclusive use.

22. B. Bouchet, "Tribus d'autrefois, Kolkhozes d'aujourd'hui," in *Des ethnies aux nations en Asie centrale*, La Calade, 1992, 55-69, has some interesting illustrations of this.

23. Central Asians not infrequently claimed to be both atheists and Muslims: these loyalties belonged to different spheres of activity and there was not felt to be any conflict between them. A similar situation is to be found amongst the Muslims of China.

24. See Bess Brown, "Political Developments in Central Asia: Some Aspects of the Restructuring Process in Turkmenistan, Kyrgyzstan and Kazakhstan in the Late 1980s," in *Political and Economic Trends in Central Asia*, ed. S. Akiner, London, 1993, 62-74.

25. Estimates of the number of people killed in the clashes between the Meskhetian Turks and Uzbeks range between 100-300; the lower figure seems to be the more likely. The incidents involving Uzbek and Kyrgyz appear to have been on a smaller scale, with fewer fatalities. However, reporting on both sides was highly partisan. Amateur video films, recording lurid scenes of brutality, were made and distributed by various factions—and denounced by their opponents as faked reconstructions. It is impossible to be certain about the details of these clashes; all that is clear is that they were extremely violent.

26. In the course of 1990, the First Party Secretaries of the Central Asian republics, starting with Islam Karimov of Uzbekistan, were transformed into Presidents following Mikhail Gorbachev's own example. Before the end of that year, Uzbekistan (20 June), Turkmenistan (23 August), Tajikistan (24 August), Kazakhstan (25 October) and Kyrgyzstan (12 December) had all made declarations of sovereignty. These were not, however, such radical steps as the terminology might imply. Similar declarations were made by Armenia and Azerbaijan. "Sovereignty" in the Central Asian republics seems to have been

interpreted as republican laws taking precedence over Union laws; political, economic and military independence was not envisaged.

27. Personal communication to the author by Abdurahim Pulatov in March 1991.

28. The author was travelling in Central Asia at the time, and in all five republics the respective declarations of independence were totally unexpected. In Kyrgyzstan and Tajikistan, even members of Parliament were taken by surprise. There were no signs of rejoicing on the streets or in private homes: it was not until the following year that "Independence Day" became an occasion for public celebration.

29. Kyrgyzstan launched its own national currency (the *som*) in May 1993. Turkmenistan followed suit (with the *manat*), but Uzbekistan, Kazakhstan and Tajikistan wanted to stay within the rouble zone. The Presidents of these republics signed an agreement to this effect with Russia at the CIS economic summit in Moscow on 7 September. However, Russia subsequently sought to impose even harsher fiscal and monetary conditions; Kazakhstan and Uzbekistan found these new demands unacceptable. The former launched its own currency on 15 November (the *tenge*) and Uzbekistan embarked on a transitional phase, preparatory to introducing its currency (the *sum*) in 1994. Tajikistan reached an agreement with Russia to retain the rouble. The value of the Kyrgyz *som* and the Kazakh *tenge* began to fall dramatically almost as soon as they had been introduced. There was also a chronic shortage of banknotes, which made even the simplest domestic transactions a problem.

30. The demographer V. Perevedentsev has calculated that in the near future, in Uzbekistan and Tajikistan, for every ten people who leave the ranks of the working age group, some 35 will enter it ("Evrazia," *Moskovskie novosti,* no. 41, 11 October 1992).

31. The Central Asian and Russian press carry frequent reports on this subject. Concern is currently focused on Badakhshan, where the civil war has almost totally destroyed the local economy. In this traditionally poverty-stricken area, the population now has few options other than to turn to the drug trade. There also appears to be a considerable through traffic of drugs from Afghanistan. The drugs are transported by lorry from Khorog down to Osh in Kyrgyzstan, and thence dispatched onwards to a variety of destinations. In the whole of 1992, Kyrgyz law enforcement operatives confiscated 3.5 kg. of smuggled opium; by September of 1993, they had already confiscated more than 70 kg. of contraband drugs (*Pravda,* 3 November, 1993).

32. In December 1993, when the author visited Kazakhstan, the "Russian question" was cited by many Kazakhs (including lawyers, journalists, academics, taxi drivers and students) as the chief threat to the future of the republic.

33. The decree to establish a National Guard was passed on 16 March 1992.

34. Nevertheless, Muslims from abroad who visit Central Asia today are constantly struck by the almost complete absence of any knowledge of even the most basic precepts of Islam amongst the local population.

35. President Akayev of Kyrgyzstan is sometimes singled out as the one leader who does not have a Communist Party background. In fact, in 1986, he, too, was holding a senior Party post. Apart from specific appointments, he, like the others, was formed in an environment in which at least superficial adherence to Communist ideology was a basic requirement for anyone with career aspirations.

36. A discussion of Chinese-Kazakh relations is beyond the scope of this paper, but it must not be forgotten that if the Russian threat to the integrity of Kazakhstan were to become a reality, it is probable that the only effective support which the Kazakhs would be likely to receive would be from the Chinese, ancient rivals of the Russians. Paradoxically, the Chinese are also seen to pose a major threat to Kazakhstan. Thus the Kazakhs must of necessity maintain a very careful balance in their relationship with their two huge neighbors.

2. The ROOTS of ISLAM in CENTRAL ASIA: A BRIEF PRIMER

Mehmet Saray

THE ROLE OF ISLAM IN CENTRAL ASIA

The Turks first adopted Islam when the Arab armies reached Talas in 751 A.D. Before Islam, Turks practiced the Göktengri religion. As a result of the similarities between the two religions, Turks began to convert to Islam in large numbers. The principles of the Qur'an provided a foundation which the Turks found attractive.

The first Muslim Turkish State, Karakhanates, was founded in 932 A.D. It was after this that an Islamic scholarly community began to form in Central Asia. These scholars of Islam had an effect not only on the Muslim Turks, but also on the other Muslim nations. Ahmet Yesevi and Imam-i Buhari were the most well-known Muslim scholars among this new group of intellectuals. It is worth examining the contribution of these two scholars. Yesevi was very successful in introducing the principles of Islam to the general population. He refrained from producing commentary on the principles of the Qur'an. Rather, his approach in explaining the principles of the Qur'an was attractive and compelling. As a result

---

Mehmet Saray is a lecturer in Russian and Eurasian Studies at Istanbul University and holds a post as Chief Advisor for Social, Education and Cultural Affairs at the Turkish International Cooperation Agency. The author of many scholarly works on Central Asian issues, Dr. Saray advises the Government of Turkey on Central Asian policy and has accompanied the President of Turkey on official delegations to the region.

of this, Yesevi became a notable figure among the Muslims. Subsequently, his friends and followers continued interpreting Islam to the others as Yesevi did. Because of the resounding successes of Yesevi, present Turkish and Kazakh authorities decided to establish a university named after Ahmet Yesevi in the city of Turkistan. Furthermore, the government of Turkey has given $15 million to restore Ahmet Yesevi's Mausoleum. As early as the late 1800s, Russian leaders understood the political potential of Vesevi's influence in establishing Islam in Central Asia. In 1876, the Russian General Skobelev, fearing the unifying role of Islam and of leaders like Vesevi amongst Muslim peoples against the invading Russians, ordered his artillerymen to destroy the Mausoleum of Ahmet Yesevi in order to contain any Islamic influence in the region. As a result of his artillery bombardment, the southwestern side of the Mausoleum was damaged heavily, damage still evident today.

The second great Islamic scholar of this period was Imami-i Buhari. Like Yesevi, Buhari was very successful in interpreting the principles of the Qur'an. Buhari collected the writings of the Prophet Mohammed and wrote a book on Islam entitled *Sahih-i Buhari*. By collecting and rewriting the original copies of the Prophet's works, Buhari established his reputation. Buhari's work remained one of the principal textbooks at the Islamic academies (the medresses) for centuries after his death. When the Russian armies moved into Central Asia in the second part of 19th century, the ideas of those two famous scholars were still embedded in the minds of Central Asian Muslims.

WHAT DID THE RUSSIANS KNOW ABOUT ISLAM?

Did the Russians understand the influence and power of Islam in Central Asia? What did they know about the Qur'an and the Prophet Mohammed?

Although the Russians were able to learn about the contents of the Qur'an by the beginning of the 18th century, Russia's real interest in Islam as a movement began in the 16th and 17th centuries when the Ottoman Empire emerged as the leader of the Islamic world. On the orders of Peter the Great, the Qur'an was translated from French into Russian by Peter Kosinov in 1716 and titled *The Law of Turks About Mohammed and al-Qur'an*. Peter the Great was suspicious about Islam and asked his friend Dimitri

Kantemir, the Moldavian King, to write a book on Islam in order to ridicule it. Kantemir completed his work, *The Book of System or the Position of Mohammed's Religion*, in 1711. The book contained false information and derogatory claims about both the Qur'an and Mohammed.

Russian studies on the Qur'an continued at the Academy of Oriental Studies, which was founded by Peter the Great but not completed until after his death in 1726. The Russian scholars at this academy translated the Qur'an from Arabic into Russian in 1790, only the second translation of the Qur'an into Russian. The title of the book was *Arabian Mohammed and His Book Qur'an*.

The University of Kazan, founded in 1804, attracted three Islamic scholars, Professor G. S. Sablukov, Professor Vladimir Solovyev and Professor Nikolai Ilminski. Prof. Sablukov translated the Qur'an from Arabic into Russian in 1878 while he was working as a lecturer. It is still considered to be one of the authoritative Russian translations of the Qur'an. However, Sabukov's work was constrained because of pressures from anti-Islamic forces. He was forced to produce two books critical of Islam: *Additions to the Translation of Qur'an* (1879) and *Information about Qur'an* (1884).

Professor Vladimir Solovyev, like Sablukov, was very successful in his early academic career. His research volume, *Mohammed: His life and Religious Orders*, was influential and caught the attention of academic circles in Russia. In his later years, however, he too was forced to write anti-Islam articles in which he attempted to prove that Islam was the religion of uncultured people.

The third and most effective Russian scholar on Islamic studies was Professor Nikolai Ilminski. Ilminski spent several years in Egypt studying the Qur'an. Because his knowledge about Islam was informed by the experience of living among Muslims, his work was more authoritative than that of his Russian contemporaries. Ultimately, however, like Sablukov and Solovyev, Ilminski used his knowledge in order to weaken Islam as a religious force. According to Ilminski, Islam was the main threat to the unity of the Orthodox Russian State. He did everything in his power and through his influence with K. P. Pobedonostsev, head of the Russian Orthodox Church, to thwart and oppress the Muslims culturally and politically. He also strived to raise the cultural level of the Orthodox Church and to bring the nominally Orthodox as well as "the defectors" into the fold.

At the end, Ilminski decided, with the help of the Ministry of Education, to take strict measures to eradicate the influence of Muslims through the Russian education system. His principal instrument was the "Kazan Baptized Tatar School" in which Orthodox Christianity and the Russian language were aggressively taught to Muslim students. The goal was to Russify and Christianize the Muslim people over a period of time. After achieving some initial success, Ilminski introduced Russo-Tatar, Russo-Kazakh, Russo-Kyrgyz, and Russo-Bashkir schools in Russian-occupied Muslim Turkic countries. At these schools Muslim children from age 6 to 18 were taught about Christianity and the Russian language. At the end of this training, the great majority of the students became converted to Christianity. However, Russia's forceful Russification and Christianization of Muslim children, provoked a negative reaction from Muslim intellectuals led by Ismail Beg Gasprinski. Gasprinski and his allies introduced a reform movement in modern and religious education by opening "Usul-i Cedid" schools throughout Turkic countries.

Gaprinski's formidable challenge weakened Ilminski's system. Some of the students in this system who attended Russo-Tatar schools abandoned Christianity and chose Islam. However, Ilminski's campaign did not stop. He began to use Turkic dialects (on local languages) as a tool to achieve his aims. This was a counter-challenge to Gasprinski's efforts to unify the many Turkic languages. When Gasprinski died in 1914 (Ilminski died in 1891), he had come close to achieving linguistic unity and the modernization of Islamic education among Turkic people.

Thirty-five years later, the Soviet authorities still relied mostly on Ilminski-trained cadres and expanded his work on national languages. At the same time, the Soviets asked the Turkic peoples to convert their Arabic alphabet into Latin. The conversion would sever the cultural association of Muslims with both Islam and Turkey. But, when Turkey accepted the Latin alphabet in 1928, the Soviets saw it as a danger to their program of diluting the influence of Islam. From 1937 to 1940 the Soviets forced the Turkic people to replace the Latin-based alphabet with Russian-based alphabets. Specially modified for each national language, these alphabets were remarkably similar to Ilminski's transcriptions. In 1938, contrary to the principles of the Communist Manifesto, Russian officially became a compulsory language for all Soviet citizens.

ISLAM UNDER THE SOVIET REGIME

The Soviets began to attack Islam as soon as the civil war was over. The Soviet attack was directed toward the basic Muslim institutions upon which Islam rested: the properties in *mainmort* (Waqfs) which guaranteed the clergy's economic power; the courts, both of the *adat* (customary law) and of the *Shari'at* (Quranic law), which enabled Islam to maintain its hold on the private life of the believers; and confessional instruction. The attack was simultaneous. The Waqfs, both public and private alike, whose revenues went to maintaining the mosques, religious schools, and hospitals, were abolished in the Muslim territories between 1925 and 1930. The first attempt was made in the Republic of Uzbekistan. By decree of the Uzbek SSR dated December 19, 1925, all waqfs situated outside towns, with the exception of orchards and vineyards, were expropriated by the People's Commissariat for Agriculture. Soon afterward the urban waqfs and those at mosques were commandeered. By 1930, the waqfs had for all intents and purposes been swept from the face of the Soviet Union. The Soviets then launched their second wave by abolishing the law of custom (adat) and the Quranic law (Shari'at), leaving the Muslims no alternative but to plead their cases at the Soviet Ministry of Justice as their only legal recourse. Soon after destroying the Islamic institutions in the Caucasus and Central Asia, the Soviets launched a new hostile campaign against Islamic customs. They had now destroyed the foundation of most Islamic life in the USSR.

In order to appreciate the extent of the damage done to Islam during the Soviet period, it is necessary to examine the components of the policy:

- The education of youth on the basis of Islam was forbidden.
- Islamic religious life (prayers, Ramadzan, Zekat, pilgrimages to Mecca) was forbidden by law.
- The publication of religious books was forbidden.
- Mosques and Madrasahs were closed, and the property of the waqfs was confiscated.
- Islamic spiritual leaders were arrested and many of them executed. Consequently, the Muslims were left without trained religious authorities.
- Muslim children were indoctrinated with anti-Islam materials as an integral part of the Soviet education policy.

In assessing the challenge to the Muslims of defending Islam, it should be emphasized that because of legal stipulations, and as a result of continually enforced anti-Islam measures by the Soviet government, Muslims were forced to defend Islam in a predominantly illegal manner and to perform their duties inconspicuously. Efforts by Soviet Muslims to save Islam took five paths:

Creed (Kalima-yi Shahadat)

The Muslims had no trained religious leaders at their disposal. Also, there was little Islamic religious writing from which Muslim youth could at least learn the meaning of Islam. Furthermore, there was no religious teaching amongst Muslims. In spite of this, Muslim elders tried to convey the fundamental principles of Islam, the Kalima-yi Shahadat, to Muslim youth. Family life was the focus of Islamic pedagogy. Children learned the Kalima-yi Shahadat and repeated it silently and constantly. Such teaching passed from one generation to another. This was seen as the preservation of Islamic tradition and as a sign of respect for the spirit of ancestors. Although the Creed (Kalima-yi Shahadat) was maintained among the Muslims, its influence diminished over time.

Prayer

Soviet law forbade prayer in mosques, and most were closed. Therefore, prayers were conducted privately and in secret. Even in the family, prayers were conducted only if the head of the family was an agent of the Communist Party. There were 24,321 mosques in Muslim portions of the USSR before the Soviets came to power. It is estimated that only 200 mosques remained open in the Soviet Union during the last several decades. Sometimes, the Soviet authorities allowed Muslims of the older generation to pray, but they had to pray silently.

Fasting

Although Soviet religious law did not mention Ramadzan, fasting was vigorously opposed by the Soviet authorities. Fasting hampered work and was, therefore, detrimental to the progress of Communism. Despite this, many Muslims fasted without drawing attention to themselves. Both the fasting festival and the sacrificial offerings donated by pilgrims were forbidden in the Soviet State; religious ceremonies were often held in closed circles. This custom also diminished in time.

The Zekat

The religious law of the Soviet Union also said nothing about the question of the Zekat. However, because of the living conditions under Communist regime, nobody was socially in a position to fulfill his obligation to the Zekat. Therefore, a regular contribution to the Zekat was almost banished from Muslim life.

Pilgrimages

Pilgrimages to the Holy City of Mecca were allowed by special permission and limited to only about 18 to 20 persons per year.

SOVIET PRACTICE TOWARD ISLAM

It is interesting to note that the Soviets practiced an intensive anti-Islam policy within the Soviet Union but encouraged a pro-Islam policy among non-Soviet Islamic countries. In the absence of opposition by the U.S. and its European allies, the Soviets easily intervened in and influenced Islamic politics. For years, the Soviets operated comfortably in Egypt, Ethiopia, Sudan, Somalia, South Yemen, Syria, Iraq, Libya and for a time in Indonesia. Soviet effectiveness and influence in Muslim countries caused great damage to Islam and to the interests of the Muslim world by undermining the cordial relations between Muslim and Western countries. The Soviets won friends or agents amongst Muslim priests and intellectuals. The Syrian, Egyptian and Libyan Muftis became defenders of Soviet policy. Some even claimed that the Muslims were free to attend their mosques and were able to conduct their religious ceremonies. In addition, the Soviets sent groups of carefully chosen people to be trained as muftis in Egypt, South Yemen, Syria, and Libya. They became tools in the hands of the Soviet authorities. The Soviet policy towards Islam continued in this manner until the rise of Mikhail Gorbachev. Gorbachev's *glasnost* and *perestroyka* policies opened new opportunities not only to the Muslims but also to the Christians of the Soviet Union. With the lifting of the Iron Curtain, the missionaries from Christian and Muslim countries began to pour into the Soviet Union. At the same time, missionary radio stations began to broadcast from European and Scandinavian countries, introducing religious teachings into the predominantly atheistic environment. Seeing this (predominantly) Christian campaign over the Soviet people, the Islamic organizations intensified their preparations for introducing Islamic propaganda into the Muslim populations of the USSR. Thus began a new rivalry centered in the Caucasus and Central Asia between Islam and Christianity over dividing the remains of the Soviet Empire.

ISLAMIC PROPAGANDA IN CAUCASIA AND CENTRAL ASIA AFTER THE COLLAPSE OF THE USSR

Caucasia

In the last years of the Soviet Union, the Caucasus became a target for Muslim countries, particularly Iran and Saudi Arabia. These two fundamentalist Muslim countries began to operate in Azerbaijan, Daghistan and the North Caucasus. Saudi activities became more pronounced in Daghistan and the Caucasus as the non-Shia Muslims were in the majority in these countries, while Iran focused on Azerbaijan, where the Shia predominated. Iran concentrated on Northern Azerbaijan for two reasons. First, some Azeris had been practicing Shiites, and the Iranian mullahs hoped to re-gain those Azeris for the Shia, which would also allow Iranian interference in Azerbaijan's internal affairs. Second, the Iranians wanted to maintain influence over the Azeris living in portions of Iranian Azerbaijan in order to prevent a split between Northern and Southern Azerbaijan. They have used two instruments to increase their influence in Northern Azerbaijan. One is money—the Iranians are spending hundreds of thousands of dollars in Azerbaijan on propaganda. Because of the weak position of the Russian ruble, the Iranian currency is more valuable among some of the Azeris. The second Iranian instrument is Allahshukur Pashazade. Mufti Pashazade has been in contact with Iranian authorities since 1985 and receives financial and political support from Tehran.

Saudi clerics travel to the Caucasus and invest there, but their influence in the area is limited. Turkey's influence in the region is limited due principally to a lack of capital.

Central Asia

The peoples of Central Asia have witnessed an interesting competition or rivalry between Muslim Countries in introducing Islam to this region. The Iranians, Saudis, Pakistanis, Aga Khan's Ismailis, and some Turkish groups are regular visitors to the republics of Central Asia. These groups target funds to the region and compete with one another in their interpretation of Islam.

Instability in Afghanistan (perpetuated by fighting among the mujahadeen groups) has created an opportunity for the Iranians, the Saudis and the Pakistanis to step into the vacuum created by the Russian withdrawal. The Afghan civil war has brought the Persian, Saudi and Pakistani religious groups into contact with Central Asian Muslims. Initially, these groups were able to send thousands of copies of the Qur'an and other Islamic reading (and modest amounts of funds) to the Central Asian republics.

The Saudis intensified their activities in Uzbekistan and were able to control a group of people through Mohammed Sadik, formerly the official and now the unofficial Mufti of Tashkent. Mohammed Sadik and a group of Turkistanis living in Saudi Arabia worked hard to obtain permission for religious activities in Uzbekistan. In addition to these unofficial religious Saudi groups, some official organizations like the Muslim World League and Islamic Bank for Economic Development began to provide funds for Islamic activities in Central Asia and Caucasia. Contrary to the principles of its establishment, the Islamic Bank provided $300,000 to each Central Asian republic for Islamic activities. The Saudis are transferring these dollars not only to encourage Islamic teaching, but also to propagate the Arab alphabet as well. This activity by the Saudis alarms Turkey and in the author's view should be resisted by the Central Asian republics. It is estimated that 70-75 percent of the people in each republic prefer to retain the Latin-based alphabet. Azerbaijan and Turkmenistan have already decided to adopt it. The Republic of Kyrgyzstan is changing its alphabet from Cyrillic to Latin, the authorities in Uzbekistan are very determined to change their alphabet to Latin in the near future, and the Kazakh authorities are willing to use the Latin alphabet as well as the Cyrillic.

With the permission of the Turkish Government I organized an official conference in Ankara in the second week of March 1993 on the common Turkish alphabet. Experts and official representatives of Kazakhstan, Turkmenistan, Kyrgyzstan,

Uzbekistan, Azerbaijan and Turkey participated in the conference. After long discussions, the participants of the conference accepted 34 letters of an alphabet to be used as a common alphabet by their countries. By this agreement, Azerbaijan and the Central Asian republics accepted the idea of ultimately converting to the Latin alphabet.

3. MOSCOW'S SECURITY PERSPECTIVE, the COMMONWEALTH, and INTERSTATE RELATIONS

RUSSIA and CENTRAL ASIA AFTER the SOVIET COLLAPSE

Eugene B. Rumer

No region of the USSR was less prepared to meet the challenge of independence and sovereignty in the wake of the Soviet breakup than Central Asia. The five Central Asian republics of the former Soviet Union—Kazakhstan, Uzbekistan, Turkmenistan, Kyrgyzstan, and Tadzhikistan—were jettisoned from the old empire in December 1991 almost against their will and without a clearly defined vision of their national interests or strategic direction, let alone plans as to how to proceed from independence toward true sovereignty. In many respects, Central Asia was no different from other ex-Soviet republics, including Russia, which lacked agreed-upon visions of national interest or strategies for domestic political and economic reforms and

Eugene Rumer is an analyst in the International Policy department at the RAND Corporation, where he has been the principal investigator on several studies examining the breakup of the Soviet Union and its implications for U.S. security interests. Dr. Rumer is the author of several RAND studies and has published articles in the *Christian Science Monitor*, and *The Wall Street Journal*, among other publications.

new foreign and security policies. Yet, the newly independent Central Asian states found themselves in a unique situation among the ex-Soviet republics, a situation stemming from the following factors:

- The lowest level of economic development in the former Soviet Union
- The cultural, political, religious and intellectual alienation from the giant Slavic and Christian Orthodox core of the old empire
- The widespread perception of Central Asia as a net drain on the rest of the Soviet economy
- The social and economic polarization of Central Asian societies.

These factors played a key role throughout the final years of the Soviet Union in the political struggle between the increasingly powerful centrifugal forces of national self-determination on the one hand, and the conservative-reactionary coalition in Moscow striving to preserve the Union at any cost on the other hand.

Although *glasnost, perestroika,* and the national reawakening that swept over the Soviet Union affected the domestic politics of the Central Asian republics, Central Asia as a block had remained the most pro-union oriented of all the Soviet republics. These nations provided Gorbachev and his unionist coalition with an important base of support in the course of the ill-fated "9+1" negotiations to save the federation in the spring and summer of 1991. No longer willing to submit to Moscow's economic and political dictate, Central Asia's political elites were nonetheless trying to hold on to the concept of a powerful union center and its economic re-distributive function which, in their view, would assure them the flow of much-needed subsidies. The union was also seen by local political elites as a guarantor of internal stability in the region because of the continuing presence of coercive instruments of the Soviet regime—the Army and the KGB.

The very reasons the political elites of Central Asia desired to preserve the union during that period were similar to that held by other republics who valued the connection with Russia. Yet many Russians questioned the value of union with less productive republics. Central Asia, as seen from Yeltsin's Moscow, was a drain on Little Russia's scarce economic resources, especially its water resources and its security, which were just beginning to return to normalcy after the Afghan adventure. Yeltsin's Russia was willing to continue relations with Central Asia, but only on conditions of mutual profitability. But it was certainly not willing to subsidize its economic development or risk the lives of its soldiers in local interethnic strife.

Prominent members of Russia's political and intellectual elite shared an unflattering chauvinistic view of Central Asia as unwashed, uncivilized and unable to tackle the challenge of independence and sovereignty, a burden that Russia should rid itself of. Russia's responsibility and interest in the region was seen by some of them as the "white man's burden" at best. Speaking at a seminar at the RAND Corporation in the Summer of 1990, the mayor of St. Petersburg, Anatoliy Sobchak, said: "I know those people, I used to live there. They understand only force and nothing else."

Others, not yet anticipating the breakup of the Soviet Union, talked about a common threat facing the "civilized" North from Southern Islamic states. The presence of that threat was reason enough to some of them for a partnership to be formed between the West and the Soviet Union. The latter's contribution to that partnership would consist of keeping an iron grip on Soviet Central Asia, thus helping in the common struggle against the tide of Islamic fundamentalism.[1]

As late as the spring of 1992, some prominent Russian academics and ideologues referred to Central Asia as Russia's "soft underbelly," finally jettisoned as a result of the dissolution of the Soviet Union.[2]

Certainly, the perception of Central Asia as an economic and security burden, as well as a culturally, religiously and politically alien territory, played an important role in its initial exclusion from the Commonwealth of Independent States signed by the leaders of Slavic and Christian Russia, Ukraine, and Belarus in December of 1991. While other republics had also not been invited to the negotiating table, none had expressed as strong a desire to preserve some form of common economic and political space as had the five reluctantly unattached and newly independent Central Asian states. Having joined the Commonwealth as a weak palliative to a union, Central Asia has pursued an all-azimuth search for a strategic direction, one consisting of attempts at strategic and economic independence, regional alliance schemes, a search for new patrons and continued close cooperation with Russia bilaterally and through the framework of the Commonwealth of Independent States.

Whereas there is little evidence that the general view of Central Asia from Moscow has changed significantly, Russia's new political and intellectual elites have displayed a much greater appreciation for its strategic and geo-political importance for their country's security and economic interests, as well as for their domestic politics. This change, arguably, is natural and should have been expected as the euphoria of victory after the August coup yielded to the realities of domestic political and economic transformation and post-Soviet settlement throughout the former USSR.

Rising from under the rubble of the Soviet empire, Russia for the first time in its modern history faced the question of its constitution and national interests outside its own empire. What is Russia without its empire? What are Russia's national interests? Russia's earnest search for answers to these questions coincided with major societal, economic and political upheavals triggered by the initiation of the Gaidar-Yeltsin reforms. These upheavals have demonstrated the uncertainty of Russia's post-Soviet choice. They have also given rise to the increasingly pronounced voices of neo-imperialism in Russian domestic politics which are advocating the preservation of "common economic space" throughout the former Soviet Union and the assertion of Russia's security interests throughout the territory of the ex-USSR.

Following the breakup of the union, there has emerged an almost reverse correlation between the mounting domestic political, economic and societal crises in Russia on the one hand and the growth of various neo-imperialist ambitions on the other hand, ranging from "enlightened" ambitions to outright neo-imperialism expressed in debates about Russia's security policy and interests.

Russia has yet to formulate a realistic strategy for the region commensurate with its means. In the present domestic upheaval in Russia, which is likely to continue well into the future, the chances for such a strategy appear slim. Russia's policy in Central Asia therefore promises to be hostage to its own unpredictable domestic political developments as well as to even less predictable and potentially less stable internal trends in the region.

RUSSIA: FROM "THE FAR ABROAD" TO "THE NEAR ABROAD"

Since the breakup of the Soviet Union, Russian policy toward Central Asia has largely been a reflection of the entire spectrum of Russia's domestic and external policies and political trends. The launching of the Gaidar economic reforms in Russia, done largely without consultation with the other republics to which its economy was so closely tied and on which the reforms were bound to have a profound impact, clearly was a snub to the leaders of the non-Slavic republics, including those in Central Asia who were not initially invited to sign the Commonwealth Declaration. Russia was asserting its independence in economic policy matters—the rest of the ex-Soviet republics could either follow or not.

Russia's ambitious pursuit of its independence and its apparent eagerness to shed its Soviet baggage was demonstrated equally in the boldness of the Gaidar plan of "shock therapy" reforms and in its quest for a new alliance with the West as the central strategic direction of Russia's foreign and security policy. The newly-independent former Soviet republics were relegated to a second tier of policy issues. Among them, Central Asia mattered even less than most. Unlike Ukraine or Belarus, its geography was irrelevant from the standpoint of close relations with the West. Intellectually and culturally, it was part of the East. Russia was seeking to establish itself as part of the West and define its interest in a close partnership with it.

The preponderance of the Euro-Atlanticist direction in Russia's foreign and security policy proved to be as short-lived as the euphoria surrounding Gaidar's reforms. As economic difficulties mounted and the consequences of economic reforms posed opportune grounds for political mobilization by the opponents of the Gaidar government, the latter's policies across the entire spectrum of foreign and domestic issues came under assault. This assault was mounted by a broad coalition consisting of a powerful lobby of industrialists; a second tier of the old *nomenclatura* and ex-Communists still occupying powerful positions throughout the country and in its legislature; right-wing xenophobic Russian nationalists; and a new circle of advocates of "great power policies" for Russia from the ranks of the democratic coalition. The first two categories mobilized in defense of their economic and political interests threatened by the Gaidar reform plans; the third never reconciled itself to the loss of the empire and the political victory of the democratic pro-Western coalition in Russia; the fourth awakened to the challenge of post-imperialism and reconstruction after its political victory over the old imperial center.

Their criticism of the Yeltsin-Gaidar agenda was made all the more possible by the declining economy, the specter of mass social dislocation as a result of further reforms, and the perceptible shortcomings of the policies pursued by the new Russian government. The same economic and political factors have contributed to an active internal Russian debate about national interests, which intensified as the victory of the "Euro-Atlanticist" pro-Western course appeared all the more tenuous amidst mounting economic and political difficulties.

The Russian foreign ministry under the leadership of Andrey Kozyrev was singled out in the course of this assault. Its policy was criticized for the following shortcomings:

- The neglect of Russia's great power status in pursuit of the "Euro-Atlanticist" course
- The neglect of Russian national interest in the "near abroad"
- The neglect of interests of Russian nationals left in the near abroad.

Kozyrev's Euro-Atlanticist strategic orientation came under particularly heavy fire because Russia, according to Kozyrev's detractors, was also an Asian power whose interests lay at least as much in Asia as in Europe, and as much in the "near abroad" as in the real, or "far abroad."[3] The critics of Foreign Minister Kozyrev and Prime Minister Gaidar have accused them of betraying Russia's interests and traditions in both Europe and Asia in exchange for promises of Western economic assistance. Gaidar and Kozyrev, it has been argued, were reducing Russia to subservience to the West and abandoning its strategic interests and spheres of influence to potentially hostile powers. The resulting vacuum, it has been claimed, will be filled by opposing forces hostile to Russia's interests.[4] Under the leadership of Gaidar and Kozyrev, it has been charged that Russia is about to trade its great power status for Western aid and slip into the category of second-rate players on the Eurasian scene.

The alternative to Gaidar's and Kozyrev's Euro-Atlanticist course urged by their critics is the "near abroad"—the "Eurasianist" school. In the critics' view, it is the locus of Russia's traditional interests and natural sphere of influence. The refocusing of Russian foreign policy on the "near abroad" has been advocated by a broad spectrum of political actors, ranging from democrats like Yeltsin's former advisor, Galina Starovoytova, to "enlightened post-imperialists" like parliamentary Foreign Affairs Committee Chairman Yevgeniy Ambartsumov, State Councilor Sergey Stankevich, the presumably centrist Civic union, as well as the notorious "red-brown" coalition.

Calls for the reorientation of Russian foreign and security policy from the "Euro-Atlanticist" direction to the "near abroad" coincided with the first assault on the Gaidar economic reform program on the domestic front, particularly its shock therapy component, which began as early as the spring of 1992. A combination of political, economic and security trends combined to bring about a perceptible shift in Russian foreign policy, which marked the beginning of Russian policy toward the "near abroad."

On Russia's domestic front, this development was the result of:

- The mobilization of the industrialist lobby in opposition to Gaidar's economic program and in defense of their vital interests—preservation of the predominant position of heavy industries in Russia's economy and restoration of the damaged economic links throughout the post-Soviet economy
- The nationalization of Russia's defense and security policy
- Early disillusionment with post-Soviet realities and a search for new platforms for domestic political mobilization.

The hallmarks of the political and policy trends in the spring of 1992 were the appointment of representatives of the industrialist lobby to key posts in the Gaidar cabinet; the establishment of Russia's own—separate from the Commonwealth—Defense Ministry and the drafting of Russia's own military doctrine; the signing by Russia of important Commonwealth and bilateral security documents; and the beginning of a consensus among Russian foreign policy experts and political analysts on a new vision of Russian national interests, distinct and different from the unabashedly "Euro-Atlanticist" vision of Kozyrev and Gaidar.

Amidst widespread predictions of the Commonwealth's imminent demise, these developments served not so much as to make the Commonwealth a more important vehicle for post-Soviet cooperation in economic and security spheres, as to make it clear that Russia's divorce from its empire would not be as quick as it seemed in the months prior to the dissolution of the Soviet Union. Furthermore, these developments also demonstrated that while the Commonwealth agreement indeed would be likely to play a significant political, legal and psychological role, Russian policy would be driven primarily by uncertain visions of national interests. The events of the spring of 1992 also drew the dividing line between the centrifugal and centripetal groupings among the Commonwealth participants. None were more firmly committed to the latter camp than the five Central Asian states.

CENTRAL ASIA: BACK TO RUSSIA

The Central Asian states' commitment to the Commonwealth and to cooperation with Russia is the result of their colonial legacy as well as contemporary political, economic and security factors both external and internal to the region. Central Asia emerged from Soviet/Russian domination badly in need of an external stabilizing presence. Impoverishment, societal divisions, and the sad and skewed economic development which was a legacy of the Soviet regime were among the few common features shared by them. In most other respects, the dividing lines crisscrossing the region and its societies outnumbered common interests and the will to tackle common challenges together. The veneer of common culture, religion and language was just that—beneath it ran inter-ethnic tensions, territorial disputes, clan and tribal rivalries and internal societal divisions. Moreover, in the spring of 1992, the list of challenges to the region's stability and security was augmented by the specter of de-stabilization from outside the political boundaries of the region—from Afghanistan—as factional rivalries following the collapse of Najibulla's regime threatened to spill over into once Soviet Central Asia.

Central Asian political elites underwent a brief period of post-independence euphoria, seeking to establish their strategic independence from Russia, to perhaps form their own regional political and security alliance and to find new partners and/or patrons elsewhere. Romantic visions of a Greater Turkestan, pan-Turkic association and partnership with or patronage of the great powers of the Middle East, the Persian Gulf and South Asia, clashed with harsh post-Soviet realities in the region. Apparently, no feasible amount of economic assistance promised by Turkey and Saudi Arabia could replace Russia's stabilizing presence in the region.

Moreover, while Central Asia's opening to the outside world promised the benefits of much-needed economic assistance, it also brought with it the unwelcome challenge of political and ideological pluralism—anathema to Central Asia's political elites which, in the words of Russian officials, remained "semi-feudal, semi-Communist."[5] The collapse of the Soviet Union revealed profound cleavages in Central Asia's societies, paradoxically strengthening important centripetal[6] forces within them.

These cleavages resulted not only from a cultural alienation between indigenous populations and millions of ethnic Russians residing in the region who have long played a pivotal role in Central Asia's economy, but also from the fact that the region's political and cultural elites had become heavily Russified and Westernized during the decades and centuries of Soviet and Russian domination. There has emerged in Central Asia a collusion of interests between the old Communist *nomenklatura*, long-dependent on Moscow for regional security and stability, and the national intelligentsia, who have extensive ties to Russia and support a policy of continuing close relations.

The formation of this de facto coalition demonstrated a profound, perhaps significant split in Central Asian societies—that between the relatively small Russified, Westernized, and secularized national political and cultural elites and the impoverished, poorly educated masses, still very much under the influence of Islam as a cultural presence and vulnerable to its penetration in the region as a political force.[7]

To the entrenched political elite, the growth of Islam as a political force would mean the end of their predominant position of power. To the intelligentsia and cultural and academic elite, it would mean a radical change of ideology (perhaps even more pervasive than the old Communist ideology), and the abandonment of cultural values and artistic freedoms they have been able to enjoy to a limited degree even before, and especially during, *perestroika*. To the average urban dwellers—Central Asia's quasi-middle class—it would also mean a fundamental departure from their way of life with its widely shared values of a consumer society.

On the other side of the Islamic divide are the masses—the uneducated poor in rural areas where Islam has always been more resilient, even during the worst years of Soviet oppression; the urban poor; the unemployed young who cannot find work in cities or in the countryside; and a segment of nationalist Islamic fundamentalist intelligentsia, including a growing number of clerics. The rural population in Central Asia on average amounts to 60 percent of the total population in the region.

In most Central Asian countries there are few overt signs of political mobilization among these segments of the population on the basis of Islam or any other ideological current for that matter. But the economic and social conditions in the countryside create a fertile environment for the dissemination of Islam and its transformation from a religious dogma into a political ideology—the answer to all ills that have plagued those societies.

In the eyes of Central Asian elites, Russia remains the only actor potentially capable of maintaining the existing degree of stability in the region. Central Asia's newly independent states are not yet capable of securing themselves, nor is any other potential patron of the region likely to play that role. To the contrary, in the view of the local political elites the opening of Central Asia to the world is likely to result in the erosion of their own political position. Closer ties to the great powers of the Persian Gulf—Iran or Saudi Arabia—would be likely to strengthen the presence of Islam as a social and/or political force, hardly a desirable outcome and a dubious price to pay for economic assistance. A further rapprochement with Turkey, on the other hand, also carries its price of potential, albeit likely to be very limited, political liberalization and exposure to more pluralistic models of political development.

The importance of Russia to the region as a stabilizing actor and the lack of alternatives to it are highlighted by the position of two regional superpowers—Kazakhstan and Uzbekistan—as consumers of security vis-a-vis Russia. Each has a unique role in and claim on the leadership in the region. Each has an equally unique and significant dependency on Russia.

For Kazakhstan, with its minority Kazakh population, its Russian and/or Russified majority, as well as extensive common border with the Russian Federation, good relations with Russia constitute the most basic precondition for its territorial integrity and survival as a state. For Uzbekistan, with its sizable—by some accounts two million or more—Tadzhik population and common border with civil war-torn Tadzhikistan and Afghanistan, Russia's military presence in the region is a crucial requirement for domestic stability.

The Commonwealth Agreement, for all its shortcomings and despite the many dire predictions of its imminent demise, is a document of unmatched political and legal significance for Central Asia. Not only did it legitimize at the time of its signing the region's ties to Russia and secure Russian military presence, but it committed its signatories to mutual respect for territorial integrity and the inviolability of the existing boundaries. Given Central Asia's arbitrarily drawn borders and scarcity of land resources, the significance of this factor cannot be overestimated.

Central Asia's search for security anchors and patrons outside the Commonwealth following the breakup of the Soviet Union was brief. The fall of Najibulla's regime in Afghanistan and the escalation of internal tensions in Tadzhikistan, both of which occurred in April of 1992, drove home the necessity to look to the North for security guarantees.

The Commonwealth summit meeting in Tashkent in May 1992 became the pivotal event in the Commonwealth of Independent States' (CIS) saga and Central Asia's efforts to restore weakened ties to Russia. It reaffirmed both Central Asia's strategic orientation to Russia and the Commonwealth and Russia's commitment to play an important role in the region. It also highlighted the trend toward the nationalization of Russia's security policy because Russia, rather than the CIS, became the guarantor of security in Central Asia.

Preceded by widespread speculation about the demise of the CIS as a result of the anticipated withdrawal of the Central Asian countries, the Tashkent summit proved the opposite. Central Asia was in the Commonwealth to stay. The Commonwealth of Independent States' collective security agreement signed in Tashkent by Russia and the majority of Central Asian states addressed the wish of Central Asia's leaders expressed candidly by Uzbek president Islam Karimov: "Russia must become the guarantor of security in the region."[8] The agreement established Central Asia's states as consumers of security and Russia as the provider of it.

RUSSIA'S INTEREST IN CENTRAL ASIA

Notwithstanding the widespread Russian image of Central Asia as a poor and backward region as well as a potential drain on Russia's meager resources, Russia's interests in Central Asia are easy to define. First among them is the presence of some 10 million

Russian compatriots relegated to the status of a "white minority" in former colonies, alien to them in terms of culture, language and religion. Their well-being and security constitutes an important domestic political issue for the Russian government. The Yeltsin government has frequently been charged with betraying Russian national interests and compatriots in the "near abroad." A large-scale exodus of Russians from Central Asia would undoubtedly create a huge political and economic problem for the Russian government and its economy, already straining under the weight of other challenges.

Despite the perception of impoverishment in Central Asia, Russia's economic interests in the region should not be underestimated. Grain from Kazakhstan; cotton, a monopoly Central Asia had in the former Soviet Union (a dubious advantage for the region in the current economic environment); a variety of ferrous and non-ferrous metals; natural gas; gas pipelines from Iran; as well as a variety of intermediate products and manufactured goods all make Central Asia an important commercial partner for Russia in a time when trade links throughout the former Soviet economy have been disrupted and industrial production is suffering from a host of other factors.

From an economic and political point of view, Kazakhstan is perhaps the single most important Central Asian state for Russia. Traditionally not included in the geographic category of Central Asia by Soviet economists and geographers, it has been combined with the other four southern states as a result of political developments. Kazakhstan's position is unique in Central Asia for the following reasons:

- It is the only Central Asian state bordering on Russia
- Its titular nationality accounts for less than half of the country's population
- Its Russian population is reported to be in excess of 6 million, largely segregated from the Kazakh population
- Large tracts of its territory are considered historically by many in Russia as traditional Russian lands
- It is home to significant ex-Soviet defense-industrial facilities, including the space launch complex and nuclear weapons testing facilities
- Ex-Soviet nuclear weapons were deployed on its territory

- Its vast agricultural areas developed during the "Virgin Lands" campaign in the 1950s are of strategic importance for grain-hungry Russia.

The internal de-stabilization of Kazakhstan is likely to entail inter-ethnic conflicts between ethnic Kazakhs and Russians and would pose a severe political, security and economic challenge to the Russian government. It would have few choices other than to intervene, as both a measure to protect expatriate Russians and to extinguish a potentially major regional conflict at its doorstep, in lands still considered by many Russians to be traditionally Russian.

Russia's security interests in Central Asia are not limited to neighboring Kazakhstan only. Discussions about Russia's national interests have rather quickly—in just a few months—produced a consensus among those concerned with the question. While many of the positions expressed in the course of these discussions have differed significantly in tone and ambition, their essence has been largely the same: Russia has always been a great power with a large sphere of influence and will remain one; and it will continue to actively pursue its interests throughout the territory of the former Soviet Union as a right or as a responsibility, a cross" laid on its shoulders by history and geography.[9] This great power vision has firmly supplanted the isolationist and retreatist mood that dominated the early post-Soviet consensus with respect to Russia's policy toward the "near abroad."

From the standpoint of Russia defined as a great power, its withdrawal from Central Asia would be inconceivable and would violate the most basic and general Russian security concerns. Russia's withdrawal from Central Asia would create a geopolitical vacuum in the region, which would then become vulnerable to penetration by, susceptible to, and the influence of hostile or potentially hostile outside powers (their competition for influence in Central Asia) as well as ideological movements hostile to Russia.[10]

Chief among these ideological movements is Islamic fundamentalism. Although the majority of responsible Russian analysts recognize that Islamic fundamentalism remains merely a specter of a powerful political force on the Central Asian scene, its potential for growth is perceived in Russia as significant. The authoritative report of the Committee for Foreign and Defense Policy, published on the first anniversary of the August 1991, coup noted, "(The threat of spread of Islamic fundamentalism in Central Asia) is evidently exaggerated. Central Asian peoples are predominantly Sunni rather than Shiia muslims."[11]

Nonetheless, Russian specialists on Islam are prone to emphasize that Islam in general, not just its fundamentalist branch, is a religion which is much more active politically in the life of societies where it predominates. Furthermore, they are fond of noting that despite the relatively small likelihood of Islamic revolutions in Central Asia, the influence of fundamentalist ideas is growing in the region. On the whole, Russian analysts tend to be rather sanguine about the short-term prospects of Islamic fundamentalism in Central Asia and its potential challenge to the region's stability and Russia's security. Most, however, emphasize the importance of Russia's continuing presence in the region as a guarantee of continuity and stability, as well as a preventive measure against the spread of hostile forces and influences.[12]

Russia's interest in controlling the spread of Islamic fundamentalism and the role of Islam in the political and social life of Central Asia has yet another—distinctly applicable to Russia—dimension. Russia's own Muslim population is estimated at more than 10 million. As the dominant religion among ethnic groups not limited to Russia's geographic periphery, the future of Islam in Russia cannot be relegated to the periphery of the domestic political and policy agenda of the country.

Russia's Muslims have experienced their own Islamic renaissance, much like other religious and ethnic groups in the former Soviet Union. Hundreds of students from Russia have been sent to study Islam in Egypt and other Islamic countries. This, however, has prompted calls for the establishment of Islamic teaching institutions in Russia, where their number and quality of instruction have been deemed inadequate by the leaders of the Muslim community.[13] They have complained about the preferential treatment accorded by the Russian government to the Russian Orthodox Church and the lack of attention to the needs of the Muslim community. The proposed remedy would lead to the establishment of a Ministry for the Affairs of Islam of the Russian Federation.[14] While Russian analysts acknowledge the low likelihood of these demands being translated into the rise of Islamic fundamentalism in Russia proper, they have expressed concerns about the growth of influence and popularity of Islamic parties in Russia's Islamic regions—Tatarstan, Chechnya, and

Dagestan.[15] They acknowledge that ethnic and regional factors play a far more important role than religious ones as the basis for political mobilization, but emphasize the latter's latent potential and its challenge to Russia's internal security and territorial integrity.[16]

Few mainstream Russia analysts have concrete policy prescriptions for dealing with the specter of a politically active Islam at home. The range of advice is limited to the politically correct recommendations of respect for and better understanding of this alien religion and culture. Nonetheless, many acknowledge that the growth of a politically active Islam in Central Asia would reverberate negatively among Russia's Islamic population. Hence, most focus their prescriptions on the external containment of this long-term challenge to Russia's security.[17]

This assessment and the overall policy prescriptions coming from Russian security analysts and students of Central Asia and Islam conform to the largely nonspecific perceptions the Russian specialists have of security challenges to Russia in Central Asia in the short-term among Russian specialists. When looking at Central Asia, most Russian mainstream strategic thinkers recognize its importance and the need for a Russian presence there, but they avoid articulating visions of specific threats to Russia's security interests. In the words of the Committee on Foreign and Defense Policy:

> Challenges to Russia from the south are not concrete and do not pose an immediate challenge to (its) security; they are dispersed and diffused. Their military-political containment should be executed through flexible application of force, capable of supporting diplomacy through the conduct of policing operations intended to separate (the conflicting factions) and peacekeeping operations, preferably coordinated in the framework of the general Euro-Atlantic community.[18]

Other prescriptions for Russian policy toward Central Asia recommended by the analytic community are merely a subset of the general recipe for greater economic and political integration within the framework of strengthening the CIS. Pursuit of confederation if often espoused by the proponents of Russia's new post-imperial course.[19]

RUSSIA'S POLICY IN CENTRAL ASIA: PRESENT AND FUTURE

Russia's policy in Central Asia has generally followed the prescriptions of academic and security specialists. Although it may be premature at this point to describe Russia's policy in the region as a pursuit of a certain strategy, their actions have been consistent with the general goal of maintaining the status quo in the region and supporting the existing regimes and boundaries. This policy has been most clearly demonstrated with respect to the civil war in Tadzhikistan. Russia has committed itself to the task of securing Tadzhikistan's border with Afghanistan. While Russia did not play an active role in the defeat of Tadzhikistan's so-called Islamic-Democratic coalition, Uzbekistan did play a crucial role.[20] Moscow in effect chose to look the other way and ignore the brutal war and Uzbekistan's participation in the conflict, which led to the restoration of the old Communist government in Tadzhikistan. Since then, Moscow has evidently chosen to support that government.[21]

"Too bad" has been the reaction of some Russian analysts, in effect arguing that stability in the region is more important than democracy.[22] Others have reacted with indignation, but they have elicited little response from the Russian government.[23]

Russia has also undertaken to normalize the situation in Afghanistan, a source of instability in the region which has threatened to spill over into Central Asia. As a containment measure, Foreign Minister Kozyrev has sought to establish closer ties with Pakistan as a power with immediate interests in and influence on Afghanistan.[24]

Iran—another important player in the region—has also been courted by Foreign Minister Kozyrev. During a visit to Tehran in April 1993, Kozyrev received assurances that Iran would not support Tadzhik refugee opposition groups in Afghanistan.[25] While the latter commitment has come into question in the Russian media, it is important to recognize that Tadzhikistan is only one issue in the broader context of Russian-Iranian relations, where common interests have prevailed with respect to the sale of Russian weapons to Iran. It remains to be seen whether or not Russia and Iran are prepared to play the carrot-and-stick game against each other and connect the two issues in the broader agenda of their relations.

Notwithstanding the general activist approach of Russian diplomacy in and around Central Asia, the future of Russia's commitment to the region remains in question, as does the region's commitment to Russia. Central to this uncertainty are the domestic political and economic situations of all the parties involved.

Russia's renewed commitment to the region has emerged amidst accelerating economic and political crises which have endangered not only the country's domestic political peace and international position, but its territorial integrity and survival as a unitary state. Thus, Russia's emergence from its brief isolationist phase and its return to great power ambitions have occurred precisely at the time when the prospects of it crumbling from within have become more plausible than ever.

The domestic political and economic environments of the Central Asian states are equally uncertain. As their economies continue to deteriorate and their societies remain polarized, prospects for maintaining social peace grow bleaker. The ability of local elites to maintain social peace and stability will remain questionable at best unless their economies improve, an equally questionable outcome.

Amidst deteriorating socioeconomic conditions, the need for external actors to take on the role of stabilizing the region is likely to grow. Will Russia be able and/or willing to play such a role? It has taken it upon itself to play that role, but its ability to do so is highly questionable. Factors discussed earlier have encouraged many Russians to argue that Moscow should adopt the stance of hegemonic great power rather than as partner. Even in a Central Asia ruled by Russian-oriented national elites, Russia's great power ambitions hardly make a solid foundation for a lasting and mutually beneficial partnership.

IMPLICATIONS FOR U.S. POLICY

Both the air of uncertainty and instability and Russia's position in and policy toward the region pose serious challenges for U.S. policy toward the five Central Asian states. While the basic goals of that policy include support for free-market reforms and progress toward some form of political pluralism, far more important goals in the short run are to avoid further bloodshed and de-stabilization in the region.

It is obvious to most observers in and outside of Central Asia that the five newly independent states are not capable of guaranteeing their own security and stability. They are caught up in a vicious circle where political reforms cannot be undertaken in light of their economic weakness, and economic reforms cannot be carried out because the socioeconomic price necessary will be deadly to the fragile political regimes. The region is crying out for an external stabilizing presence and economic support.

This situation calls for caution and realism in the conduct of U.S. policy toward the region. Caution is required so as to not upset the fragile political balance in the region. Realism is required because however the existing regimes in Central Asia may differ from the norms of political pluralism and the principles of the Universal Human Rights declaration, they may be the only viable alternative to further chaos and bloodshed in the region for a considerable time to come.

Another reason to be realistic about the limits of U.S. policy and influence in Central Asia is that no matter how objectionable the U.S. may find Russia's policy in the region—especially if Russia pursues the hegemonic ambitions of some of its more nationalist politicians—the region is not likely to occupy a prominent place on the U.S. foreign policy agenda. The Yugoslav crisis has demonstrated the lack of U.S. and European political support for long-term and large-scale involvement in the name of upholding an uncertain peace in faraway regions. If any power is going to sustain a long-term stabilizing presence in the region, it will be Russia. There are no alternatives to its presence there, which is also welcome by the existing political regimes.

Realism in U.S. policy toward Central Asia does not have to mean that the region is to be removed from the U.S. foreign policy agenda. The United States has a number of options available of pursuing its general goals of improving the stability and security of Central Asia and encouraging its transition to a more open political system and market-oriented economy.

Economic assistance to Central Asia is a key instrument in the arsenal of U.S. foreign policy that would meet the constraints of realism; recognize the fact that Russia is likely to remain the principal stabilizing presence in the region; help stabilize it; and assist its political-economic transformation.

Given the fiscal constraints on U.S. foreign aid programs, U.S. assistance to Central Asia is likely to be limited. However, the region's underdeveloped economy, poverty, and weak socioeconomic infrastructure offer rich targets of opportunity that promise appreciable payoffs even from limited investments. Projects in the areas of primary health care delivery, the improvement of sanitary conditions, water conservation and irrigation appear to be most promising from the standpoint of improving the quality of life for vast sectors of the rural and urban population. Such projects can be undertaken in collaboration with international aid organizations and friendly regional powers, taking advantage of considerable local technical expertise and abundant and inexpensive labor in the region.

If successful, this approach would help alleviate some of the underlying causes of social instability in the region, thus creating healthier conditions for political and economic transformation. It would not undermine Russia's position in Central Asia, thus threatening to de-stabilize the region further. And it would permit U.S. foreign policy toward the former Soviet Union to avoid the appearance of Russo-centricity and recognize Moscow's legitimate interests there, but not neglect a region whose geopolitical significance in the post-Cold War world is likely to increase in the years to come.

NOTES

1. Interviews, Moscow & Leningrad, 1990 & 1991.
2. Discussion at the Gorbachev Foundation, Moscow, May 12, 1992.
3. The term "near abroad" refers, quite condescendingly, to the former Soviet republics other than Russia. It underscores their tenuous position as independent sovereign states.
4. See for example the writings of one Natalia Narochnitskaya, Deputy Chairman of the Constitutional-Democratic Party and foreign policy expert of the "Russian Unity" bloc. "Osoznat' Svoyu Missiyu," *Nash Sovremennik*, no. 2, 1993; "Natsional'nyy Interes Rossii," *Mezhdunarodnaya Zhizn'*, no. 3-4, 1992. See also, Yevgeniy Ambartsumov, Chairman of the Foreign Affairs Committee of the Supreme Soviet, "Interesy Rossii Ne Znayut Granits," *Megapolis Express*, May 6, 1992.
5. "My — Pravitel'stvo Bednogo Gosudarstva," *Moskovskiye Novosti*, April 26, 1992.
6. The term "centripetal" in this context is used to denote pro-Russian and pro-Moscow tendencies.
7. Tadzhikistan has been the one notable exception to this pattern. Tadzhikistan's democratic coalition, including representatives of its national intelligentsia, has aligned itself with the Islamic movement in the course of its civil war. However, Tadzhikistan's political picture has been extremely complicated by ethnic, clan and regional rivalries which cut across the religious and cultural divides, thus defying attempts at analysis along the lines of class and ideological divisions. The pattern referred to above may well be typical of Central Asian

societies not yet touched by the widespread violence of civil war. In the unfortunate event of further de-stabilization of Central Asia, the de facto coalition may well fall apart as a result of the old elites' fear of any political pluralization and will likely crack down on intelligentsia-based democratic movements.

8. Vitaliy Portnikov, "Govorit' o Granitsakh—Znachit Razorvat Srednyuyu Aziyu," *Nezavisimaya Gazeta*, May 15, 1992.

9. On this subject see for example: Narochnitskaya, op. cit.; E. A. Pozdnyakov, "Sovremennyye Geopoliticheskiye Izmeneniya i Ikh Vliyaniye na Bezopasnost' i Stabil'nost' v Mire," *Voyennaya Mysl'*, No. 1, 1993; "Rossiya—Velikaya Derzhava," *Mezhdunarodnaya Zhizn'*, #1, 1993; K. Pleshakov, "Missiva Rossii. Tretlya Epokha," *Mezhdunarodnaya Zhizn'*, #1, 1993; Andranik Migranyan, "Podlinnyye I Mnimyye Orientiry Vo Vneshney Politike," *Rossiyskaya Gazeta*, August 4, 1992; Sergey Stankevich, "Fenomen Derzhavy," *Rossiyskaya Gazeta*, June 23, 1992; Yevgeniy Ambartsumov, "Interesy Rossii Ne Znayut Granits," *Megapolis-Express*, May 6, 1992; "Strategiya Dlya Rossii," *Nezavisimaya Gazeta*, August 19, 1992; A. Vladislavlev & S. Karaganov, "Tyazhkiy Krest Rossi," *Nezavisimaya Gazeta*, November 11, 1992.

10. "Strategiya Dlya Rossii," *Nezavisimaya Gazeta*, August 19, 1992.

11. Ibid.

12. A. Malashenko, "Novaya Rossiya i Mir Islama," *Svobodnaya Mysl'*, no. 10, 1992; "Chto Ostaetsya Musul'manam?" *Nezavisimaya Gazeta*, January 6, 1993; "O Tadzhikistane bez Pristrastiya," *Nezavisimaya gazeta*, March 3, 1993.

13. M. Zargishiyev, "S Pomoshch'yu Allakha po Puti Koranicheskoy Istiny," *Nezavisimaya Gazeta*, April 2, 1993.

14. Ibid.

15. A. Malashenko, "Novaya Rossiya i Mir Islama," *Svobodnaya Mysl'*, no. 10, 1992.

16. Ibid.

17. Interviews, Moscow, May-June 1992; Santa Monica, September 1992.

18. "Strategiya Dlya Rossii, *Nezavisimaya Gazeta*, August 19, 1992.

19. Ibid; "O Suti Kontseptsii Vneshney Politiki Rossii," *Mezhdunarodnaya Zhizn'*, no. 1, 1993; V. Chernov, "Natsional'nyye Interesy Rossii i Ugrozy Dlya Yeyo Bezopasnosti," *Nezavisimaya Gazeta*, April 29, 1993.

20. See: A. Dubnov, "Katastrofa v Tadzhikistane, o Kotoroy v Rossii Pochti Nichego Ne Znayut," *Novoye Vremya*, no. 4, 1993.

21. M. Yusin, "Rossiya Delayet Stavku na Novoye Tadzhikskoye Rukovodstvo," *Izvestiya*, April 14, 1993.

22. A. Malashenko, "Chto Ostaetsya Musul'manam?" *Nezavisimaya Gazeta*, January 6, 1993.

23. Dubnov, op. cit.

24. A. Nadzharov, "U Rossii Novaya Aziatskaya Politika," *Nezavisimaya Gazeta*, April 16, 1993.

25. M. Yusin, "Rossiya Delayet Stavku na Novoye Tadzhikskoye Rukovodstvo," *Izvestiya*, April 14, 1993.

SECURITY CONCERNS of the CENTRAL ASIAN STATES

Bess A. Brown

In the aftermath of the dissolution of the Union of Soviet Socialist Republics (USSR) and the creation of the Commonwealth of Independent States (CIS), security and national defense have not been the top priorities of the new countries of Central Asia. Of far more immediate concern were the creation of viable national economies and the quest for foreign recognition. Prior to the collapse of the USSR, each of the Central Asian republics had begun a tentative search for contacts with the outside world and had taken the first steps toward ending the domination of its economy by the ministries in Moscow—however, none of these states had advanced in the process far enough to be truly independent. For the new states of Central Asia, the most important issues in the first 3 years of independence were coping with the economic decline resulting from the rupture of Soviet-era ties and maintaining political and social stability in a region with little or no tradition of statehood. The dominant internal security issues for the Central Asian leadership are the avoidance of social and political unrest fueled by anger over high inflation rates and sinking living standards and the suppression of regional, ethnic, or clan antipathies emerging after decades of repression.

The establishment of national security became paramount to the Central Asian states in mid-1992 when civil war broke out in Tajikistan, fueling fears of Islamic fundamentalism, particularly

Bess Brown, a Senior Research Analyst for Central Asia at the Research Institute of Radio Free Europe/Radio Liberty, has written for *Central Asian Survey* and the *RFE/RL Research Report*. Dr. Brown received her Ph.D. in Uralic and Altaic Studies from Indiana University.

acute in Uzbekistan, and regional de-stabilization that would discourage foreign investors in Kazakhstan and Kyrgyzstan. These three states, along with many Tadzhiks, then looked to Russia for help in coping with the crisis. Even prior to the outbreak of the war in Tajikistan, all the Central Asian countries had turned to the Russian Federation for assistance in creating defense establishments. Despite this, the Central Asians have not been wholehearted supporters of a unified CIS military structure, preferring instead to conclude bilateral agreements with Russia on military assistance or to join with Russia in the defense of the Tadzhik-Afghan border against attacks of Tadzhik Islamic oppositionists and their fundamentalist Afghan supporters. The heads of state of Uzbekistan, Tajikistan, Kazakhstan, Kyrgyzstan, and Russia signed an agreement on August 7, 1993 to cooperate in protecting the Tadzhik-Afghan border, referring to the common border of the Commonwealth but making no pretense that the defense force would be a CIS effort.[1] For the Central Asians, the Commonwealth is an economic lifeline, not a defense alliance.

CENTRAL ASIA AND THE CIS

The leaders of the Central Asian republics of the USSR were taken by surprise by the announcement in early December 1991 that the heads of state of the Russian Federation, Ukraine, and Belarus had agreed to create a commonwealth that would mean the demise of the Soviet Union but would apparently not include the non-Slavic states. All the Central Asian republics except Kazakhstan declared their independence in the months after the August 1991 coup in Moscow; but, with the possible exception of Uzbekistan, all appeared to see their independence as a means of maximizing their maneuvering room vis-a-vis the central authorities in Moscow rather than as a statement of intent to try to "go it alone." None could imagine simply being "let go" by the center, but in December they were abruptly faced with the reality that Moscow, as the center of the USSR, had ceased to be a political entity.

Despite their distress at being excluded from the discussions that led to the creation of the CIS by Russia's Boris Yeltsin, Ukraine's Leonid Kravchuk, and Belarus' Stanislau Shushkevich on December 8, 1991, the Central Asian leaders who gathered in Ashkhabad a few days later to decide whether to seek membership in the new body were not prepared to beg for admission at any price.[2] One of the conditions they placed on their admission to the CIS was that the three Slavic states accept the Central Asians as founding members with equal rights. The Central Asian states had developed a degree of self-confidence during their last years as part of the USSR, while reasserting traditional values and reaching out to foreign states for investment to supplement or replace the slowly failing economic support from Moscow. It was unclear, however, what options the Central Asians believed they had at that point other than membership in the CIS.

The leaders of the Central Asian states have attempted to create mechanisms to coordinate regional economic relations and development, but despite announcements that the groundwork had been laid for a Central Asian "common market," the practical results have been limited at best.[3] The differences among the five states, which were already considerable, have rapidly increased since independence. Each country has gone its own way in foreign policy, plans for economic reform, political orientation, and security policy. In May 1993 Kazakhstan's President Nursultan Nazarbaev stated that there would be no confederation or other unitary state structure in the Central Asian region because "everyone wants to live in his own room, not a communal apartment."[4] If, in the discussions of regional economic cooperation, there have been proposals for creation of a regional military force or even regional coordination of defense planning, they have not been acted upon. Part of the reason may be the perception by the Central Asian leaders that their defense needs and interests differ too greatly for coordination to be practical.

The inability of the Central Asian states to create a regional entity as a substitute for the CIS does not mean that they have been satisfied with the way the Commonwealth has developed. Their exclusion from the negotiations that formed the CIS was a bitter blow particularly to Kazakhstan's Nazarbaev because during 1990 and 1991 he had played a prominent role in attempting to formulate the shape of whatever union, confederation or commonwealth would replace the centralized structures of the USSR. Nonetheless, Nazarbaev has been one of the most vocal proponents of a more formal structure for the CIS and one of the few leaders to support a post-Soviet Commonwealth.[5] He has repeatedly demanded that the member states agree to create coordinating structures to help restore the economic ties that had previously bound the former Soviet Union together. According to Nazarbaev, there is little point in the existence of the CIS without such structures to at least enforce trade agreements between Commonwealth states.[6] In this sentiment Nazarbaev has been echoed by Kyrgyzstan's President Askar Akaev, whose country has been one of those to suffer most severely from the rupture of Soviet-era economic relations.[7]

In spite of their disappointment with the ineffectiveness of the Commonwealth, four of the five Central Asian states—Kazakhstan, Uzbekistan, Kyrgyzstan and Tajikistan—signed the CIS Charter in January 1993, which Nazarbaev interpreted as a vote, albeit of limited force, for cooperation.[8] Continuing economic setbacks throughout 1993 further convinced the Central Asian leaders—as well as those of most other Commonwealth member states—that there was no practical alternative to Nazarbaev's vision of the CIS as an economic association, and in September 1993 all but Turkmenistan signed on as members of a CIS economic union.[9] Turkmenistan, which has been drifting away from the Commonwealth largely because of its own relative economic success, is an associate member of the union in keeping with its president's reluctance to participate in any collective decisionmaking within the CIS framework. He insists, however, that his country will remain a member of the Commonwealth.[10]

CENTRAL ASIA AND CIS SECURITY

Initially, the new states of Central Asia (with the exception of Kyrgyzstan) announced that they would create their own defense establishments, recognizing that defense is one of the requirements of national sovereignty. Because of the pressure of more immediate needs, however, the details of national defense were left to be worked out later in agreements among CIS member states or in bilateral agreements with the Russian Federation. Every one of the Central Asian states turned to Russia for assistance in creating a military establishment and entered into bilateral agreements under which the Russian military provides advice and equipment. These agreements were generally expressed in terms of relations between equal sovereign states; there was no question of subordination to the Russian military structure. The CIS unified command affected primarily Kazakhstan, which participated in the unitary CIS control of strategic nuclear missiles. Apart from the nuclear issue (which evaporated with the removal of nuclear warheads from Kazakhstan's missiles), it is unclear what military role the CIS would retain.

At the CIS summit in Tashkent in May 1992, all the Central Asian states except Turkmenistan signed a collective security agreement with other CIS members. The most concrete results of this pact were the agreement in January 1993 that Uzbekistan, Kazakhstan, and Kyrgyzstan would join with Russia in setting up a volunteer peacekeeping force for Tajikistan, and one they signed with Tajikistan in August 1993 to defend the Tadzhik-Afghan border against incursions from Afghanistan. Protection of the Tadzhik-Afghan border has been the only over arching regional security issue to affect the Central Asian states——and not all of them agree on its significance. Turkmenistan's President Saparmurad Niyazov has said that Afghanistan poses no threat to his country, nor does the threat of Islamic fundamentalism which has so worried his Uzbek counterpart. The Turkmen leader has been reluctant to join in any regional security arrangements.

KAZAKHSTAN

Kazakhstan, the largest of the Central Asian states and the second most populous after Uzbekistan, was the last of the republics of the former Soviet Union to claim independence (on December 15, 1992), doing so almost a week after the creation of the Commonwealth and the demise of the USSR. Kazakhstan was also among the last republics to assert its sovereignty even though its president, Nursultan Nazarbaev, had been a vocal and articulate supporter of maximum control of the republics over their own resources and economic, social and political policies.

Demographic realities have played a major role in defining the limits of Kazakhstan's independence. Russian peasants began to settle the region that is now the Republic of Kazakhstan in the 18th century, following the establishment of Russian forts as defense lines advancing southeastward into the Kazakh steppes. The greatest influx of Russian settlers occurred, however, in the 1950s in connection with Nikita Khrushchev's "Virgin Lands" development scheme. This plan made Kazakhstan into one of the primary grain-growing regions of the USSR, but it left an ethnic imbalance: in the republic that bore the name of the Kazakh people, the Kazakhs were a minority. This was not only because of the settlement of non-Kazakhs, but also because of the loss of up to half the Kazakh population in the famine that accompanied Stalin's collectivization in the early 1930s. Kazakh demographers are convinced that had their nation not lost so many in the famine years, they would have outnumbered the Russians despite the Virgin Lands scheme. Not until 1989 did the Kazakh population of Kazakhstan exceed the Russian population.

As a result of historic settlement patterns, the northern regions of Kazakhstan (and also the capital, Almaty) are primarily Russian, while the southern parts of the country are primarily Kazakh. Therein (in the view of much of the Kazakh intellectual and political elite) lies the most acute danger for their country—if the Russian people in the north become dissatisfied with their status as citizens of an independent Kazakhstan, they could demand that the northern regions of Kazakhstan become part of the Russian Federation. Therefore, one of the policy cornerstones of Kazakhstan's present government is avoiding interethnic friction that could disaffect the Russian population. Kazakhs hold most of the important government posts, including the ministries of defense, foreign affairs, and chairmanship of the National Security Committee (formerly the KGB), but the Prime Minister is a Russian, Sergei Tereshchenko.

The demographic makeup of Kazakhstan also has dictated a close association with the Russian Federation, seen as inevitable by Nazarbaev and his government team. However, some of the more nationalistically minded Kazakh political groups criticize the relationship with Russia, but they have no practical alternative to offer. In March 1993 Kazakhstan and Russia concluded a series of wide-ranging agreements, including the intent to cooperate militarily, set up a joint defense zone and coordinate the use and the conversion of military-industrial installations.[11] Nazarbaev commented that Kazakhstan's government already regards the territory of the two countries as a joint defense zone, and that in view of the close relationship between the two states, the creation of mixed military units should be considered.

Despite the overwhelming importance of the relationship with Russia, the dominant issue in Kazakhstan's security policy since independence until recently had been the presence on its soil of strategic nuclear missiles inherited from the Soviet military. Kazakhstan's leadership went on record as accepting unified CIS control of nuclear weaponry,[12] but despite the appeals of numerous foreign officials, Kazakhstan was as reluctant as Ukraine to hand over the missiles to Russia. Early in 1992 one official explained that Kazakhstan has two large nuclear-armed neighbors—Russia and China—and saw in the missiles a guarantee of its own security. Subsequent agreements with Russia and an agreement with China on a mutual reduction of the military presence on the Chinese-Kazakhstan border seem to have reduced the fears that Kazakhstan might be under threat from its nuclear-armed neighbors.[13] Nazarbaev, during a visit to Washington in May 1992, stated that Kazakhstan was seeking security guarantees from Russia, the US and China before it would agree to give up its nuclear weapons.[14]

After the foreign ministers of a number of Western states visited Alma-Ata in early 1992 to persuade Kazakhstan to either hand over the missiles to Russia or destroy them, Kazakhstan declared its intention to sign the Nuclear Non-Proliferation Treaty as a non-nuclear state, and it signed both the START-1 Treaty and the Lisbon Protocol. According to the (then) CIS Commander-in-Chief, Evgenii Shaposhnikov, Kazakhstan's Supreme Soviet ratified the latter two agreements.[15] Kazakhstan was initially reluctant to sign the Non-Proliferation Treaty as a nonnuclear state[16] but did finally sign the agreement in 1994. In November 1992, U.S. experts visited Kazakhstan to discuss the technical aspects of destroying the missiles within the country rather than shipping them back to Russia.[17] Nazarbaev stated that Kazakhstan would need both U.S. funding and technical help to destroy the missiles,[18] an argument Kazakhstan officials used throughout 1993. This continual temporizing on the issue of giving up the missiles indicates that Kazakhstan's policymakers found it very difficult to reconcile themselves to the potential loss of their nuclear status in the world community.

However, Kazakhstan's earlier status as a nuclear power was particularly ironic in view of the environmental damage the country sustained from the Soviet Union's nuclear weapons testing program. One of the first and most influential non-Communist political organizations to appear in Kazakhstan was the antinuclear Nevada-Semipalatinsk Movement, which experienced its greatest triumph when the nuclear weapons test site was shut down after the August 1991 coup. The weapons tests left behind a legacy of shattered health and nuclear waste dumps that were patiently sought and catalogued by a government-sponsored geological expedition whose report appeared in early 1993. Kazakhstan's leadership had to weigh the antinuclear convictions of many citizens against the influence Kazakhstan gained from its possession of nuclear weapons.

It seems certain that most citizens of Kazakhstan prefer a non-nuclear status for their country. The exception has been some of the more hot-headed Kazakh nationalist groups, who demanded Nazarbaev's resignation after he initially promised his Washington hosts that Kazakhstan would give up the missiles. Several times during 1992 rumors surfaced inside and outside the CIS that Kazakhstan was selling, or considered selling, nuclear weapons or weapons components to states such as Iran or Iraq; in each case the rumors proved unfounded and officials in Kazakhstan suggested that the stories were being circulated in order to demonstrate that Kazakhstan could not guarantee the security of its nuclear arsenal.

Kazakhstan's military doctrine, anchored in a series of laws on military policy and organization adopted by the country's Supreme Soviet at the end of 1992, rejects the first use of weapons of mass destruction and declares that Kazakhstan's defense posture shall be committed purely to the protection of the country's independence and territorial integrity.[19] Like the other Central Asian states except Tajikistan, Kazakhstan assumed control over all the military forces, installations, and property of the CIS Armed Forces stationed on its soil in mid-1992, an arrangement later approved by the CIS collective security agreement.[20] In August 1992 Nazarbaev issued a decree creating border troops from the border guard units of the Eastern Border District, which then ceased to exist.[21] In addition to setting up its own army, Kazakhstan declared its intention to establish its own navy and claimed part of the Caspian Sea fleet.[22] Kazakhstan's armed forces are allowed to participate in peacekeeping missions, but as a result of a December 1992 law on military structure, the president may authorize their use in such missions only with the agreement of the Supreme Soviet.[23] Nazarbaev agreed early in 1992 to allow Kazakhstani troops to participate in a CIS peacekeeping force in Tadzhikstan, but the necessary approval of the legislature was given only in April.[24] The peacekeeping force was Kazakhstan's first military venture outside its own territory.

Nazarbaev has an affinity for multinational security mechanisms. Even before Kazakhstan became an independent state, Nazarbaev floated a scheme for an Asian equivalent to the Conference on Security and Cooperation in Europe (CSCE). In early 1992 Kazakhstan joined the CSCE along with the other successor states to the USSR, but Nazarbaev has continued to seek support for his Asian security plan.[25] Two preparatory meetings of potential member countries were held in 1993, but interest in actually setting up an Asian security structure seemed to be limited. In late 1992, the Kazakhstani president assured NATO Secretary General Manfred Woerner that Kazakhstan wants to be a stabilizing force in world affairs.[26] All evidence indicates that Kazakhstan's leadership takes very seriously the country's role as a major player on the Eurasian, if not the world, scene. But its independence of policy and action remains restricted by its special relationship with Russia, which affects Kazakhstan's security policy at least as much as any other aspect of the country's existence.[27]

KYRGYZSTAN

The small and mountainous state of Kyrgyzstan shares some of the ethnic characteristics of Kazakhstan. A third of the population is non-Kyrgyz, and Kyrgyzstan's president, Askar Akaev, has sought to create a multinational government for his multinational state. Akaev is the only Central Asian head of state who does not have a high-level Communist Party career behind him—he is a physicist who lived for many years in Leningrad and who has committed himself to creating a Western-oriented democracy in Kyrgyzstan. Some members of the Kyrgyz nationalist opposition have accused Akaev of using authoritarian methods to reach his goals, but on the whole Kyrgyzstan has made great strides toward political liberalization and economic reform under his guidance. Both democratization and Akaev's ambitious privatization scheme have been endangered by the social and political stresses caused by the severe decline in living standards following the breakdown of Soviet-era economic ties.

Kyrgyzstan is they only CIS country without its own army, and Akaev has publicly boasted about this.[28] It has no Ministry of Defense—defense functions are carried out by the State Committee on Defense. The relatively minor role of national security reflects Akaev's own determination that Kyrgyzstan will avoid all military blocs—he envisages Kyrgyzstan as the "Switzerland of Central Asia."[29] Economic reality is also a factor: the country has little ability to support a large military establishment. Apparently, however, in 1993, 78 percent of the population felt that an army was a necessary part of state sovereignty.[30] During 1993 the Kyrgyzstan government began the formation of a national army.

During 1992, Kyrgyzstan committed to drastically reducing the number of troops on active service on its territory.[31] Despite stating that former Soviet troops would not be put under Kyrgyzstan's jurisdiction, Akaev issued a decree in June 1992 taking over the military units stationed in the country.[32] At the same time, Kyrgyz Vice-President Feliks Kulov enunciated Kyrgyzstan's military doctrine as "armed neutrality," adding that the number of existing troops could be reduced by half without endangering Kyrgyzstan's security, and that the country's defense needs could be met without expensive equipment.[33]

When Kazakhstan took over what had formerly been the USSR's eastern border region, Kyrgyzstan found itself without leadership, support, or even medical supplies for its border guards, and the Kyrgyz government appealed to Russia for help. Under an agreement between the two countries signed in October 1992, Russian border troops assumed the responsibility for guarding Kyrgyzstan's borders until other arrangements could be made.[34] This understanding was followed in April 1993 by an agreement on military cooperation between the two countries. Under the terms of this agreement, Kyrgyzstan will permit Russia to operate a naval communications center on Kyrgyz territory. The Interfax news agency commented that Kyrgyzstan readily agreed to host Russian military installations because they create badly needed jobs at defense plants in the Central Asian state.[35] Shortly after the agreement was signed, Akaev stated that he hoped Russia would soon remove its troops from Kyrgyz soil.[36] Akaev's wish for the removal of Russian troops may have been less an expression of unhappiness at their presence than a reflection of his realization that the presence of troops further burdens an economy that is already in desperate straits, and for whose presence there is little need because of the lack of a credible threat from outside the CIS. The only apparent threat to Kyrgyzstan that may have called for military action was the possibility that the fighting in neighboring Tajikistan in 1992 might have spilled across the border. Apparently some forces of the Tadzhik opposition took refuge in Kyrgyzstan in January 1993 when pro-government forces triumphed in the civil war.[37] Kyrgyzstan has been reluctant to become involved in Tajikistan, however; the country's legislature refused to send peacekeeping troops in the fall of 1992, and border guards from Kyrgyzstan who had been sent to the Tadzhik-Afghan border were then withdrawn in March 1993. In August 1993 Kyrgyzstan agreed with Russia, Kazakhstan, Uzbekistan, and Tajikistan to organize a common defense of the Tadzhik-Afghan border, and border guards from Kyrgyzstan have subsequently served there without apparent objections from the Kyrgyz parliament.

The official reaction of the Kyrgyz government to military exercises that troops from Uzbekistan conducted in Kyrgyzstan's Osh Oblast in March 1993 without proper permission from Bishkek is indicative of the country's security priorities—while Kyrgyzstan's independent press raised a scandal over the unauthorized incursion of Uzbek troops, the Kyrgyz government tried to hush up the incident, fearing complications with neighboring Tajikistan.

UZBEKISTAN

The most populous state in Central Asia, Uzbekistan sees itself as the region's natural leader, a view not shared by its neighbors. Uzbek assertiveness has been a major factor militating against regional cooperation. Uzbekistan's relations with Moscow were affected in the last years of the Soviet Union by a growing perception in the Central Asian republic that the demand for ever greater cotton production had ruined its environment and the health of many of its people and had deformed Uzbekistan's economic development.

The former Communist Party leadership still dominates political life in the country—former Communist Party chief Islam Karimov has been president since 1990; he maintains an authoritarian rule by pointing out the dangers of social and political instability. There is some validity to his arguments. In 1989, bloody riots erupted in Uzbekistan's Fergana Valley, followed by sporadic attacks on Russians in various parts of the republic. When prices were freed throughout the CIS in January 1992, Uzbekistan was the only Central Asian state to experience street violence.

Karimov fears not only violence caused by economic and social hardship, however. He reacted to political unrest in neighboring Tajikistan by first trying to seal the common border. Later he branded as Muslim fundamentalists the Tadzhik opposition coalition of nationalists, democrats and Islamists, saying that they posed a threat to all of Central Asia and beyond. The creation of a coalition government in Tajikistan, in which non-Communist opposition forces received a share of power, represented a major threat to Uzbekistan's conservative ruling elite in Karimov's view, and he set about trying to undermine the Tadzhik government. As pro- and anti-Communist forces battled each other in southern Tajikistan during the last 6 months of 1992, Karimov appealed to the CIS and even the United Nations for help in limiting the damage and preventing the involvement of Muslim fundamentalist forces in Afghanistan sympathetic to Islamic groups in Tajikistan. The specter that Karimov conjured up of a repetition of the war in Afghanistan on Commonwealth soil brought home to other CIS states the magnitude of the danger and led to Russia, Kazakhstan and Kyrgyzstan agreeing to send volunteer peacekeeping troops to Tajikistan.

In January 1992 Uzbekistan set up a national guard formed from its own Ministry of Internal Affairs troops.[38] Development of a defense establishment and military doctrine proceeded slowly as other concerns, especially economic and social issues, took precedence. During the summer of 1992 the Uzbek legislature specified that the country's armed forces would consist of land and air units, air defense forces, a special task force and a national guard.[39] The same law also specified that Uzbekistan would be a neutral state whose military establishment would exist for purely defensive purposes. Uzbekistan's military doctrine was formed in January 1993, but the country's military establishment was already taking an active role outside the country's borders, helping Tajikistan's conservative government mop up opposition resistance.[40]

Karimov stated in September 1992 that, in the face of threats from Tajikistan and from revolutionary Afghanistan via Tajikistan, Russia had become the chief guarantor of Uzbekistan's security and stability.[41] Responding to Karimov's eagerness for increased cooperation between the two countries, Russian Defense Minister Pavel Grachev visited Tashkent in February 1993 to explore the possibilities for an agreement on military cooperation, including the use of strategic installations. According to Grachev, agreements were envisaged by both sides on joint mobilization plans and joint Russian-Uzbek maneuvers.[42]

Without the impetus provided by events in Tajikistan, it seems doubtful that Uzbekistan would have been interested in such close military cooperation with the Russian Federation. The Uzbek leadership continues to be suspicious of Russia because of criticism in the liberal Russian press of Karimov's authoritarianism and intolerance of opposition, and also of the Uzbek role in the Tadzhik civil war. Many Russian liberals are convinced that Tajikistan's conservative government could not remain in power without Uzbek support. According to Russian sources, on many occasions in 1993 Uzbekistan's air force carried out attacks on Tadzhik opposition forces fighting the government. Karimov has played a pivotal role in convincing the Russian government and the leaders of neighboring Central Asian states that the security of the entire Commonwealth is dependent on sealing the Tadzhik-Afghan border against raids by the Tadzhik opposition and their Afghan supporters. In the view of many Central Asian observers, Karimov fears less for the security of the CIS than he does for the stability of his own authoritarian rule that might be effectively challenged by Uzbek Muslim forces supported by Islamic groups in Tajikistan or Afghanistan.

TURKMENISTAN

Soon after Turkmenistan was recognized as an independent state by the outside world, foreign observers assessed it as the Central Asian country most likely to extricate itself from the economic decline that affected the rest of the CIS, based on Turkmenistan's possession of the proven resources of natural gas and petroleum. In the first two years of its independence, Turkmenistan had already made a number of deals to build pipelines to ship its gas to likely customers in Europe, India, and even Southeast Asia. Many foreign firms have bid on petroleum exploration rights, and exploratory drilling is underway in several parts of the country.

Turkmenistan's high degree of success in integrating itself into the world economic community is a major element in President Saparmurad Niyazov's independent-minded approach to the CIS. He says that his country intends to remain a Commonwealth member despite not joining the CIS economic union set up in September 1993, but he has been unwilling to join any collective agreement, including the one on collective security, preferring that all relations with other CIS states be conducted on a bilateral basis.[43]

In June 1992 Turkmenistan signed a bilateral accord with Russia under which the Russian Ministry of Defense would assist in setting up a national army in Turkmenistan, providing equipment, training, and funding.[44] This army was to be under joint Russian-Turkmen command and could not become involved in military actions without the agreement of both countries. According to Niyazov's close associate and deputy prime minister of Turkmenistan, Valerii Otchertsov, the Russian Foreign Ministry rejected a proposal by officials in Turkmenistan for a joint army.[45] By April 1993, there were 60,000 troops stationed in Turkmenistan, of which 15,000 were under direct Russian command, and the remainder were under joint command. Few Turkmen were in the officer corps, and 300 men had been sent to Turkey for training. Niyazov, describing Turkmenistan's military establishment to a delegation from the World Economic Forum, announced that he planned to ask NATO for help in training Turkmen officers.[46] He explained his country's lack of concern about defense matters by saying that he could not imagine a threat to Turkmenistan's security for at least the next 10 years. The civil war in Tajikistan, according to the Turkmen leadership, poses no threat to Turkmenistan, which is immune to Muslim fundamentalism, despite its proximity to Iran and increasingly close relations with that country.

TAJIKISTAN

The only non-Turkic-speaking state in Central Asia, Tajikistan was the poorest of the former republics of the USSR. It is the only one of the new Central Asian countries to experience large-scale violence since independence. The civil war that erupted there in mid-1992 and the threat of intervention from Afghanistan have provided a graphic illustration of Russia's role as a stabilizing force within the CIS, at least in the view of some member states, particularly Uzbekistan.

In early 1992 Tajikistan's Communist-ruled government announced that, like its neighbors in the region, it would turn to the Russian Federation for help in creating military forces. These plans were forgotten in the political tumult that began that March and continued until May, when a coalition government was installed in power. Former Communists held a majority of the seats in the new government, but one-third of the seats were given to members of opposition nationalist, democratic and Islamic parties and movements. The support for these opposition groups was rooted in certain regions of the country; their opponents were characterized as pro-Communist, but it is probably more accurate to describe them as anti-opposition. Because of regional antipathies, these forces rejected a coalition government that included the former opposition, and by early June 1992 fighting had broken out between the supporters and opponents of the new government.[47]

During the 6 months of fighting in the latter half of 1992, the Russian 201st Motorized Rifle Division, stationed in Tajikistan under an agreement with Russia, played a prominent if largely non-combatant role. The division was commanded by a Tadzhik general, M. Ashurov, who ordered his troops to stay out of the fratricidal fighting. The Tadzhik nationalist-democratic-Islamic opposition accused the Russian troops of clandestinely supplying weapons to the pro-Communists. Ashurov and his subordinates insisted that if any of their weapons came into the hands of either side, it was because they had been stolen. Reports from Tajikistan indicated that such thefts were fairly common, as were reports of Russian troops selling their weapons. In late 1992 Russian sources reported that the 201st had reluctantly begun recruiting inhabitants of Tajikistan to fill out its ranks. While the 201st was trying to maintain neutrality, the Russian border guards who had been stationed on the Tadzhik-Afghan frontier and who remained in place at the request of Tajikistan's government after the country became independent, fought almost daily battles with Tadzhiks who had slipped into Afghanistan to supply themselves with weapons from the Afghan resistance.

Uzbekistan was particularly concerned about the regional security aspects of the Tadzhik civil war, but Kyrgyzstan also reported incursions into its territory by armed groups from the neighboring state. Kyrgyzstan's Vice-President Feliks Kulov attempted to mediate in the civil war and earned himself a reprimand from the country's Supreme Soviet for offering Kyrgyz troops as peacekeeping forces as early as the fall of 1992. The legislature voted resolutely that no Kyrgyz troops would be allowed to become involved in Tajikistan.

Unable to prevail over its opponents or devise a peace plan that would be acceptable to those who sought a restoration of pro-Communist forces, the coalition government resigned in November 1992, opening the way for a return to power of the conservatives who had been supported by Uzbek President Karimov. Liberal Russian sources have claimed that Tajikistan's present regime is dependent on Uzbekistan to remain in power. A Russian who had been employed in Uzbekistan's Ministry of Defense, Aleksandr Shishlyannikov, was appointed Tajikistan's Minister of Defense. Tajikistan's present leadership makes no secret of its dependence on Russian and Uzbek military as well as humanitarian assistance. Popular opinion of the government's need for outside support is unrecorded; the once-vocal opposition is in prison, silenced or has fled the country. Despite frequent assurances by government officials that resistance has been nearly wiped out within Tajikistan, pockets of resistance continue to exist in the Pamir mountains in the southeastern part of the country. Throughout the summer of 1993 Tadzhik government troops skirmished with resistance groups in an attempt to open the road from Dushanbe to Gorno-Badakhshan, an autonomous region high in the Pamirs that has tended to support the opposition. The leadership of the region promised the Dushanbe government it would disarm the opposition if Tadzhik government troops stayed out of the Pamirs; incursions by government forces into the region worsened relations and strengthened Badakhshani antipathy to the conservative government.

After gaining power in November 1992, Tajikistan's conservative leadership planned to form a national army from the troops of the so-called Popular Front of Tajikistan, one of the main pro-Communist forces during the civil war. This plan seems to have had limited success because the National Front, a loosely organized guerrilla group, was largely the creation of one man and lost what little discipline he had been able to impose on it after he was killed. By late 1993 Tajikistan's army was largely a Russian and Uzbek creation with Tadzhik recruits.

Despite the continued presence inside Tajikistan of anti-Communist, pro-Islamic forces, the government perceived Afghanistan as the source of the greatest danger after mopping-up operations in the early part of 1993. Former Afghan resistance fighters were accused by Russian border troops and Uzbek officials of running training camps and providing weapons to Tadzhik oppositionists who had taken refuge across the border. Some 300,000 Tadzhiks fled to Afghanistan in January and February of 1993, fearing the wrath of the restored conservatives in the new government; by September the Tadzhik leadership had had very limited success in persuading the refugees to return home. The government's reasoning on the refugee issue was easy enough to follow—the Tadzhik refugees in Afghanistan were likely to be recruited by the Tadzhik Islamic opposition for a holy war against the Dushanbe regime.

Not all Central Asians perceive the civil war in Tajikistan as a meaningful threat. For Uzbekistan's Karimov, it is the region's most important security concern. But for most other Central Asian leaders, economic decline, falling living standards, and the desperate need for foreign help to extricate their countries from the wreckage of the Soviet system are far more immediate issues than Afghanistan and an Islamic fundamentalism that few see as a danger to their own societies.

NOTES

1.   ITAR-TASS, August 7, 1993.
2.   See Shirin Akiner, *Central Asia: New Arc of Crisis?*, Royal United Service Institute for Defense Studies, 1993; Bess Brown, "Central Asia," in *RFE/RL Research Report*, February 14, 1992.
3.   See Bess Brown, "Regional Cooperation in Central Asia?" *RFE/RL Research Report*, January 29, 1993.
4.   ITAR-TASS, May 5, 1993.
5.   *Literaturnaya gazeta*, September 2, 1992.
6.   For example, *Izvestiya*, September 15, 1992; *Pravda*, December 10, 1992; KazTAG report of January 27, 1993.
7.   DPA, October 6, 1992.
8.   AFP and Reuter, April 16, 1993. Nazarbaev made the remark to journalists after a CIS summit in April that was held to try to strengthen the Commonwealth.
9.   ITAR-TASS, September 23, 1993.
10.   For example, his statement to the Canadian ambassador on his refusal to attend the October 1992 CIS summit in Bishkek, reported by Interfax on October 7 and the statement of First Deputy Foreign Minister Boris Shikhmuradov in *Izvestiya*, October 6, 1992.
11.   *Kazakhstanskaya pravda*, March 9, 1993.
12.   Nazarbaev in *Le Monde*, September 27, 1992.
13.   Xinhua, November 24, 1992.
14.   *Washington Post*, May 6, 1992.
15.   ITAR-TASS, January 21, 1993.
16.   For example, Nazarbaev in the U.S, Vice President Erik Asanbaev in Great Britain, Reuter, November 20, 1992.
17.   KazTAG-TASS, November 5, 1992.
18.   Interfax, February 19, 1993.
19.   *Krasnaya zvezda*, January 28, 1993; *Nezavisimaya gazeta*, December 24, 1992.
20.   *Izvestiya*, May 12, 1992.
21.   Izvestiya, August 26, 1992.
22.   Interfax, April 5, 1993.

23. Interfax, December 21 and 22, 1992.
24. Interfax, April 13, 1993.
25. *Nezavisimaya gazeta,* October 9, 1992.
26. KazTAG-TASS, November 4, 1992.
27. See Kazakhstan's Minister of Defense, Sagadat Nurmagambetov, on the special relationship with Russia, KazTAG-TASS, December 23, 1992.
28. Kyodo News Agency, April 23, 1993.
29. Interview in *Slovo Kyrgyzstana,* February 14, 1992.
30. *Svobodnye gory,* February 23, 1993.
31. Interfax, March 25 and November 5, 1992; *Kazakhstanskaya pravda,* June 3, 1992.
32. KrygyzTAG-TASS, June 1, 1992.
33. *Kazakhstanskaya pravda,* June 3, 1992.
34. Radio Rossii, November 8, 1992 and *Slovo Kyrgyzstana,* February 16, 1993.
35. Interfax, April 9, 1993.
36. Kyodo News Agency, April 23, 1993.
37. *Nezavisimaya gazeta,* January 13, 1993.
38. *Izvestiya,* January 30, 1992.
39. Interfax, August 6, 1992.
40. *Izvestiya,* December 10, 1992; *Krasnaya zvezda,* January 21, 1993.
41. *Liberation,* September 8, 1992.
42. ITAR-TASS, February 3, 1993.
43. Interfax, March 24, 1993.
44. *Nezavisimaya gazeta,* June 16, 1992.
45. Author's discussions.
46. Interfax, April 22, 1993.
47. For accounts of the civil war in Tajikistan, see Bess Brown, "Tajikistan: The Fall of Nabiev," *RFE/RL Research Report,* September 25, 1992; "Tajikistan: The Conservative Triumph," *RFE/RL Research Report,* February 12, 1993; "Tadzhik Opposition to Be Banned," *RFE/RL Research Report,* April 2, 1993.

CENTRAL ASIA:
EMERGING MILITARY-STRATEGIC ISSUES

Maxim Shashenkov

The five republics of Central Asia—Kazakhstan, Uzbekistan, Kyrgyzstan, Turkmenistan and Tajikistan—that have recently emerged as independent nations, are today undergoing a process of fundamental change and transition. They are searching for new identities, determining their place and role in the region and the world, and trying to define new relations among themselves and with other states. Recent military-strategic developments are an integral part of this overall transition. They reflect the numerous complexities and problems of the current situation in the region and are increasingly influenced by emerging domestic and regional dynamics of local politics.

It is clear that the future of the national armed forces and the shape of military-strategic relations in Central Asia will be fashioned primarily by general political developments in this region. Security links with Russia, as well as Russian strategy toward the region, will also remain at the heart of the regional military-strategic agenda for many years to come.

Maxim Shashenkov is completing his doctoral studies at Nuffield College, Oxford University, where he is the recipient of a Soros scholarship.   He has been an editor in the African department at the TASS news agency and is the author of *Security Issues of the Ex-Soviet Central Asian Republics* (1992). Mr. Shashenkov studied at Moscow State University, where he received a degree in Oriental History from the Institute of Asian and African Studies.

At present, the Central Asian states are just beginning of the process of creating their own armies and developing their own strategies, threat perceptions and military doctrines. At this stage, it seems important to not restrict a regional military-strategic analysis to a pure military framework (military balance, troop deployments, etc.), but to link it to emerging trends in the domestic and regional politics of the Central Asian states. Thus, the purpose of this paper is to present a general overview of some of the most salient tendencies in the evolution of Central Asian military-strategic issues in the context of local politics and Russian-Central Asian relations. Many of the phenomena, associations, and trends described here are likely to be of a transitional nature because of the extreme political fluidity which marks the politics of this region.

CENTRAL ASIAN REPUBLICS AND THE COMMONWEALTH OF INDEPENDENT STATES: MILITARY DEBATES

The break-up of the USSR has unleashed a complex mosaic of republican interests, geo-political needs and quests for status. It has also necessitated the regionalization of republican security perceptions and concerns. Russia, because of its "heartland" position, was strongly committed to keeping an integrated defense complex on its western and southern perimeter, but it could not prevent the inevitable fragmentation. In the first 2 months following the creation of the Commonwealth of Independent States (CIS) in late December 1991, Russian President Boris Yeltsin sought to preserve the centralized command network and "common military-strategic space" of the CIS. Ukraine, however, acted quickly to secure control over the military stationed on its territory and to declare its independence in the military sphere. Moldova, Azerbaijan and Belarus shared a similar vision of their military future, preferring to create national armed forces.

In early May 1992, Russia itself, alarmed by the rapid "nationalization" of military properties in the European and the Caucasian regions of the CIS and dissatisfied with the prospect of sharing "common-purpose forces" with potentially unstable and economically underdeveloped Central Asian republics, opted for setting up her own national armed forces.

Throughout this period (December 1991 - April 1992), the linchpin of the entire CIS military debate hung on Russian-Ukrainian relations while the impact of the Central Asian "five" on the discussions remained limited. From the beginning, the Central Asian republics sided with Russia, arguing first in favor of preserving single union armed forces and subsequently for close military-strategic cooperation and alliance between the CIS member-states. The military discussions prevailing at that time indicated that there was little divergence in their positions on crucial military-strategic issues. The claims of Central Asian officials usually did not go beyond requesting changes in the role of their draftees, observing the humane conditions of the military service and guaranteeing that young Central Asians would not be sent to perform their service in hot spots. The main disagreements between Russia and Central Asia concerned the question of financing the single armed forces: initially,all the Central Asian republics, with the exception of Kazakhstan, demanded that, since they received subsidies, they should contribute little or nothing to the military budget.[1]

These positions reflected the general "pro-integration" policy of the bulk of the Central Asian ruling *nomenklatura*, which, unlike most of the colonial countries of Asia and Africa, had no experience in a wide-scale political and military struggle for independence and remained loyal supporters of the single Union until the final collapse of the USSR. Indeed, Central Asia has passed through a process of "passive decolonization," with independence thrust upon the region virtually overnight. This occurred against a background of heavy economic, financial and military dependence on the center. As a result, the bulk of Central Asian ruling elites were reluctant to see the breakup of traditional (and beneficial for them), all-Union structures and ties, and they feared that this process would disrupt domestic and regional stability. For them, Russia remains the only force capable of guaranteeing a certain degree of stability and order in Central Asia. More important, a belief still exists there that Russia will eventually come to rescue current "pro-Russian" ruling authorities if they are openly challenged by Islamist or nationalist opposition.

In addition, throughout 1992, steady changes in Russian foreign policy toward the greater assertiveness in the "near abroad," caused renewed emphasis on Russian security concerns and geo-political interests in the ex-Soviet republics. Also, those in

Central Asia who worried about Moscow's "turning its back" on the Muslim South were reassured by the Russian/CIS conduct in Tajikistan that Russia was moving toward a more active and direct involvement in their region. A rising collusion of interests between Central Asian ex-Communist elites, who are in need of an outside stabilizing force, and the Russian government, which due to its security considerations is more eager today to play the role of active *status quo* guarantor in the region, has become the most significant and important phenomenon in current Russian-Central Asian relations. This "elite factor" is a key to understanding the roots and the rules of the emerging Russian-Central Asian strategic partnership.

Since the breakup of the Union, the newly acquired independence of the Central Asian republics has created a new domestic and regional dynamic. As individual Central Asian republics began to formulate their "national" security priorities and interests, the erosion of Central Asia's unity of views on military issues became unavoidable. Natural differences between the five, determined by their different resources and capabilities, geo-strategic position, domestic situation, and perceived status and role, resulted in a noticeable differentiation of approaches to the military-strategic questions.

Although all of the newly independent states continued to place a major emphasis on the Russian commitment to their security, Kazakhstan and Uzbekistan, the two largest states in the region and rivals for the status of regional "power center," have proved to be more assertive concerning their military requirements and more inclined to establish their own armies in the event of the failure to preserve the single CIS armed forces.

As a precondition for this step, Kazakhstan, late in December 1991 and followed by Uzbekistan in January 1992, placed all its troops stationed on their territories, with the exception of strategic forces, under republican national jurisdiction.[2] Uzbekistan appeared to be the first in Central Asia to argue in favor of having a separate national army within the structure of the CIS joint armed forces and setting up a republican defense ministry separate from that in Moscow. In April 1992, Kazakh President Nursultan Nazarbayev signed a decree authorizing the withdrawal of the 40th Russian army, which had fought in Afghanistan and was subsequently stationed in Kazakhstan, from the command of the Central Asian Military District and its subordination to the

Kazakh government.[3] The Russian move toward a separate army in May 1992 was quickly followed by the decision of Kazakhstan and Uzbekistan to set up independent republican armed forces.

The three other Central Asian states—Turkmenistan, Kyrgyzstan and Tajikistan—were, on the whole, much more reticent on defense issues, preferring to share with Russia the burden of financing and maintaining the troops deployed on their territories. Tajikistan and Kyrgyzstan, which ranked among the poorest Soviet republics, scarcely possessed sufficient resources to start their own military programs.   In Tajikistan, growing domestic instability occupied the attention of President Nabiyev and his government. In a situation of deepening regional/clan fragmentation and the rise of local opposition to the traditional political and economic dominance of Khujent-Kulyab clans, most of the old Soviet ruling elite in Tajikistan sought to preserve Russian military commitment to their republic.

In the beginning of 1992, the Kyrgyz authorities on several occasions expressed their desire to refrain from setting up their own armed forces and to settle for the creation of a small national guard. President Askar Akayev and his close associates promoted a vision of Kyrgyzstan as the future Switzerland or Singapore of Central Asia. The republic's stand on military-strategic issues at that stage was spelled out by Akayev: "We are for a neutral Kyrgyzstan and do not intend to enter any military blocks. We do not want to create our own army, and we are not thinking of taking into our jurisdiction military formations stationed on the republic's territory."[4]

Turkmenistan's first steps in the military sphere also reflected the new individuality and distinctiveness of the military-strategic outlook of this newly independent republic. Two elements in the position of Ashqabad were particularly indicative and significant. First, Turkmenistan, on whose territory a large part of the Turkestan Military District's units and weapons were deployed, announced that their numbers far exceeded its own defense requirements and that it did not lay claim to all the troops stationed on the republic's territory. The financing of these troops was calculated to be too heavy a burden for the Turkmen economy.[5] Secondly, early in 1992, Ashqabad articulated its preference for bilateral military agreements with Russia. In February, President Supurmat Niyazov emphasized that if the idea of the CIS single armed forces failed, his republic would "be in favor of concluding a defense alliance with Russia."[6]

By the time of the fourth CIS summit, held in mid-May 1992 in Tashkent, where a "collective security" agreement was concluded, a great degree of ambiguity surrounded the fate of the "Soviet" military in Central Asia. While Uzbekistan and Kazakhstan had already taken all troops (except strategic units) stationed in their territories under their jurisdiction and declared the creation of their own armies, in Tajikistan, Turkmenistan, and Kyrgyzstan, the status of locally based military forces was not settled. Russian Defense Minister General Pavel Grachev proposed granting "Group of Forces" status to military units in those three republics, which would then allow them to be considered part of the Russian army.[7] However, this proposal was later rejected by Turkmenistan, which insisted on having "joint troops" under joint command and finance with Russia.[8] These issues of "Soviet troops" were finally decided at the end of May and in June 1992 through bilateral negotiations between Russia and Turkmenistan and between Russia and Kyrgyzstan.

TASHKENT COLLECTIVE SECURITY AGREEMENT

The creation of its own national armed forces made it easier for Russia to formulate and advocate its national interests within the CIS and in Central Asia. Cautious criticism of the prospect of sharing strategic and "common-purpose" troops with Central Asians and the warnings of non-profitability for Russia of such arrangements gave way to a growing recognition of the necessity to keep Central Asia within the Russian military-political sphere of influence and to support the existing *status-quo* in the region. On the one hand, the fall of the Najibullah regime in Afghanistan and civil war in Tajikistan, with its negative impact on the situation in the region, made politicians, academics and military officials in Russia more assertive regarding emerging and potential volatile strategic threats to their country emanating from Central Asia and the CIS southern "underbelly." On the other hand, growing centrifugal tendencies within the CIS and the attempts of Ukraine, Moldova, and Azerbaijan to dilute close military relations with Russia prompted Moscow to try to save what it could of common military space and structures of the Union. In Moscow, the military authorities spoke of Russia's vital interests in keeping its air-defense complex, space monitoring installations and existing military infrastructure intact. In the context of rising regional instability, the Central Asian governments also perceived a distinct advantage in allying themselves with Russia.

The Collective Security Treaty, signed at the fourth CIS summit in Tashkent in May 1992, was aimed at providing an important multilateral umbrella for military cooperation between the signatory states and legitimizing Russia's military-strategic commitment to each of the participants. In fact, it serves as a general cover for a genuine coordinating mechanism that would function on a bilateral level and secure Russia's role as a security guarantor for other signatory countries. Moreover, the agreement provides Russia with an important mechanism to wield significant influence over Central Asian states' military development and activities and helps to preserve old links and channels for the supply of weapons, military hardware and spare parts to these republics.

Six states—Russia, Kazakhstan, Uzbekistan, Kyrgyzstan, Tajikistan and Armenia—signed this agreement, in which aggression or the threat of aggression against any member was to be regarded as aggression against all signatories. The six republics confirmed their commitment to refrain from the use of force in their interstate relations and from entering military alliances directed against other participating states.

The treaty established a Collective Security Council (CSC) consisting of each of the heads of state and the Commander-in-Chief of the CIS joint armed forces. The CSC was to be responsible for the coordination of the joint activities of the member-states in the field of security.[9] The Collective Security Treaty was signed for a period of 5 years and was open to other CIS republics.

This agreement clearly has all the features of a Russian-Central Asian alliance, and its "southern/Central Asian orientation" is well reflected in the list of its participants. Armenia's decision to join the treaty was mainly prompted by the difficult geo-strategic position of this republic and the constant threat of a full-scale war with Azerbaijan.[10]

Turkmenistan abstained from signing the Collective Security Treaty, pointing to its absurdity at a time when the "joint army of a commonwealth is being torn apart by conflicts."[11] Instead, Turkmen officials continued to give priority to bilateral military cooperation with Russia in the framework of a "joint armed forces." This position was strictly in line with Ashqabat's preference for bilateral rather than multilateral agreements and its reluctance to see the CIS develop into anything more than a purely economic association. Turkmenistan was also negative about involvement in existing or potential "hot spots" in the CIS, or even in Central Asia, and refused to participate in any CIS peacekeeping forces. Richly endowed with gas and oil and having better prospects for internal stability than any of its fellow Central Asian republics, Turkmenistan is circumspect in avoiding any "unnecessary" commitments to other CIS or Central Asian states.

MULTILATERAL MILITARY COOPERATION: JOINT ARMED FORCES (JAF)

The formation of new structures and institutions of the proclaimed collective security organization is in early stage. Since May 1992, there have been more declarations than real action in bilateral and multilateral cooperation between Russia and the four Central Asian republics or among the Central Asian states themselves. Despite the fact that roughly 100 different military-strategic agreements and records have been signed by the CIS, the bulk of these remained on paper only, while the Commonwealth lacked any effective mechanism for their implementation and the promotion of military cooperation.[12] In March 1993, Marshal Yevgenii Shaposhnikov, (then) Commander-in-Chief of the CIS Joint Armed Forces, admitted that despite signing the Tashkent agreement, there had been little further "rapprochement" between the signatory states.[13]

The overall picture of military cooperation in the Central Asian and other CIS states is further complicated by a lack of clarity regarding the interrelation and interaction of different forms and structures of such cooperation—bilateral agreements, Commonwealth agreements, the Tashkent Treaty, and similar agreements signed by only six or seven CIS members. The concept of CIS military security was originally designed as a "collective defense" for all 11 CIS members. Consequently, emerging command and control structures of the CIS Joint Armed Forces (JAF) (High Command, Council of Defense Ministers and others) were to incorporate all 11 CIS members, not all of which sought close-tied multilateral military cooperation. The divergence of views within the CIS seriously damaged the effectiveness of ongoing negotiations on military-strategic issues. The "pro-integration" position of the "Tashkent six" in the military-strategic sphere was effectively obstructed by other CIS states, Ukraine, Moldova, and Turkmenistan in particular, which retarded the progress of the Tashkent process. The "Tashkent six," in fact, proved to be subordinate to Moscow's efforts to maintain a wider military-political alliance within the framework of the Commonwealth (including, Belarus and other CIS members if possible).[14] In the end, as Colonel-General V. Samsonov, (then) Chief-of-Staff of the JAF in the CIS, acknowledged in February 1993, the JAF simply did not exist in reality.[15]

At the same time, a steady merging of the Tashkent process with the JAF agreements package and ideas has occurred. Only participants in the "collective security" treaty were invited to the February 27 meeting of the CIS Defense Ministers Council in Moscow. Remarkably, in its editorial, the Russian army's daily *Krasnaya Zvezda* called this meeting a watershed, saying that after this the "Tashkent six" would begin to work on further consolidation and deepening of their military-strategic cooperation, while the other states would search for other ways to secure themselves.[16] The fact that only seven CIS member-states (the "Tashkent six" plus Belarus) put their signatures to the CIS Charter in Minsk in January 1993 suggests the united acceptance of the "collective security" approach. This process is likely to lead eventually to the final crystallization of a "two-speed" CIS in the military sphere as advocated by Nazarbayev,[17] with the finally established JAF confined in all probability to only the six signatory states of the Tashkent Treaty.[18] Belarus has endorsed some CIS military agreements, and the Belarus parliament has voted for the republic's inclusion in a CIS collective security agreement signed in Tashkent.[19] At the same time, Belarus has strong reservations against participating in peacekeeping forces and CIS collective forces.

During the past year, a concerted effort was made to develop the concept of the CIS Joint Armed Forces, to determine its structure and functions and to set up appropriate command and control structures. According to Lieutenant-General Ivashov, (then) Secretary of the CIS Council of Defense Ministers, the Joint Armed Forces, which are in a process of creation, will be composed of (1) strategic nuclear forces, (2) collective peacekeeping forces and (3) collective forces for the prevention of conflicts at CIS external borders. Their numerical strength was left to be defined, given the lack of unity between CIS members regarding the JAF structure and composition.[20] By the middle of February 1993, only Kazakhstan had announced its readiness to allocate a contingent to the CIS forces for the prevention of conflicts on the external borders.[21] Questions of financing of the JAF were not settled.[22] There is a range of problems and difficulties surrounding the issue of the CIS peacekeeping forces.

Moreover, even the six participants in the "collective security" agreement do not have the same views on the structure, control or command system of the defense union. Initially, two of them—Russia and Uzbekistan—favored the Warsaw Pact model; the others—Kazakhstan, Kyrgyzstan, Tajikistan and Armenia— preferred to organize the collective defense according to the NATO pattern. The latter argue that only the NATO model will guarantee real equality among all the participants, will keep in check any imperial ambitions from the Russian side and will allow the CIS JAF High Command to evolve into a truly interstate military-political coordinating body.[23]

Later, Russia occupied a more flexible position on the NATO/Warsaw Pact issue; but at a May 1993 meeting of the CIS Council of the Defense Ministers, the Russian representative General Boris Gromov categorically rejected a draft treaty on the CIS JAF proposed by Marshal Shaposhnikov and his staff. By contrast, the other five Tashkent Treaty signatories backed Shaposhnikov and his proposals. The main reasons given by the Russian delegation to explain its refusal to approve this draft included: (1) a strong objection to the idea of the transfer of the command and control of the strategic forces to the CIS JAF High Command; and (2) a fear that the creation of the JAF might provoke a negative reaction by NATO and Eastern European countries.[24] This position reflected a growing concern within the Russian military that the transfer of too much power and authority to the CIS JAF's command structures (which will have a Central Asian majority over Russia—4 to 1) would substantially reduce Russia's freedom of manoeuvre and could open an important Central Asian channel of influence in Russia's military-strategic decisionmaking process.

MULTILATERAL SECURITY COOPERATION IN CENTRAL ASIA

Although military-strategic questions were included in initial discussions on regional cooperation in Central Asia, the five states have been far more successful in endorsing agreements on economic, social and political issues than in the sphere of defense.

A first attempt to create a Central Asian multilateral forum for solving political and ethnic conflict was evident in the April 1992 summit of the Central Asian republics held in the Kyrgyz capital, Bishkek. The participants adopted a joint declaration recognizing the inviolability of existing borders in Central Asia. This declaration also obliges the five countries to pursue a coordinated policy in the sphere of regional security, arms control and the reduction of military forces in their territories.[25]

The rapidly deteriorating situation in Tajikistan gave new impetus to the discussions on Central Asian military cooperation, which was seen as a threat to the stability of the entire region. A summit meeting of Central Asian leaders in Alma-Ata in November 1992 was dedicated entirely to the Tajik conflict and possible joint initiatives in ending the hostilities. Among other proposals, the issue of bringing into Tajikistan military units from Kazakhstan, Uzbekistan and Kyrgyzstan was raised during the consultations.[26] It was announced that the defense ministers of Kazakhstan, Uzbekistan, Turkmenistan, Tajikistan, and Kyrgyzstan were to meet to discuss ways of normalizing the situation in Tajikistan.[27] Despite the participation of Russian Foreign Minister Andrei Kozyrev, the Alma-Ata meeting carried a strong Central Asian regional accent and paved the way for further intra-regional discussions in the field of security and defense. After the January 1993 Tashkent summit of the heads of Central Asian states, Nazarbayev spoke of the possibility of setting up a Central Asian "defense union" as a continuation of full-fledged regional economic, social and political integration.[28] This statement, however, seems to be more of a message to Russia to pay more attention and respect to Russian-Central Asian defense cooperation than an expression of serious plans to create a genuine Central Asian defense alliance.

On the whole, effective development of a regional security framework on the foundation of only Central Asian states is unlikely in the near future, given the strong military and economic dependence of each of these countries on Russia. However, this does not exclude the possibility of setting up an institutional framework for Central Asian defense cooperation. Central Asian regional military cooperation will probably intensify if a more cautious approach towards Russian involvement in local conflicts in Central Asia or along former USSR southern frontiers prevails in Moscow. As a prelude to such a scenario, the CIS debates over the Tajik civil war were most significant. The Central Asian states, Uzbekistan in particular, urged Moscow to play a more active role, particularly in Tajikistan, while the Russian leadership remained hesitant and ambivalent for some time concerning the military means of resolving the Tajik situation.

BILATERAL MILITARY COOPERATION

Parallel to the emerging Commonwealth multilateral defense structures, a process of increasing the bilateralization of relations between member states in the spheres of defense and security has been under way since the spring of 1992. This has been reflected, in particular, by a series of agreements on friendship, cooperation and mutual assistance signed in 1992 by Russia with Kazakhstan (May 25), Uzbekistan (May 30), and Kyrgyzstan (June 10); a Russian-Turkmen agreement on friendship and cooperation (June 8); and a more recent Russian-Tajik package of military agreements (May 25, 1993).

The first three agreements, in fact, legitimize the Russian military-strategic alliance with Kazakhstan, Uzbekistan, and Tajikistan each on a bilateral basis. They hold that the signatory states should preserve a joint military-strategic space, cooperate closely in guaranteeing a reliable defense and give each other a right to use military installations and bases on each others' territories in case of war or the threat of war. The signatory states are to refrain from taking part in any military alliance directed against another state or allowing their territories to be used as a staging area for aggression against another state.[29] The treaty between Russia and Turkmenistan, although less comprehensive, confirmed close-tied military cooperation between the two states.

The bilateralization of relations between Russia and the Central Asian states helps Moscow to compensate for the weakness of a multilateral CIS military structure and to overcome a constant conflict of interests between the eleven members of the Commonwealth. At the same time, as one Russian study of the evolution of the CIS concludes, bilateralization "to some extent undermines plans to consolidate the CIS," since it "only exposes the relative nature of the multilateral agreements."[30] Indeed, the most effective results for Russian-Central Asian defense cooperation have been achieved through bilateral negotiations. Routine questions are also dealt with exclusively through bilateral agreements.

Since the spring of 1992, military-strategic cooperation between Russia and Kazakhstan has been wide-ranging, intensive, and fruitful. Both sides have agreed to pursue a coordinated policy in the spheres of security, disarmament, and arms control; to coordinate their scientific and production activities in the military sphere; and to cooperate in the conversion of defense enterprises, the development of dual-purpose high-tech production facilities and the export of defense goods. Russia and Kazakhstan have also endorsed agreements on the joint maintenance and use of the Baykonur cosmodrome and the Semipalatinsk testing ground, joint use of military-industrial complexes of the two states, joint development of existing systems for training officers, and the preservation of existing procedures for military service for officers. The Russian side has undertaken to train representatives of Kazakhstan in its military academies and colleges. Substantial numbers of junior military specialists for the Kazakh army (especially, for Air Defense, the Air Force, and communications units) will continue to undergo their training in Russian military centers.[31] Some of these points are to be reconfirmed in a comprehensive Treaty on Military Cooperation between Russia and Kazakhstan, which the presidents of the two countries are to sign in the future.[32]

Although bilateral activities between Russia and Uzbekistan and between Kyrgyzstan and Tajikistan have been more modest in scale and intensity than the Russian-Kazakh military dialogue, they also confirm the tendency toward the increasing bilateralization of Russian-Central Asian defense cooperation.[33] Turkmenistan has been building its defense system on the basis of bilateral ties with Russia.

Most significantly, the bilateralization process further underpins and strengthens Russia's central position and leading role in the emerging network of military-strategic ties in post-Soviet Eurasia. Russia remains the single most important military-strategic partner for all of the Central Asian republics. This picture might change in the future, but, so far, the development of vertical military ties between the Russian Federation and the Central Asian states (some of which were inherited from the Soviet past) have largely out-paced earlier signs of an establishment of horizontal links between the Central Asian "five."[34] The consolidation of the vertical military-strategic ties between Russia and the other participants in the Collective Security Treaty are seen by many senior Russian military men as the most efficient, realistic and beneficial way of tackling the problems of a new defense alliance. By shifting the context for discussion of the major issues of military cooperation from a multilateral to a bilateral basis, Russia appears to be in a better position to influence its Central Asian partners, to shape their independent military development and to keep them within Moscow's military-strategic sphere of influence.

At the same time, the lack of an official basis for bilateral horizontal ties between the newly-independent states in Central Asia will hardly constitute an obstacle to military involvement in one another's domestic conflicts, to the creation of new military alliances or to the movement of weapons, mercenaries and ammunition across the region's frontiers. Indeed, in post-Soviet Central Asia, with its artificial boundaries and divided ethnic groups, there is little likelihood that the existing states will quickly become self-sufficient and viable entities. Any "internal" conflict could, therefore, spread into neighboring states and engulf larger areas of the region. To prevent the further worsening of a "domestic" conflict, neighboring states will be prompted to use force to liquidate what is perceived as a direct threat to their own survival. The close involvement of the Uzbek military on the side of the People's Front formations in the Tajik civil war provides an insight into the forms and ways of potential military "interaction" in the region.[35] Such scenarios present difficult policy choices for other participants in the Tashkent Collective Security Treaty, particularly for the Russian Federation.

PEACEKEEPING IN CENTRAL ASIA

At their summit meeting held in Kiev on 20 March, 1992, 10 of the 11 CIS members signed an agreement on "Groups of Military Observers and Collective Peacekeeping Forces in the CIS," which set the terms and basic conditions of peacekeeping operations in the Commonwealth. The prevention and settlement of inter-ethnic, religious and political conflicts within the CIS were proclaimed to be the major objectives of these forces. The agreement said CIS peacekeeping units should be formed on a voluntary basis and should be sent to potential "hot spots" only if requested, and only if a cessation of hostilities between rival groups was in place. The consent of all members of the CIS Council of Heads of State was stressed to be a necessary precondition for the dispatch of the troops.[36]

From the beginning, the leaders of four Central Asian states—Kazakhstan, Uzbekistan, Kyrgyzstan and Tajikistan—have been among the most enthusiastic supporters of plans to set up CIS peacekeeping forces. Nazarbayev was the first to propose the creation of such forces.[37] In July 1992, Islam Karimov, the president of Uzbekistan, while hosting a meeting of CIS foreign and defense ministers in Tashkent, initiated a wide-ranging discussion of the security problems of the southern frontiers of the CIS and, in the "Central Asian context," called for more efficient and rapid measures to deploy inter-republic peacekeeping units. To this end, the Tashkent meeting endorsed a working protocol on CIS peacekeepers which called upon its signatories to create and train a special military contingent for peacekeeping operations, as well as groups of military and police observers.[38] At the Bishkek CIS summit in September 1993, the responsibility for the command, preparation, and training of the CIS peacekeepers was given to the High Command of the CIS Joined Armed Forces.[39]

In Central Asia, Tajikistan was the first conflict where Commonwealth peacekeepers were due to be deployed.[40] However, after several months of discussions and negotiations, few of the original plans and goals were achieved. Furthermore, Tajikistan has revealed many of the real and potential problems and dangers surrounding any CIS (i.e. Russian-Central Asian) peacekeeping mission in this region.

First, the neutrality and actual ability of a Russian-Central Asian peacekeeping contingent to act in line with the rules and regulations of UN-type peacekeeping operations are doubtful. Equally, there are questions about its capability to bring long-term and widely accepted stability and peace to the areas of conflicts in the region. Many of the Tajiks, the only non-Turkic nation in Central Asia with a strong historical fear of being overwhelmed by the Turkic majority, did not welcome the plan to deploy troops from other Central Asian republics in Tajikistan. Long-suppressed historical rivalries, ethnic frictions and sympathies have re-emerged with new strength in post-Soviet Central Asia, making any military involvement of one state, even under the auspices of the "CIS peacekeeping force," in the internal fighting of another to be a very complicated and dangerous exercise.

Moreover, each of the newly independent Central Asian republics is a multi-ethnic entity with artificial frontiers and the potential for border disputes with its neighbors. The arrival of a military formation from a nearby state that has a corresponding ethnic minority into an area of conflict could harm inter-ethnic relations there and jeopardize the very purpose of their mission. This was the case with the Russian and Uzbek military in Uzbekistan, which failed the neutrality test and put additional strain on already fragile ethnic relations, especially between the Tajiks and Uzbeks.

Second, the complexity of the Tajik conflict, as well as the emerging intrastate and regional dynamics of Central Asian politics, has revealed certain weak points in the Russian-Central Asian alliance. Its coherence was challenged by the emerging divergence of views and perceptions of the Tajik war and the differences in the decisionmaking process. Russia and Uzbekistan displayed the strongest support and readiness to take part in a CIS inter-republic peacekeeping mission in Tajikistan. Significantly, both Russia and Uzbekistan can be justly described as the most "interested parties," as the states most closely involved in the conflict in Tajikistan. *Inter alia*, Moscow is seriously worried about the fate of the 300,000-strong Russian community in this republic.[41] The civil war in Tajikistan, accompanied by the progressive clan-regional fragmentation of this country, poses the most serious threat to the survival of the current Uzbek regime. Tajiks, of whom substantial numbers reside in Uzbekistan, have a long tradition of friction with Uzbeks, who were their overlords in pre-Soviet days. The prospect of the emergence of the "Tajik factor," caused by continuing conflicts in Tajikistan and Afghanistan, is a source of concern to Tashkent. The fact that around 23 percent of Tajikistan's population are Uzbeks caused the Uzbek authorities to take effective measures to stop the fighting in the neighboring republic. In addition, the Tajik war constantly fans the spread of Islam as a political force, which is perceived by the ex-communist ruling elite in Uzbekistan as a potentially fatal opponent.

The governments of Kazakhstan and Kyrgyzstan, although alarmed by the dangerous sources of instability on their doorsteps, have had to cope with strong internal opposition to their peacekeeping involvement in Tajikistan. Initial enthusiasm and full-scale support for the military mission aimed at bringing peace to Tajikistan has evolved into a more cautious approach by both Alma-Ata and Bishkek. In addition, the more liberal political systems of these states, compared to Uzbekistan, allowed the opposition to exercise strong influence on the decisionmaking process.

In the autumn of 1992, the then-acting president of Tajikistan, Iskanderov, insisted that peacekeepers for his republic be comprised of only Kyrgyz and Kazakh troops.[42] This idea was supported by the CIS meeting in Bishkek. In October 1992, however, an absolute majority at a closed sitting of Kyrgyzstan's parliament voted against sending a Kyrgyz battalion into Tajikistan. They pointed out that all CIS states, not only Kyrgyzstan, should contribute their troops to this operation.[43] In Kazakhstan, the parliamentary faction, which categorically opposed the introduction of Kazakh troops into Tajikistan, has also proved to be very influential.[44]

In November, after another appeal by the Tajik Supreme Soviet for peacekeeping forces to be sent into the republic, representatives of the Russian, Kazakh, Uzbek, Kyrgyz and Tajik defense ministries met in the Uzbek town of Termez and agreed to send a multinational peacekeeping contingent of 3,500 to 5,000 men to Tajikistan. However, this agreement was subject to ratification by the parliaments of these states. This jeopardized any chances for its effective and rapid implementation because of strong parliamentary opposition in both Kazakhstan and Kyrgyzstan.[45] In February 1993, Kyrgyzstan finally sent its peacekeeping battalion only to withdraw it several months later after six soldiers deserted to Afghanistan.[46]

Finally, the evolution of the situation in Tajikistan and the Tajik-Afghan border has put new requirements on the roles and functions of CIS peacekeepers, which is likely to lead to deeper and larger-scale involvement. Originally designed as a small military contingent brought in to separate rival Tajik groups, the Commonwealth peacekeeping corps is perceived by the present Tajik leadership as a much-needed guarantor against rebel attacks by the defeated "Islamic-democratic" opposition and the Afghan *mujahedeen* from their camps in northern Afghanistan.[47] They were to be deployed along the republic's border with

Afghanistan. Thus, the Commonwealth operations in Tajikistan fell more in line with the Tashkent agreement on collective security than with the Minsk agreement on peacekeeping in the CIS.

These difficulties, however, are unlikely to distract Russia from its attempts to take the lead in regional peacekeeping operations and to establish itself as the guarantor of peace and stability in the territory of the former Soviet Union. Peacekeeping is increasingly viewed by the Russian military as an important means to legitimize the defense of the country's strategic interests in the CIS and to reinforce its own prestige, status, and role in post-Soviet Russia.

NATIONAL ARMIES OF THE CENTRAL ASIAN REPUBLICS

Reluctantly driven into the process of military fragmentation, the Central Asian republics appeared to be the least prepared of the former Soviet republics to assume the responsibilities of their own defense. The republican armed forces are still in an embryonic stage. Since the early summer of 1992, when the Central Asians began to organize their own armed forces, independent military construction has been largely confined to the development of new local command and control structures and the elaboration and adoption of new military doctrines, packages of "military laws," and general plans for future military construction. Little has been done on the ground. Troops are led by predominantly Slav officer corps, undergoing the old training courses, learning the same military regulations, and wearing old uniforms.

The troops stationed in Central Asia suffer from problems common to other armies emerging from the wreckage of the mighty Soviet army—psychological and organizational disarray, wide-spread desertion, difficulties with the supply of spare parts and ammunition, resulting from the breakup of traditional military-industrial ties, low salaries, and a steep decline in the prestige and social status of military service, compounded by budgetary shortfalls and economic hardship. These difficulties are worsened by the growing fluidity of the officer corps, persistent attempts by Slav officers to transfer to their native republics, a dire shortage of local expertise, a very high rate of desertion and uncertain prospects for political stability in some Central Asian republics.

On the whole, there is no likelihood that the five Central Asian republics will quickly become self-sufficient militarily. Armies are expensive and consume badly needed resources. All five Central Asian republics are closely tied to Russia in terms of military equipment, the supply of spare parts, logistic support and military training. As long as present elites continue to rule the Central Asian republics, they are likely to seek Russian assistance in military development and to build their security on the basis of multilateral and bilateral links with the Russian Federation.

Similarly, Central Asian armies need time to become "Central Asian," i.e., to train their own officers, to create their own military colleges and centers, to sort out questions of military supplies, to develop national symbols and loyalty, and to cultivate their own culture of military-civilian relations.

The issues of erecting military institutions are likely to be particularly significant and pressing in Kazakhstan and Uzbekistan. The prospect of ethnic tensions and conflict in Kazakhstan, which is almost equally divided between Russians (38 percent of the population) and Kazakhs (40 percent),[48] engulfing the republic's armed forces is most worrisome. Moreover, the Kazakh army today is almost entirely under the command of Slav officers. Only three percent of the officer corps of the 40th army, which has become the backbone of the new republican armed forces, are ethnic Kazakhs.[49] The rank and file of these troops also reflect the multi-ethnic composition of the country's population. Whether the Slav community will use their positions in the army, along with their hold on the economy, to neutralize the Kazakhs' increasing control of government and administrative structures in rising competition for power is not yet clear. However, it is unrealistic to expect the Kazakh authorities to maintain full control over their military if nationalist impulses become dominant in Kazakhstan.

Understandably, Alma-Ata has to be very cautious in its independent military building program. To preserve domestic stability and to prevent dangerous politicization of his army, President Nazarbayev advocates a close military-strategic alliance with Russia and has made far-reaching proposals on further integration of the Russian-Kazakh defense "axis."[50] Kazakh military doctrine anticipates close interaction with other CIS states which participate in the Tashkent Collective Security agreement. The strategic line of the republic's defense is based on close coordination and cooperation with the Russian army on the basis of a collective defense. In addition, Russia will contribute to the establishment of the Kazakh armed forces.[51]

At the same time, the Kazakh officials are well aware of the vital importance of steady "Kazakhization" of the armed forces in Kazakhstan. For the past months, much attention has been paid to the questions of training and preparing ethnic Kazakh officers and military specialists. Most senior Kazakh military officials consider this to be their most urgent problem. In August 1992, a treaty was signed with Russia on training Kazakh military staff. It mandates that more than 450 representatives from Kazakhstan will study in Russian military colleges and academies in the next five to six years. Some of the Kazakh officers will undergo their training in the United States. Along with these steps, the Alma-Ata military officer cadet academy (one of only two military higher educational establishments in the republic) is to be transformed into a multipurpose military training institution. Military faculties structured on the basis of Kazakh universities will also be established.[52]

Currently, the main difficulties seriously affecting the combat readiness and general conditions of the Kazakhstan army are the migration of non-Kazakh officers (mostly Ukrainians, Byelorussians and Russians), a 30 percent manpower shortage,[53] high draft avoidance, and substantial budget problems. After the collapse of the Soviet Union, 1,517 officers left the republic, another 836 expressed their desire to serve in their "native" republics.[54] In 1993 Kazakhstan's parliament became a scene of lively debates about the military budget, which revealed certain contradictions in the views of different layers of society on military issues. In the end, slightly more than 69 billion rubles were allocated for the defense expenditures in 1993 out of an overall budget of 722 billion rubles.[55]

In accordance with published documents, the army of Kazakhstan will consist of ground forces, an air force, antiaircraft defense troops, and naval units. At the end of 1992, Alma-Ata officially laid claim to its part of the Caspian flotilla, which will constitute the Kazakh Naval Force.[56] Kazakhstan has also created its own border guard troops, internal troops and a national guard.[57] For the time being, the Kazakh borders will be protected by joint Russian-Kazakh forces.

In the long term, the optimal size of the army is envisioned to vary from 0.5 percent to 0.9 percent of the total population (about 45.000 men), while by the end of 1993, the Kazakh armed forces will be reduced to the level of 170,000 men.[58] In the next several years, Kazakhstan's military leadership plans to pursue two fundamental goals in their armed forces development: (1) a steady shift to a voluntary army; and (2) equipping the Kazakh army with highly maneuverable armaments, including combat aircraft and helicopters. Taking into consideration the country's geography, the mobile, highly trained units, capable of rapid deployment in any part of the Kazakh Steppes, are seen as a major element of the future armed forces.[59]

The Uzbek authorities also have very serious reasons to be concerned about the conditions, morale, loyalty and readiness of their newly born armed forces. On many occasions in the past, Islam Karimov, President of Uzbekistan, has made it clear that he would not hesitate to use force if a "Tajik scenario" develops in his republic. The Uzbek ruling establishment will increasingly seek the support of the army, police and security services against its domestic opponents, which are mainly of nationalist or Islamist character. Furthermore, the proximity of Tajikistan and the strong historical, ethnic and cultural interrelation of Uzbekistan and Tajikistan urge the Uzbek officials to be sensitive to the republic's military requirements. A question for President Karimov and his associates is how capable the Uzbekistan army will be in fulfilling, if necessary, important internal functions such as supporting the president and destroying any armed domestic opposition, or in conducting low-intensity warfare in Tajikistan or on the frontier with Afghanistan.

As in the case of Kazakhstan, the close military alliance with Russia and the progressive "nationalization" of the armed forces appear to be the cornerstone of the Uzbek military policy. The present Uzbek leadership wants Russia to maintain its military-strategic commitment to the *status-quo* in Central Asia.[60]

Uzbekistan is committed to preserving a "single defense space" with Russia, including joint defense, coordination of military doctrines and legislation, combat and mobilization training, the promotion of military-technical cooperation, and the holding of joint military exercises. In a gesture of good will, 5,000 conscripts from Uzbekistan joined the Western Group of Forces of the Russian army in 1993.[61]

As with the rest of the region, the national composition of the newly created Uzbekistan army is a source of many problems and difficulties. The officer corps remains overwhelmingly Slavic (70 percent), while more than 70 percent of the soldiers come from Uzbekistan.[62] A language problem has become very acute; Slav officers are encouraged to learn the Uzbek language, while a substantial proportion of the Uzbek recruits, who do not possess an adequate knowledge of Russian, spend much time trying to learn it in order to communicate with their commanders. The situation is further complicated by the severe friction and even sporadic fighting between the Uzbek soldiers drawn from different parts of Uzbekistan, especially between "eastern" and "western" Uzbeks.[63]

In 1993, the backbone of the active Uzbek Ground Force consists of two brigades: a national guard brigade of 2,000 men based in Tashkent, and a motorized rifle brigade in Termez on the border with Afghanistan.[64] The Uzbek Defense Ministry began to recall officers of Uzbek nationality (more than 4,000 of them are presently serving in Russia) back to their native republic. There are also plans to restructure and reform three military colleges functioning in Uzbekistan in order to train more military specialists at home. The first military school for Uzbek youth was founded in Fergana.[65]

Tashkent aims to have a mobile and combat-ready army, which will number not more than 30-35,000 men. So far, there has been little talk of a voluntary army, and Uzbekistan's Law on Defense proclaims universal military service to be an underlying principle of its military doctrine. The republic's armed forces will include ground forces, an air force, an anti-aircraft defense force, special forces and a national guard. Uzbekistan has also announced the creation of its own border guards and internal security troops.[66]

Up until the early summer of 1992, the Kyrgyz authorities were reluctant to establish a separate armed forces for the republic. On a number of occasions, President Akayev and his close associates pointed out that the CIS security agreements provide Kyrgyzstan with firm and sufficient guarantees of security and defense. He also mentioned that his republic planned to limit itself to setting up a national guard of about 800 men. At the same time, Bishkek announced that it would attempt to maintain political neutrality on military questions.[67]

However, the ongoing preparations for separate armies in the other Central Asian republics and substantial pressure from Moscow (which preferred to avoid ambiguity on the status of troops deployed in Kyrgyzstan and refused to finance the troops stationed in the republic) prompted the Kyrgyz leadership to review their initial approach to the military issues and to begin building a Kyrgyz army. At the request of Marshal Shaposhnikov, (then) Commander-in-Chief of the CIS JAF, President Akayev signed a decree transferring troops stationed in Kyrgyzstan to the jurisdiction of this republic.[68]

The 8th motorized rifle division based in Bishkek and Rybachy, together with a mountain brigade of 500 to 600 men in Osh and a regiment of the internal troops, became the core of the Kyrgyz armed forces. In 1993 the Kyrgyz army numbered approximately 15,000 men, of whom 4,500 are officers. There were also 3,000 border guard troops in Kyrgyzstan. Since the autumn of 1992, Russia has covered 80 percent of the cost of the border protection in the republic.[69]

The Kyrgyz government plans to have a small, combat-ready "self-defense force" of 8,000 men in the future. Over the long run, the Kyrgyz "self-defense" troops will become a highly professional voluntary mechanism. There is also a project to create a reserve system for the armed forces. At the same time, Bishkek is seeking close defense cooperation with other participants under the Tashkent Collective Security Treaty.[70]

In May and June of 1992, intensive bilateral negotiations and consultations took place between Russia and Turkmenistan over the fate and new arrangement of the substantial part of troops and armaments of the Turkestan Military District (four divisions), which were based on Turkmen territory. Late in May, the Turkmen officials proposed to Russia that all military units in Turkmenistan would be under "joint control." This formula of Russian-Turkmen "joint troops" envisioned the joint finance, supply and staffing of the military units deployed on the territory of Turkmenistan. The Turkmen proposal also mentioned that Slav officers serving in the "joint forces" could maintain the citizenship of their own states.[71]

In subsequent negotiations, Russia initiated a more precise division of functions between the two states. A bilateral defense protocol, signed early in June, proclaimed that Turkmenistan would set up its own national armed forces "under the joint command of the Russian Federation and Turkmenistan."[72] All major questions such as the strategic tasks of the troops in Turkmenistan and their movements, military training and maneuvers would be decided through bilateral consultations between the Russian and Turkmen military officials. The sides also share the burden of financing and maintaining these troops.[73] Two divisions based in Kushka and Kyzylarvat will constitute the backbone of the Turkmen army.[74] Jurisdiction over the air defense forces (two regiments in

Ashqabat and Nebit-Dage), a number of air force units and a training division in Ashqabat was passed to Russia. These troops remain within the command of the Russian army.[75] In July 1992, the formation of a national guard of 1,000 men was announced in Ashqabat.[76] In March 1993, the Turkmen government concluded an agreement with their Russian counterparts on the creation of the Turkmen Naval Forces, which will function under the joint command.[77]

Interethnic and intertribal contradictions in the Turkmen army have been on the rise since independence. While 90 percent of the soldiers and sergeants in the military units are Turkmen, more than 90 percent of the officers are ethnic Slav. Some cases of Turkmen draftees refusing to obey Russian officers were reported. Furthermore, in the summer of 1992, the fighting between Turkmen soldiers of different tribes led to 18 deaths. Draft avoidance in Turkmenistan is the highest in Central Asia, with some regiments lacking 40 percent of their draftees. The result is very low discipline and morale in the units of the Turkmen army.[78]

Turkmenistan aims to have an army of 28,000 men.[79] In the future, the Turkmen army will recruit on a voluntary basis. The contract system of military service has already been introduced in a number of units.[80]

The victory of the People's Front of Tajikistan (PFT) over the so-called "Islamic-democratic" opposition, first in Dushanbe and later in the bulk of the territory of Tajikistan in late December 1991 to early 1992, signaled the return to power of the remnants of the ex-Soviet Tajik political elite, largely recruited from the Khujent and Kulyab regions. In terms of the strategic outlook of Tajikistan, it meant the revival of a strong pro-Russian/pro-CIS orientation and, even more, the emergence of a significant military-political dependence on neighboring Uzbekistan, which made a large contribution to the PFT's victory over the so-called "Islamic-democratic" forces.

New Tajik authorities were quick to announce the creation of the first five battalions of the Tajik regular troops on the basis of the PFT military formations. Military advisers from the CIS JAF (primarily from the Russian 201st division and Uzbekistan) were invited to supervise and assist local "field commanders" in the creation and deployment of these troops. At the same time, Imamali Rahmonov, Chairman of the Supreme Soviet of Tajikistan, announced his country's full adherence to the CIS Collective

Security Treaty and urged Russia and other members of the Tashkent treaty to provide immediate military support to his country, particularly in sealing the Tajik-Afghan border. An ethnic Russian, Alexandre Shishlyannikov, who was born in Uzbekistan and had long experience in serving in the Turkestan Military District, was appointed as the Minister of Defense of Tajikistan.[81]

For the time being, the major problems for the Tajik armed forces remain the guerilla warfare with the remnants of the "Islamic-democratic" armed groups, which retreated to the high mountain areas of the southeastern part of Tajikistan, and the border clashes with hostile Tajik and Afghan fighters and weapons smugglers. To fulfill these functions, the emerging Tajik military will have to rely heavily not only on Russian and CIS support, but also on the so-called "voluntary army," mainly recruited from among the pro-government Tajiks of Kulyab and the Kurgan-Tyube region. The creation of strong defense lines along the republic's southern borders are seen as one of the major military priorities. To overcome another serious problem—the tremendous shortage of command expertise—the Tajik Defense Minister has begun to recall about 200 reserve officers. In January 1993, the Tajik High Command-Engineering College accepted the first 150 military cadets into newly established 8- to 9-month military courses to prepare junior officers for the armed forces.[82]

In the future, Tajikistan plans to have a small, but mobile armed force of 20,000 men. These will include ground forces (several motorized rifle and one mountain brigade) and an air force.[83]

THE RUSSIAN-CENTRAL ASIAN MILITARY-STRATEGIC PARTNERSHIP: PROBLEMS AND PROSPECTS

Central Asia presents Russia with a number of difficult dilemmas and problems. Few people doubt that stability in this region, which borders Russia from the south and is home to millions of Russians and Russian-speaking people, is of vital importance to Russia's own well-being, security, and territorial integrity.

The issues at stake in current Russian debates on Central Asia deal with "how" and "at what cost" Russia can secure its interests in these areas. Is Moscow in a position to play a stabilizing role in Central Asia or is the disruption of this region and the emergence of a new "arc of crisis" on the Russian southern borders inevitable?

Can Moscow stabilize this region without getting closely involved in internal disputes or even in fighting in the Central Asian states? Can Russia afford to spend badly needed resources on the support of certain regimes or military operations in Central Asia? What are the most flexible and beneficial forms and structures of Russian-Central Asian military-strategic cooperation? Is the Tashkent Treaty a "trap" or a significant achievement of Russia? The debates in Moscow continue, and these issues are likely to remain on the agenda for many years to come.

In reality, however, recent developments in Russian policy suggest that its leadership has opted for a closer involvement in Central Asian affairs and the promotion of full-scale military-strategic cooperation with the present Central Asian regimes. Russian military and political support for the ex-Communist elites from the Khujent/Kulyab clans, which defeated the so-called "Islamic-democratic" opposition and seized power in Tajikistan in December 1992, clearly indicates where Russian preferences are. Stability, the rights of ethnic Russians in the region and the closure of the CIS frontiers rather than a turbulent "democratic" transformation are Moscow's primary objectives in Central Asia. The region is increasingly seen as within the Russian/CIS vital sphere of interest, with Russia having a legitimate responsibility and obligation for the stability and peace in these areas. In general, this shift toward a more active policy in Central Asia has been in tune with the overall refocusing of the Russian foreign policy on the "near abroad" and its renewed emphasis on further political, economic and military-strategic integration and consolidation of the Commonwealth of the Independent States. Moscow has announced that the curtailment and regulation of armed conflicts in the territory of the former USSR was in Russia's vital interest, and Russia would play the role of the rightful guarantor of military and political stability of the territory of the former USSR.[84]

Many senior Russian military officials and specialists look upon the Tashkent Collective Security agreements as a first step toward creation of a close military-political alliance within the framework of the CIS and the fulfillment of Russia's security requirements.[85] The southern orientation of this military-political alliance is seen as inevitable and highly important for the Russian state in a changing geo-political environment. Instability in "the South," Islamic fundamentalism, and a bloc of hostile Islamic states are new codewords, a strategic vocabulary used by many top Russian

110

military officials to refer to their primary enemy.[86] These views hold that Russia should quickly cement its military relations with the Central Asian states, try to prevent the spread of Islam in its southern underbelly, work to preserve the *status-quo* in Central Asia and, if necessary, back the existing pro-Russian regimes against domestic and internal Islamic and nationalist opposition. In other words, as the moderate Russian newspaper *Izvestia* puts it, Russia is called upon to play the role of a "Eurasian gendarme" with legitimate rights to take military action in nearby post-Soviet states or in Central Asia in the event of extreme de-stabilization.[87]

Since the CIS JAF and the CIS "collective security" mechanism has not yet materialized fully, it is difficult to assess its "pluses" and "minuses." At the same time, the first attempts to construct and develop new Russian-Central Asian military-strategic relations have revealed numerous problems with any cooperative arrangement. Several points seem to be of crucial importance. First, the major challenge to the proposed "Russian-Central Asian axis" is the political environment within each of the Central Asian states themselves, over which Moscow will have less and less influence in the future. The present ex-Communist *nomenklatura* might be a transitional phenomenon in many parts of Central Asia. At the same time, the opposition groups are more nationalistic, militant and anti-Russian, demanding "real independence" from Moscow, the withdrawal of remaining "Soviet troops" and the creation of truly independent national armed forces. Indeed, if the current Central Asian ruling authorities fail to mobilize resources to address pressing economic and social problems in their countries and are replaced by more nationalist or Islamic leaders, political events in Central Asia will rapidly progress beyond the currently emerging military-strategic configuration in the CIS, disrupting it and demanding an overall reassessment of the military environment in the region.

Moreover, the emergence of a new type of leadership in only one or two Central Asian states would split the current regime/elite coherence of ex-Soviet Central Asia and would be likely to initiate a process of realignment in the region, linking it to existing religious, ethnic or political rivals in the Near East.

Second, the Tashkent agreements were formulated and structured as a collective defense system against challenges from outside the CIS. In reality, it can serve as a deterrent to countries bordering Central Asia from the south from military involvement in ex-Soviet areas. Meanwhile, in the immediate future, internal unrest, clan/regional strife and possible disputes between various Central Asian states are likely to take precedence over any external threat. In this regard, the Russian-Central Asian defense arrangement is simply incapable of halting intra-state clan/regional and ethnic conflicts in these areas. Thus, increased pressure on the internal policing functions of local militaries and Russian/CIS peacekeeping or peacemaking operations to stay out of intra-CIS upheavals, together with the CIS role in border protection, can be expected to become a primary focus of military-strategic developments in these areas in the near future.

Third, the more resources, energy and effort Russia spends on building and developing the CIS "common military-strategic space," the greater the future temptation will be for Moscow to intervene in Central Asia on the side of their clients and partners in collective security arrangements, particularly if they are challenged by domestic opposition that is anti-Russian in its outlook and supported from abroad. Hence, this is well understood in Central Asia; local authoritarian leaders like Islam Karimov and Imamali Rahmonov are likely to remain enthusiastic supporters of close military-strategic cooperation in the CIS framework. On the other hand, many Russian analysts warn today about this "trap" and the dangers of steady Russian involvement in Central Asian domestic interclan and interregional fighting, inherent in the provisions of the Tashkent Treaty. The current dispute between the General Staff of the Russian army and the High Command of the CIS JAF reflects the ongoing debate about the limits and conditions of the Russian military commitment to Central Asia. The Russian military authorities will continue to press for more favorable and flexible structures and procedures for the CIS JAF and its command, which will provide Moscow with a senior role and greater freedom to determine the rules, conditions and scale of its military engagements in existing and potential "hot spots" on the territory of the CIS.

Fourth, if the CIS JAF and its command/control structures are finally established, the emerging Commonwealth military/political bureaucracy is likely to evolve into a strong lobby within a Russian/CIS decision-making mechanism, arguing for a more active policy in Central Asia and possibly in adjacent Near Eastern countries. Moreover, the collective decisionmaking of this NATO-type alliance will determine the increasing impact of the Central

Asian states (Kazakhstan, Uzbekistan, Kyrgyzstan, and Tajikistan), which constitute a majority of the four out of seven potential participants (plus Russia, Armenia and Belarus), on the agenda, strategic orientation, and main concerns of the CIS military-strategic alliance.

In conclusion, Russians have chosen democratic changes and wide-ranging political and economic reforms as the way to rebuild and regenerate their country. To achieve these goals, Russian strategists and politicians say their country needs a "belt" of good-neighborliness, a stable and friendly environment, and peace and tranquility on its borders, including in the increasingly unpredictable south. Here is where the Russian dilemma lies. For the moment, Moscow does not see any alternative to its policy of actively maintaining the status quo, a close military-strategic alliance with authoritarian local leaders and selective military involvement as the keys to preserving stability in the region. As a result, Russia will be seen as an outside force resisting change, trying to stop or at least slow the process of regional transformation. The risk is obvious: the local counter-elite, if in power, will perceive Russia as an unfriendly and neo-colonialist state. The potential advantage, many Russians will argue, will be in preventing the negative impact of Central Asian disruptive changes and of limiting the spill-over effects of the local conflicts, which could destabilize regions within the Russian Federation in the next several years, affecting the pace of Russia's own domestic reforms.

NOTES

1.	Radio *Mayak*, November 29, 1991, BBC Summary, SU/1245, December 3, 1991

2.	*Moskovskii Novosti*, August 9, 1992, 6-7.

3.	*Izvestia*, April 21, 1992, 2.

4.	*Slovo Kyrgyzstana*, February 14, 1992, BBC Summary, SU/1307, February 19, 1992.

5.	*Channel 1 TV*, February 2, 1992, BBC Summary, SU/1297, February 6, 1992.

6.	Ibid.

7.	*Krasnaya Zvezda*, May 15, 1992, 1.

8.	*Nezavisimaya Gazeta*, June 5, 1992, 1; *Nezavisimaya Gazeta*, May 27, 1992, 3.

9.	*Rossiyskaya Gazeta*, May 23, 1992, BBC Summary, SU/1389, May 25, 1992. The text of "collective security" treaty see: *Krasnaya Zvezda*, May 23, 1992, 1.

Central Asia: Emerging Military-Strategic Issues

10.   Armenia's calculation of using the Tashkent agreement as a badly needed military-strategic outlet to Russia and a larger CIS alliance was, however, overestimated. Russia, along with its four Central Asian partners in "collective defense," refused to get involved in the battle between Armenia and Azerbaijan. Armenia's appeal to send peacekeepers into the battle areas was also rejected.

11.   *Krasnaya Zvezda*, May 8, 1992, BBC Summary, SU/1386, May 21, 1992.

12.   Interview with Yevgeniy Shaposhnikov, Commander-in-Chief of the CIS Joint Armed Forces, *Moskovskii Novosti*, February 7, 1992, 11. See also Shaposhnikov's complaints about the lack of real cooperation between the CIS member states, *"Russia" TV channel*, January 12, 1993, BBC Summary, SU/1587, January 15, 1993.

13.   *Literaturnaya Gazeta*, March 17, 1993, 11. See also interview with Marshal Shaposhnikov, *Nezavisimaya Gazeta*, January 21, 1993, 3.

14.   On the desirability of a CIS military bloc see interview with Lt-Gen Leonid Ivashov, Secretary of the Council of Ministers of Defense of the Commonwealth countries, *Krasnaya Zvezda*, November 24, 1992.

15.   *Krasnaya Zvezda*, February 17, 1993, 2.

16.   *Krasnaya Zvezda*, March 2, 1993, 1. Russian Defense Minister Pavel Grachev, answering a question on the desirability of the CIS military integration after the CIS summit in Minsk in January 1993, also pointed out: "We do not lose optimism and believe that some form of cooperation, at least between the six states, which signed a collective security treaty in Tashkent, will remain." See *Krasnaya Zvezda*, January 23, 1993, 1.

17.   President Nazarbayev's answer at the press conference after the Minsk summit in January 1993, *Ostankino Channel 1 TV*, January 22, 1993, BBC Summary, SU/1595, January 25, 1993. The Kazakh president suggested that the seven states that have signed the CIS Charter should be considered the integrator of the CIS in many spheres, including the defense union.

18.   Ukraine is eager to leave the common strategic area of the CIS following the removal of the nuclear weapons from its territory. Moldova and Azerbaijan are not participating in the development of CIS military cooperation.

19.   Kathleen Mihalisko, Belarus: Neutrality Gives Way To "Collective Security," *RFE/RL Research Report* 2, no. 17, April 23, 1993, 24-31.

20.   *Krasnaya Zvezda*, July 3, 1992, 1, 3.

21.   Interview with Col.-Gen. Samsonov, ibid.

22.   By the end of January 1993, Ukraine, Moldova, Tajikistan and Turkmenistan had not even paid their portions to finance the creation and maintenance of the High Command of the CIS JAF. See *Krasnaya Zvezda*, January 23, 1993, 1.

23.   *Krasnaya Zvezda*, March 2, 1993, 1.

24.   Marshal Shaposhnikov's plan originally envisioned a two-staged building of the CIS JAF. In the first stage (1993-1994), it was suggested the general troops be set up which would serve as cover, and simultaneously as a mobile force in limited armed conflicts at the outer borders of the CIS. The second stage was to embrace the period from 1995 to 1996, or, the final formation of the JAF by drawing from different portions and branches of the armed forces and by the creation of administrative bodies and a command-control structure. In peace time, all JAF units were to remain under the subordination of national military departments, and only in case of war would they act under the CIS banner. See *Moskovskii Novosti*, May 23, 1993, 10.

25.   *Izvestia*, April 23, 1992, 1; *ITAR-TASS World Service* in Russian, April 22, 1992, BBC Summary, SU/1363, April 24, 1992.

26.   *Pravda Vostoka*, November 7, 1992, 1, 2.; *KAZTAG TASS* via *ITAR-TASS* News Agency, BBC Summary, SU/1531, November 6, 1992.

27.   *Interfax* News Agency, January 12, 1993, BBC Summary, SU/1587, January 15, 1993. Marshal Shaposhnikov, C-in-C of the CIS JAF expressed his doubts whether the meeting would take place at all. See *Ibid.* I have not found any reports of it being held. *Interfax,* however, confirmed that there was a plan to convene this meeting on January 15. Referring to "well-informed" sources the agency cited, that the Tajik conflict "may be qualified as intra-regional, in view of which the states of the region will try to settle it without military assistance from the CIS." See *Interfax* News Agency, January 7, 1993, BBC Summary, SU/1580, January 7, 1993.

28.   *Nezavisimaya Gazeta*, January 6, 1993, 3; *Nezavisimaya Gazeta*, January 5, 1993, 3. In their later statements, Central Asian leaders insisted that the proposed regional integration of their states does not at all contradict, but substitutes for cooperation within the framework of the Commonwealth. The idea of a Central Asian defense union seems to have been initiated by President Nazarbayev. In general, the strategy of the Kazakh leadership is based on the full support of two instruments of integration—the Commonwealth and the Central Asian regional alliance. The skillful balancing between/within these two mechanisms is believed to allow Kazakhstan to achieve three fundamental sets of policy objectives: (1) to preserve internal inter-ethnic tranquility between Kazakh and Slavs communities; (2) to counterbalance the Russian might in the CIS, to create insurance against the reemergence of Russian imperial tendencies and to acquire important leverage of influence over Russian policy; and (3) to create for Kazakhstan a regional power center in a new Eurasian geo-political environment.

29.   For the text of the Russian-Kazakh agreement see: *Kazakhstanskaya Pravda*, July 23, 1992, 2. The agreements with Uzbekistan and Kyrgyzstan are reported to be very similar to the Russian-Kazakh treaty, which was concluded first.

30.   *The Commonwealth of the Independent States: Developments and Prospects.* Report of the Center of International Studies (Moscow: Moscow State Institute of International Studies, September 1992), 11.

31.   Interview with Major General Alibek Kasimov, Chief-of-Staff of the Armed Forces of Kazakhstan, *Krasnaya Zvezda,* March 17, 1993, 1, 2; *KAZTAG* News Agency, September 9, 1992, BBC Summary, SU/1487, September 16, 1992; *Kazakh Radio*, October 10, 1992, BBC Summary, SU/1510, October 13, 1992; *Krasnaya Zvezda,* August 19, 1992, 3; *Krasnaya Zvezda*, August 20, 1992, 2; *Izvestya*, August 21, 1992, 1.

32.   *Krasnaya Zvezda*, March 2, 1993, 1.

33.   An example is the Russian Defense Minister's trip to Uzbekistan and Tajikistan in February 1993. In Tashkent, he discussed with the Uzbek military authorities a wide range of issues, including joint utilization of the strategically important facilities deployed on Uzbek territory, military-technical cooperation, and the mutual supply of foodstuffs, spare parts and material goods. Plans for joint planning for combat and mobilization training and the holding of military exercises involving units of the Russian and Uzbek armed forces were also under consideration. See *ITAR-TASS* News Agency, February 3, 1993, BBC Summary, SU/1605, February 5, 1993; *Krasnaya Zvezda*, February 5, 1993, 1; *Krasnaya Zvezda*, February 2, 1993, 1.

34.   There have been very few bilateral agreements between the Central Asian states in the military sphere. As a rule, they are more general declarations than agreements on specific military questions. Thus, bilateral treaties on friendship, cooperation and mutual assistance signed by several countries in the region declare the signatories' adherence to a unified defense policy. The Kyrgyz-Uzbek treaty, for example, obliges the two states to maintain security in the region, to pursue a unified defense policy and to come to the assistance of each other, including military help, in case of an attack. See *Channel 1 TV*, September 29, 1993, BBC Summary, SU/1501, October 2, 1992. In August 1992, Uzbekistan and Kyrgyzstan signed a protocol of intention to cooperate in military affairs. It calls on the defense ministries of the two states to develop a mechanism for mutual assistance and cooperation. See *Krasnaya Zvezda*, August 18, 1992, 1.

35.   In the Russian mass media, there have been several reports revealing some facts of the Uzbek army's interference in the ongoing war in Tajikistan. Many groups of the People's Front's (PF) fighters are said to be trained by Uzbek officers, and some of them received regular payments from Uzbekistan. There is information about the involvement of Uzbek military aircraft and helicopters in bombing the positions of so-called "Islamist-democratic" opposition in Tajikistan. Also, Tashkent has supplied weapons and ammunition to the PF military formations. See, *Nezavisimaya Gazeta*, December 12, 1992, 3; *Nezavisimaya Gazeta*, December 11, 1992, 3; *Nezavisimaya Gazeta*, January 29, 1993, 3; *Interfax* News Agency, January 14, 1993, BBC Summary, SU/1588, January 16, 1993.

36.   Suzanne Crow, "The Theory and the Practice of Peacekeeping in the Former USSR," *RFE/RL Research Report* 1, no. 37, September 1992, 32; *Krasnaya Zvezda*, April 17, 1992, 3.

37.   Interview with Deputy C-in-C of the CIS JAF, Col-Gen. Boris Pyankov, *Krasnaya Zvezda*, October 15, 1992, 2.

38.   *Krasnaya Zvezda*, July 17, 1992, 1; *Krasnaya Zvezda*, July 18, 1992, 3; *Moskovskii Novosti*, June 26, 1992, 3; Suzanne Crow, ibid, 33.

39.   Interview with Col.-Gen. Pyankov, *Ibid*. Accordance to Pyankov, the peacekeeping regiments of the republics will be subordinated to the military command of their national armed forces, while being simultaneously under the operational control of the High Command of the CIS JAF. He mentions, that Russia is ready to allocate 2-3 regiments, Uzbekistan - one regiment, Kyrgyzstan - one battalion. Some CIS states (Ukraine, Belarus) are not going to have such permanent contingents for peacekeeping operations, but if necessary, will establish them for "accomplishment of tasks required in a concrete situation;" *ITAR-TASS* News Agency, October 13, 1992, BBC Summary, SU/1512, October 15, 1992.

40.   Before Tajikistan, peacekeepers already operated in South Ossetia, Moldova's "Dniester Republic" and Ingushia. Yet they were not, strictly speaking, a "Commonwealth peacekeeping force:" the decisions on their dispatch were adopted by the countries involved in the conflict rather than by the CIS Council of Heads of State; the CIS contingent had not been shaped by that time. Tajikistan was supposed to be the first conflict area where "commonwealth peacekeepers" would be deployed. See *ITAR-TASS*, ibid.

41.   Russian Deputy Defense Minister, Col.-Gen. Vladimir Toporov was most explicit on the purposes of Russia's military involvement in Tajikistan, saying that the presence of the Russian troops was necessary "not because we want to make war but because Russia can hardly provide everything necessary for the upkeep of 300,000 Russians who live in Tajikistan." See *ITAR-TASS* News Agency, October 7,

1992, BBC Summary, SU/1507, October 9, 1992.

42. *Krasnaya Zvezda*, October 14, 1993, 3; *Interfax* News Agency, October 8, 1992, BBC Summary, SU/1508, October 10. This stand was influenced by Tajik internal politics. Iskanderov's nomination to the post of acting president occurred as the result of the removal of ex-president Nabiyev by forces of the so-called "Islamic-democratic" opposition. His tenure in power reflected an attempt to forge a new balance of clan-regional interests after the *status-quo* was disrupted by the dissolution of the USSR. Thus, he tried to reconcile the demands of influential officials in Khujent and Kulyab to introduce the CIS troops and the objections of Davlat Usman and Tajik *Qazi* Hajji Akbar Turanjanzadah to Russian and Uzbek interference in the internal affairs of Tajikistan.

43. *Krasnaya Zvezda*, October 16, 1992, 3; *KYRGYZTAG* via *ITAR-TASS* News Agency, October 14, 1992, BBC Summary, SU/1513, October 16, 1992. In April 1993, Kyrgyzstan even withdrew its battalion from the Afghan-Tajik border which was sent there in the autumn of 1992 to strengthen the Russian border guard detachment. In accordance with Felix Kulov, Vice-President of Kyrgyzstan, the republic now intends to send its soldiers to serve in "hot sports" only on a voluntary basis. See *Nezavisimaya Gazeta*, April 2, 1993, 3.

44. *Krasnaya Zvezda*, February 27, 1993, 2.

45. *Interfax* News Agency, December 1, 1992, BBC Summary, SU/1552 i, December 1, 1992; *ITAR-TASS* News Agency, December 8, 1992, BBC Summary, SU/1560, December 10, 1992; *Krasnaya Zvezda*, February 27, 1993, 2. By the end of December 1992, only the Uzbek parliament had agreed to send the peace-keeping troops to Tajikistan. See *Nezavisimaya Gazeta*, December 26, 1992, 3.

46. *Nezavisimaya Gazeta*, April 23, 1993, 3.

47. The CIS summit, held in January 1993 in Minsk, once more confirmed that Russia, Uzbekistan, Kazakhstan and Kyrgyzstan, would send a 500-strong battalion to Tajikistan. After the summit, the new Tajik president Imamali Rahmonov, speaking on the decision to dispatch the CIS peacekeepers, stressed that it was important to make it clear to Afghanistan that Tajikistan was not alone and that all CIS countries were working together to protect its borders. See *Interfax* News Agency, January 23, 1993, BBC Summary, SU/1597, January 27, 1993.

48. *Strategic Survey 1991-1992*, Brassey's for the IISS, London, 1992, 151.

49. *Krasnaya Zvezda*, July 2, 1992, 2. A "cadre hunger" is particularly severe with higher-ranking officers. The Kazakh statistics show that for the past 74 years only three representatives of the Kazakh nation have managed to graduate from the Military Academy of the General Staff and only two were able to qualify for the degree of the candidate of military science. See *KAZTAG* New Agency, November 23, 1992, BBC Summary, SU/1552, December 1, 1992.

50. For example, President Nazarbayev initially suggested that Russia and Kazakhstan should set up joint military units and contingents in order to promote the unity of the two armies. See *ITAR-TASS* News Agency, February 26, 1993, BBC Summary, SU/1627, March 3, 1993, *Kazakhstanskay Pravda*, May 14, 1992, 2.

51. *KAZTAG* News Agency, November 23, 1992, BBC Summery, SU/1552, December 1, 1992; *Krasnaya Zvezda*, December 24, 1992, 3; *Krasnaya Zvezda*, May 27, 1992, 1.

52. Interview with Major General Kasimov, ibid; *KAZTAG* News Agency, November 23, 1992, ibid; *Channel 1 TV*, February 23, 1993, BBC Summary, SU/1625, March 1, 1993.

53. *KAZTAG* News Agency, January 15, 1993, BBC Summary, SU/1593, BBC Summery, January 22, 1993.

54. *Krasnaya Zvezda*, January 1, 1993, 1.

55. *KAZTAG* News Agency, January 15, 1993, ibid; *Krasnaya Zvezda*, March 10, 1993, 1; *Interfax* News Agency, January 25, 1993, BBC Summery, SU/1598, January 28, 1993.

56. *Krasnaya Zvezda*, January 28, 1993, ibid, *ITAR-TASS* News Agency, November 25, 1992, BBC Summary, SU/ 1552, December 1, 1992.

57. *Krasnaya Zvezda*, July 15, 1992, 3; *Krasnaya Zvezda*, December 16, 1992, 3.

58. *KAZTAG* News Agency, November 23, 1992, ibid; *Krasnaya Zvezda*, July 2, 1992, 2.

59. Ibid.

60. The idea of a "common threat" to Russia and Uzbekistan often appears in the official statements of the Uzbek president. For example, in October in his interview to *Interfax*, President Karimov called Russia the guarantor of stability in Central Asia. Russia, in his opinion, should look after its interests in Central Asia, and, most importantly, to combat "the powerful offensive of pan-Islamism in the South." See *Interfax*, October 8, 1992, BBC Summary, SU/1508, October 10, 1992.

61. *Krasnaya Zvezda*, January 30, 1993, 3.

62. *Krasnaya Zvezda*, July 16, 1992, 2.

63. *Srednya Aziya. Spravochnye Materialy. Istoriya. Economika. Politika.* (Moskva: Institut Gumanitarno-Politicheskyh Issledovanii, 1992), 39, 40; *Krasnaya Zvezda*, July 9, 1992, 3.

64. *Srednya Aziya*, ibid.

65. *ITAR-TASS* News Agency, February 3, 1993, BBC Summary, SU/1605, February 5, 1993; *Krasnaya Zvezda*, July 16, 1992, ibid; *Krasnaya Zvezda*, August 18, 1992, 3.

66. *Pravda Vostoka*, August 6, 1992, 2; *Russia's Radio*, May 19, 1992, BBC Summary, SU/1385, May 20, 1992.

67. *Russian Television*, May 28, 1992, BBC Summary, SU/1395, June 1, 1992; *Pravda*, May 19, 1992, 2; *Krasnaya Zvezda*, June 2, 1992, 1.

68. *Krasnaya Zvezda*, ibid.

69. *Srednya Aziya*, ibid, 62-63.

70. In the opinion of President Akayev, Kyrgyz participation in CIS collective security does not contradict its proclaimed neutrality. This approach, however, differs from that of other signatory states, Russia, Kazakhstan and Uzbekistan, where many politicians and military officials are more inclined to consider the Tashkent Treaty as a first step towards creation of a future close military-political alliance. See *Nezavisimaya Gazeta*, February 17, 1993, 3.

71. *Nezavisimaya Gazeta*, May 27, 1992, 3.

72. *Krasnaya Zvezda*, June 2, 1992, 3; *Krasnaya Zvezda*, June 10, 1992, 1.

73. *Krasnaya Zvezda*, May 26, 1992, 3.

74. *Nezavisimaya Gazeta*, ibid.

75. *Srednya Aziya*, ibid, 107.

76. *Krasnaya Zvezda*, July 16, 1992, 3.

77. *Nezavisimaya Gazeta*, March 17, 1993, 3.

78. *Srednya Azya*, ibid, 107-109; *Nezavisimaya Gazeta*, May 27, 1992, 3; *Nezavisimaya Gazeta*, August 14, 1992, 3

79.   *Postfactum* in English, May 26, 1992, BBC Summary, SU/1393, May 29, 1992.

80.   *Turkmenistan State News Agency*, October 22, 1992, BBC Summary, SU/1527, November 2, 1992.

81.   *Krasnaya Zvezda*, March 19, 1993, 2; *Krasnaya Zvezda*, February 16, 1993, 3; *Tajik Radio*, Dushanbe in Russian, January 19, 1993, BBC Summary, SU/1594, January 23, 1993.

82.   *Krasnaya Zvezda*, March 19, 1993, *ibid; Krasnaya Zvezda*, January 20, 1993, 2.

83.   *Krasnaya Zvezda*, March 19, ibid.

84.   See Jogh Lough, ibid, *Nezavisimaya Gazeta*, April 30, 1993, 1, 3; *Rossiiskie Vesti*, December 3, 1992, 2.

85.   See, for example, Interview with Lt.-Gen. Ivashov, Secretary of the CIS Council of Defense Ministers, *ITAR-TASS*, November 24, 1992, BBC Summary, SU/1547, November 25, 1993; Marshal Shaposhnikov "National and Collective Security in the CIS," *Krasnaya Zvezda*, September 30, 1992, 2-3; Sergei Rogov, "What place in the world will we occupy?" *Krasnaya Zvezda*, March 25, 1993, 1-2.

86.   See Marshal Shaposhnikov, ibid; *Krasnaya Zvezda*, April 21, 1992, 3, *Krasnaya Zvezda*, April 9, 1992, 3; or Pavel Grachev's statement on the "Islamic threat" to the CIS, *Nezavisimaya Gazeta*, May 7, 1993, 3; RFE/RL News Briefs: 8-12 February 1993, *RFE/RL Research Report*, vol. 2, no. 8, 1993, 8.

87.   *Izvestia*, August 7, 1992, 6.

4. SECURITY IMPLICATIONS of the COMPETITION for INFLUENCE AMONG NEIGHBORING STATES

CHINA, INDIA, AND CENTRAL ASIA

Ross H. Munro

On the Eurasian landmass, two great historic events are underway:

- The continuing collapse of Russian imperialism and the Soviet Communist system
- China's apparently irrevocable economic and military takeoff on a trajectory that will bring it to full-fledged superpower status early in the next century.

While the implications of the first event for Central Asia are being widely discussed and intensively examined, the implications for the region of the second event are being largely overlooked. Indeed, most current surveys of the international ramifications of the emergence of the five newly independent Central Asian republics deal cursorily, occasionally not at all, with China;

Ross H. Munro has been Coordinator of the Asia Program at the Foreign Policy Research Institute in Philadelphia since 1990. Prior, he had a distinguished career with TIME magazine, serving as Bureau Chief in Hong Kong, New Delhi, Bangkok, and Washington, DC. An expert on East and Southeast Asia, Mr. Munro's articles have appeared in Foreign Policy and Commentary.

therefore this paper will attempt to demonstrate why an economically dynamic and militarily ascendant China must be considered a major player in the region, clearly outranked in importance only by Russia.

It is also important to examine India's role in the region. In this case, the country's modest standing in the surveys is quite justified. Indeed, we intend to argue that even the usual, cautious assessments of India's importance in the region fail to take into account the depths of India's current domestic and international weakness, which in turn is due to an extent to the collapse of the Soviet Union and the end of the Cold War. We will suggest that India's role in Central Asia is a minor and declining one.

CHINA AND CENTRAL ASIA

Since the Soviet Union began to unravel, China's interests in Central Asia have been repeatedly characterized as "primarily defensive—to stop instability from spilling over into Chinese Turkestan,"[1] the Xinjiang Uighur Autonomous Region that, despite its name, is a part of China that is tightly controlled by Peking. In a narrow sense, this is accurate. Although all nation-states try to guard their sovereignty and territorial integrity, few put quite as much emphasis on it as the People's Republic of China. While Hong Kong, Taiwan, and Tibet are most often cited in this connection, the Chinese often have Xinjiang in mind as well. Indeed, Chinese rulers have considered Xinjiang a territorial integrity issue for centuries. This century alone has witnessed at least two serious attempts by Xinjiang's Turkic Muslims to win effective independence from China. Most recently, from 1989 until 1991, unrest intermittently reached serious, and in one or two pockets, insurrectional proportions[2] among elements of the Turkic Muslim population, who officially constitute 60 percent of the population.[3] Nevertheless, it seems in retrospect that both the Chinese authorities and foreign analysts may have over-estimated the significance of these disturbances.

That the Chinese overreacted, there is little doubt. But given the other events that were occurring at the time of the disturbances, the Chinese response is completely understandable. The spring of 1989 was dominated by the demonstrations on Tiananmen square that ended in violence on June 4. We know now that the Chinese leadership really didn't regain its balance and self-confidence before late 1991. Simultaneously, the Soviet Union was unravelling, prompting predictions that Leninism was doomed everywhere, including China. With the formal breakup of the Soviet Union following the failure of the hardliners' coup attempt in August 1991, the five Central Asian republics were in effect set loose. This prompted analysts worldwide to opine that the situation in Central Asia was not only fluid, but volatile. China was not immune to such speculation, particularly when the unrest in Xinjiang suggested that the forces of instability in the former Soviet Union had somehow already leapfrogged the border.

Until spring 1992, the Xinjiang media carried several articles attacking "splittists," "separatists," and other subversives in the Xinjiang Uighur Autonomous Region. Equally intriguing were articles repeatedly exhorting local militias in Xinjiang to do their jobs vigilantly and well, particularly in securing the border areas. Xinjiang officials openly acknowledged that they were concerned about the impact of the breakup of the Soviet Union[4] and that Chinese troops were reinforcing Xinjiang's border with what was then still Soviet Central Asia.[5]

It must be assumed that their words and actions reflected genuine and widespread alarm among Chinese authorities, but there was also another political element at work. The demands for tighter controls clearly reflected, at least in part, the Chinawide effort by conservatives to reassert their influence in the wake of the Tiananmen incident. It should be noted, for instance, that previous calls for tightening up militia work in China could often be explained only as part of a more general political clamp down. Significantly, as the political climate in China changed in the first half of 1992 to the obvious detriment of conservative forces, reports in the Xinjiang media about unrest and militia-building declined dramatically. A March 1992, speech by Xinjiang's government leader denouncing "splittists"[6] seems to have been the last hurrah of the hard line in Xinjiang. After that, references to "splittists" and to militia-building dried up, while news of economic reform and development, including many reports of Xinjiang's burgeoning trade ties with its Central Asian neighbors, dominated official media reports from the region.

Several other factors, some probably more important than the workings of domestic Chinese politics, also explain why the alarm of Chinese authorities over the situation in Xinjiang and Central Asia didn't last. One was that the wave of Muslim unrest itself evidently quickly subsided. This in turn probably can be largely attributed to China's long-term approach to minority issues. Since 1949, except during the Great Leap Forward and the Cultural Revolution, China's minority policies have arguably been among the world's most sophisticated, although not the most benign. Peking, on the one hand, deliberately leaves no doubt about its willingness to use force to quell anything smacking of ethnic separatism. On the other hand, Peking assiduously recruits, coopts, and rewards members of non-Han Chinese groups who are able or ambitious. There are minority quotas for higher education and for government employment as well as a network of minorities institutions that recruit and reward future co-opters with lifetime sinecures.[7] Meanwhile, Peking continues to promote the movement of Han Chinese into Xinjiang and other minority regions in order to tilt the population ratio against the non-Han. As recently as December 1991, it was reported that China was moving Han Chinese farmers and forestry workers to areas along Xinjiang's border with Kazakhstan and Kyrgyzstan, presumably in order to stabilize the frontier.[8] This adroit mix of policies has been largely successful in Xinjiang and the rest of China—with the partial and unique exception of Tibet—in limiting restiveness and revolt among the nation's ethnic minorities.

Of more recent relevance was the realization by relieved Chinese leaders that neither pan-Turkic nationalism nor militant Islam was about to sweep the Central Asian republics. That in turn meant that neither force posed a serious and immediate threat to Xinjiang itself. The ruling secular elites of all five republics made their hostility to militant Islam very clear. Iran, apparently wanting to work for now with those elites and to avoid confrontation, was being notably cautious. Moreover, China remained on good terms not only with Iran, but also Pakistan, where a political movement, Jamaat Islami, was also circumspectly promoting militant Islam in Central Asia. China has long appeared to be more concerned about pan-Turkic nationalism. China views Turkey with suspicion, not only because organizations promoting a separate Turkic state in China have long been based in Istanbul, but also because of the pan-Turkic element inherent in Turkey's primarily cultural approach to the five republics. But here also, the foreign message was not falling on fertile soil in the five republics, where attitudes toward Turkey often seemed wary.

Satisfied that they weren't facing any serious and immediate danger from Central Asia, the Chinese leadership has been able to formulate a regional policy for the long term. With considerable confidence, we can infer China's Central Asian policy from its actions and words. China recognizes that it has a strong national interest in the long-term stability of the Central Asian republics since that should help inhibit the growth of both militant Islam and pan-Turkic nationalism, which would threaten Xinjiang. China's other highly complementary goal is to increase Chinese political and economic influence in the five Central Asian republics, starting with the three that border on China.

The strategy China has chosen to pursue its goals in Central Asia can be seen as a natural spinoff of the economic development strategy that China reaffirmed and dramatically accelerated in 1992 at the urging of Deng Xiaoping. It should be recalled that a key part of Deng's "pitch" to China's Communist Party leaders was that their counterparts in the erstwhile Soviet Union had lost power largely because they had failed to deliver economic growth and a decent standard of living. China's communists would suffer the same fate, he argued, unless they were willing to adopt market-oriented economic growth policies, which they did.

Likewise, by pursuing trade and investment opportunities with its Central Asian neighbors, China helps strengthen their fragile economies. This responds to what Central Asian leaders consider their most basic need. It is not cultural, linguistic or religious "aid" that Central Asia's elites crave; it is economic development. Observes Nancy Lubin: "Growing poverty, unemployment and economic inequality are viewed by Central Asians as key causes of the tragic conflicts that have already occurred in the region and as catalysts for future conflict."[9] The Chinese clearly have a similar view, believing that economic development offers the region the only possibility of limiting future ethnic and religious conflict.[10] Thus the Chinese authorities endorse increased trade and investment in the Central Asian republics as one means of assisting them.

Of course, China intends to do well by doing good. Almost by definition, increased Chinese trade and investment in Central Asia mean increased Chinese influence. Furthermore, given the mutual benefit inherent in market transactions, Chinese trade and investment in Central Asia also help China's domestic economy, particularly the neighboring Xinjiang economy. Indeed, with China's economy already one of the world's largest and fastest growing, both sides should quickly and substantially gain from China's economic offensive in Central Asia.

China's emerging, economics-based approach to Central Asia is best understood by first examining the dramatic developments in its relations with Kazakhstan since 1991. We will look briefly at China's economic ties with the other four republics. But China-Kazakhstan relations deserve close attention, not only because they are the most advanced and extensive, but also because the relationship provides us with ample illustrations of China's overall approach to Central Asia.

Although available statistics are far from satisfactory, they leave no doubt that China's bilateral trade with Kazakhstan has been soaring since early 1992. Reports from the Chinese news agency, Xinhua, indicated that Xinjiang's total foreign trade in 1992 increased to more than US $500 million. Exports and imports going through regular channels jumped by 130 percent, to about US $300 million.[11] Meanwhile, during the first 11 months of 1992, what China classifies as local or border trade, much of it barter, almost quadrupled to US $220 million.[12] Those statistics apparently cover all neighboring countries, including Pakistan and Mongolia, as well as the three adjoining Central Asian republics. But other reports left no doubt that Xinjiang's trade with Kazakhstan was responsible for much, possibly most, of 1992's growth. Xinhua reported that, by late 1992, 50 percent of Kazakhstan's imports of consumer goods—a broad category that includes food, clothing and household goods—were from China.[13] (In the spring of 1993, there were peeved acknowledgements of this fact in the Russian media.) The most basic Chinese products—such as soap, matches and cooking pots—are prized among Asia's poor for their quality and value. A small percentage of Kazakhstan's imports were financed by 30 million Yuan in commodity credits from China,[14] a form of aid that several countries are extending to the republics. The strong interrelationship between the two economies was highlighted when China turned to Kazakhstan for industrial commodities it badly needed such as fertilizer, steel, and ores. To put this in perspective, we estimate, admittedly with only fragmentary data, that China's two-way trade with Kazakhstan in 1992 alone quite possibly exceeded Turkey's trade with all five republics combined.

Further evidence of China's burgeoning trade relationship with Kazakhstan came in a May 1992, report that "a network of Chinese shops" had opened in the republic.[15] By April 1993, Xinhua reported, China had established 150 small joint ventures in Kazakhstan as well.[16] The month of June 1992, witnessed the first train to travel the full length of a rail line linking Xinjiang's capital of Urumqi to the Kazakh capital, Alma Ata.[17] Construction of that rail line had begun in 1956! Daily air service was also instituted between the two capitals.[18] More cross-border roads were opened, including one through the border town of Horgos, where a Hong Kong businessman reportedly built a US $55 million international trade center.[19] That investment exemplified yet another advantage that China enjoys vis-a-vis Central Asia: it can tap into the capital and business experience of all of Greater China, and it doesn't end there. The business communities in Hong Kong and Taiwan can also act as a bridge to world capital markets.

The increase in transportation links between Xinjiang and Kazakhstan was apparently largely responsible for an almost doubling of the number of "foreign tourists and business people" visiting Xinjiang in 1992. Their numbers increased that year to 230,000, 90 percent of them from neighboring countries, compared with 100,000 in 1991.[20] Most of the new arrivals appeared to be "shoppers" from Kazakhstan and the two other Central Asian republics bordering on Xinjiang, Tajikistan, and Kyrgyzstan.

Going in the opposite direction to work in Kazakhstan were hundreds of Chinese experts and technicians. Although we have seen no specific cases cited in the Chinese or Central Asian media, there's little doubt that some of these Chinese are replacing departing Russians. The Chinese experts may prove to be yet another nice "fit" between China and the Central Asian republics. China is potentially an ideal provider of low-cost, low-tech solutions the republics can use in agriculture, industry and infrastructure development. Similarly, the Chinese may prove to be the most experienced and empathetic advisers for Central Asian republics so poorly prepared for the privatization of land and the transition to a market economy. China rightly represents to the impoverished republics an excellent example of successful economic transition and growth.

Clearly, there are strong constituencies in both China and Kazakhstan that favor closer relations between the two countries in almost every field. Evidence of this emerged after talks between Chinese Premier Li Peng and Kazakhstan Premier Tereshchenko in Peking in February 1992. A joint communique noted that agreements had been signed in the areas of trade, scientific and technological cooperation, communications and transport, personnel exchanges and the establishment of a joint committee for the development of further ties.[21] By late 1992, Alma-Ata Radio was reporting that a "treaty on cooperation and military assistance between Kazakhstan and China is expected to be signed in the near future."[22] Although little more has been heard of this proposed treaty, such an announcement by a Government radio station strongly suggests that elements in Kazakhstan see closer ties with China as a way of reducing the influence of Russia, which still bases large numbers of its armed forces on Kazakh soil. More broadly, it alerts us to watch for increased Chinese political and military influence in Central Asia, following on the heels of its growing economic role in the region.

Another, largely unnoticed, exchange between Xinjiang and Kazakhstan was the exodus of tens of thousands of ethnic Kazakhs from Xinjiang. While it was reported in December 1992, that 60,000 Kazakhs had moved to Kazakhstan from Mongolia and from other parts of the Commonwealth of Independent States,[23] the movement of another 30,000 from Xinjiang remained unpublicized outside Kazakhstan itself.[24] Both the Chinese authorities and ethnic Kazakh authorities in Kazakhstan appear to be facilitating this movement, which simultaneously increases the ratio of Hans to non-Hans in Xinjiang while increasing the percentage of Kazakhs in Kazakhstan. Thus the arrangement serves the presumed interests of both the Chinese Government as well as the interests of ethnic Kazakhs in reducing ethnic Russian influence in Kazakhstan.

China's ties with the other four Central Asian republics are less developed but far from insignificant. The second most extensive set of ties are with Kyrgyzstan, which also shares a long border with Xinjiang. China has sent agricultural experts there, extended credits of US $5.7 million,[25] and begun to purchase small amounts of electricity from the republic.[26] There have also been references in the Chinese media to the two countries organizing the joint economic development of neighboring *oblasts*, or administrative divisions, on the border.[27]

128

In August 1992, China proposed exploring the possibility of exploiting four rivers whose waters flow through both Xinjiang and Kyrgyzstan.[28] By January of 1993 the two countries had already reached an agreement to "jointly build a water conservancy works over the Horgos River along the border."[29] The article implied that all the potential uses of the river—irrigation, hydro power, flood control and navigation—would be pursued. All such proposals should be carefully watched for their political implications. Water is a vital and scarce resource in Central Asia, and potential conflict between upstream and downstream users is already a serious concern. In fact, at the moment, this appears to be the only immediate issue where China could find itself in conflict with one or more of the five republics. One possible source of conflict, analysts believe, is that a river development agreement between China and Kazakhstan or Kyrgyzstan could harm the interests of a downstream user such as Uzbekistan.

With Tajikistan, the third Central Asian republic on which Xinjiang borders, China has signed 10 cooperation agreements in the past two years. China has also granted Tajikistan US $5 million in credits.[30] These announcements aside, we find little evidence of an extensive bilateral economic relationship. This may well prove to be a temporary situation, due largely to the turmoil that has afflicted Tajikistan since 1992. China is clearly concerned about events in Tajikistan, but it appears to have kept its distance awaiting the emergence of a more stable government there.

It is difficult to obtain data on China's trade ties with Uzbekistan and Turkmenistan. Given the inroads of Chinese goods in widely separated areas of the former Soviet Union during the past two years, we can assume that trade between China and these two republics is growing rapidly, albeit from a very modest base. It is possible that the dearth of information reflects a desire of the authorities in those two republics to avoid provoking the anti-Chinese sentiment that is common among ethnic Russians there. In the case of Uzbekistan, there is a need for further research to obtain hard information about the relationship. In March, 1992, Uzbekistan's leader, Islam Karimov, visited Peking where he signed 14 bilateral agreements,[31] but we have not seen any reports about progress made under their rubric. China's relations with Turkmenistan are obviously at an early stage. It wasn't until November 1992, that President Niyazov visited Peking, where he signed eight cooperation agreements and a joint communique.

Nevertheless, there was preliminary but intriguing talk of ambitious transportation projects that would link these two relatively distant republics with Xinjiang. In 1992, Mitsubishi proposed a Turkmenistan-China gas pipeline,[32] while Uzbekistan expressed interest in discussing a Tashkent-Xinjiang railway.[33]

Proposals such as these mesh with repeated calls in China during the past several years for a modern-day version of the ancient Silk Road that linked China with Central Asia and the West.[34] Although it may initially strike many as romantic boilerplate, such Chinese rhetoric is highly significant. China sees a new Silk Road of modern railways and highways as a transmission belt that could project Chinese wealth and influence far westward, not only through Central Asia but to Iran and the Middle East. While most discussions of Central Asia's future physical links with the outside world focus on a north-south axis, the logic of east-west links is often overlooked. It could well include establishing a modern railway that would directly link Central Asia, through China, with a port on the Pacific Ocean. A new Silk Road of modern railroads and highways that would effectively give China a land route far to the west, ultimately to Europe and to an Iranian opening on the Persian Gulf, would have enormous strategic consequences, possibly comparable to the impact that the advent of the Suez and Panama Canals once had.

There is also increasing talk of pipelines that would bring Central Asian petroleum to China and other destinations in industrialized East Asia. Meanwhile, China is aggressively trying to discover and develop its own oil resources in Xinjiang. With China likely to become a net oil importer,[35] the prospect of a multi-billion dollar pipeline that would bring petroleum to eastern China from Xinjiang and ultimately Central Asia seems increasingly likely. Of all the players in Central Asia, possibly only China—or rather Greater China, perhaps working with South Korea or Japan—will prove to have the access to world financial markets and multinationals' technology that is needed to transform such ambitious ideas into reality.

By helping create even modest versions of a modern Silk Road—linking, for example, Xinjiang with Uzbekistan and Turkmenistan—China would be helping to break down the walls constructed by the Soviet Union to isolate the Central Asian republics from each other. Ironically, China would thus in a sense be fostering pan-Turkic relations, but this potential negative

130

apparently fades in the face of what China could gain. As we have already indicated, China's growing role in Central Asia will reduce both the absolute and relative influence that Russia wields in the five republics. Clearly, China and the non-Russian ethnic groups in the republics have a mutual interest in building economic ties that achieve this. One of the great uncertainties of this region is whether Russia and the ethnic Russians who reside in Central Asia will eventually make a major attempt to confront and resist China's growing economic power. It is not inevitable; both sides have strong interests in avoiding a conflict that could easily expand and escalate. Despite deep antipathy for China in some Russian circles, and persistent suspicion in China regarding Russia's motives, the two countries are almost compelled to continue to pursue rapprochement and to avoid military competition. As Leszek Buszynski observes, "a troubling discrepancy between obvious geopolitical need and political preferences will continue to plague the Moscow leadership's relationship with China."[36] One manifestation of this is Russia's almost reckless abandon in selling advanced weapons systems to its erstwhile arch-foe.

While Russia is preoccupied by internal priorities and its resources are already stretched beyond the limit, China wants to continue shifting the focus of its military resources away from Russia. China is focused more on the south—Taiwan, the South China Sea and Southeast Asia. While tensions may abound, China as well as Russia will try to avoid any serious clash over Central Asia. For its part, China could find itself in a difficult, probably no-win situation if, for example, ethnic Russians and Russified Kazakhs staged a coup in Alma Ata to halt the trend toward the emergence of a genuinely Kazakh nation-state with close ties to China.

But there's no uncertainty about China's intention, and ability, to play a major role in Central Asia for the foreseeable future. Even if China's vision of a modern Silk Road is never realized, an economically dynamic and militarily ascendant China seems destined to exert tremendous influence over neighboring Kazakhstan and Kyrgyzstan. This is still not widely appreciated. If the petroleum sector is excluded, China's investments in Central Asia will probably soon outrank that of the United States, Turkey, Iran, or Saudi Arabia, general regarded as the other most likely investors. Clearly all future assessments of the role of outside players in Central Asia must treat China seriously indeed.

INDIA AND CENTRAL ASIA

India's initial reaction to the emergence of the five newly independent Central Asian republics in 1991 was, like China's, largely defensive in nature. It immediately realized that its long-term foe, Pakistan, would no longer be virtually shut out of the region as it was for decades when the Soviet Union and India were allies. Pakistan confirmed India's suspicions by moving rapidly on several fronts to develop relations with the new republics. What alarmed India most were proposals, enthusiastically supported by Pakistan, to create a bloc incorporating the five republics as well as Iran and Pakistan. Suddenly India seemed to be facing the prospect of a South and Central Asian Islamic bloc united by religion and, ultimately, antipathy for Hindu India.

India's highly skilled diplomats responded with a flurry of activity aimed at supporting the republics' pragmatic and secular leaders in their determination to resist the encroachments of militant Islam. The spring of 1992 witnessed the arrival in New Delhi of the leaders of Kazakhstan, Kyrgyzstan, and Turkmenistan. They were treated royally but were given very little to take back home. A cash-strapped Indian Government, its budget vetted by the International Monetary Fund, could offer only training programs and, in some cases, trade credits. Agreement was reached with Uzbekistan for a "balanced trade turnover" of US $75 million in February of 1993.[37] The same month, India extended US $5 million in credit to Tajikistan in addition to 8.5 tons of medical supplies.[38] Much of the Indian activity in Central Asia apparently amounted to an effort to rescue or shore up trade ties from the Soviet era that are now in jeopardy, particularly with defense factories that manufacture spares and components of Soviet weapons already in India's military inventory.

In the final analysis, it was the overall weakness of India's economy, and not just the budgetary straits the New Delhi government was in, that limited India's ability to make an impact on the new republics. In sharp contrast to China, India's economy after four decades of autarky and government regulation is simply not competitive in world markets. Thus it has little to offer the republics and, indeed, may be losing ground there. For instance, when India still enjoyed a de facto strategic alliance with the Soviet Union, it exported garments and other consumer goods to what was in effect a captive Soviet market that included the southern tier republics. But now China is offering cheaper and better quality consumer goods, including Hong Kong-designed and Chinese-made garments, to the five republics.

After the spate of activity, the inevitable letdown soon followed. Izvestiya reported that Kyrgyzstan's leaders were deeply disappointed with India's decision not to set up a full-fledged embassy and with its inability to offer much more than training programs. "Everything indicates that Kyrgyzstan's hopes of establishing wide-ranging economic relations with India are not materializing," the Russian news agency reported.[39] Since mid-1992, India's concern about the region has declined as it became obvious that Pakistan's dreams of an Islamic bloc encompassing Central Asia were not going to be realized in the foreseeable future. In interviews with members of India's foreign policy community in late 1992, few expressed strong interest or concern about the region.

But their relaxed attitudes may prove misplaced. While their judgment that militant Islam is not about to gain a foothold in the region may well prove to be accurate, few Indian analysts have absorbed the implications of China's growing influence in the region. An economically dynamic China has the resources and imagination to grasp the opportunity to expand its influence far to the west, ultimately at the expense of India, among others.

NOTES

1. *The Economist*, 26 Dec 1992.
2. "Tomur Dawamat's Speech at Party Meeting," Xinjiang Ribao, Urumqi, 29 Jul 1990. Cited in FBIS-CHI-90-201, 17 Oct 1990. The head of the Xinjiang regional government described the outbreak of violence in Baren Township in 1989 as a "counterrevolutionary armed rebellion."
3. This figure is inflated. Indeed, some Sinologists suspect that Han Chinese now form a majority in Xinjiang if one technically counts "temporary" residents, including military personnel as well as some Chinese in civilian jobs who retain an official residence elsewhere in China.
4. "Xinjiang Chairman Tomur Dawamat Says the Situation in the Region is Very Stable Despite Separatist Attempt," Ta Kung Pao, Hong Kong, 25 Mar 1990, FBIS-CHI-90-058, 26 Mar 1990.
5. "Xinjiang Prepares for Crackdown on Separatists," *Agence France Presse*, Hong Kong, 13 Mar 1990, FBIS-CHI-90-049, 13 Mar 1990.
6. Mar 92, 77.
7. For detailed data on the results of Xinjiang's efforts to recruit minority groups into the regional government and to facilitate their entrance into institutions of higher education, see Xinjiang Ribao, 29 Jul 1990, op. cit.
8. *South China Morning Post*, 12 Dec 1991.
9. Nancy Lubin. "Dangers and Dilemmas: The Need for Prudent Policy Toward Central Asia," *Harvard International Review* (Spring 1993).

10.   For a typical Chinese view of Central Asia, see "Central Asia on the Rise," *Beijing Review*, Aug 3-9, 1992, 12.

11.   "Xinjiang Gives 1992 Import, Export Statistics", *Beijing Xinhua*, 19 Jan 93, FBIS-CHI-93-017, Jan 28 93, 45.

12.   "Xinjiang's Border Trade Volume up 359 Percent," Xinhua Domestic Service, 21 Dec 92, FBIS-CHI-92-252, 31 Dec 92, 57.

13.   "China Provides Half of Kazakhstan's Imports," *Beijing Xinhua* 27 Oct 92, FBIS-CHI-92-210, 29 Oct 92

14.   "Package of Joint Documents Signed With PRC," *Moscow TASS International Service* 26 Feb 92, FBIS-SOV-92-039 27 Feb 92, 67.

15.   "Trade Talks Held With Xinjiang-Uighur Delegation," Alma-Ata Kazakh Radio Network 9 May 92, FBIS-SOV-92-092, 12 May 92, 55.

16.   "Kazakh Minister Seeks Economic Ties With China," *Beijing Xinhua*, 30 Apr 92, FBIS-CHI-93-082 30 Apr 93, 7.

17.   "Rail Link With PRC City Inaugurated," Moscow Teleradiokompaniya Ostankino Television First Program Network, 23 Jun 92, FBIS-SOV-92-124, 26 Jun 92, 81.

18.   "Air Route Opens Between Beijing, Alma-Ata," *Beijing Xinhua* 17 Dec 92, FBIS-CHI-92-246, 22 Dec 92, 6.

19.   "Faster Economic Development Seen in Xinjiang," *Beijing Xinhua*, 4 Nov 92, FBIS-CHI-92-214, 4 Nov 92, 53.

20.   "Xinjiang Reports Tourism Boom," *Beijing Xinhua*, 4 Jan 93, FBIS-CHI-93-001 4 Jan 93, 74.

21.   "Kazakh Prime Minister, Delegation Continues Visit," *Beijing Xinhua*, 28 Feb 92, FBIS-CHI-92-041 2 Mar 92, 10.

22.   "Military Treaty With China in `Near Future,'" Alma-Ata Radio, Alma-Ata World Service, 15 Dec 92, FBIS-SOV-92-242, 16 Dec 92, 43.

23.   "Authorities Agree to Take Refugees From Tajikistan," *Moscow ITAR-TASS*, 22 Dec 92, FBIS-SOV-92-247, 23 Dec 92, 69.

24.   Travelers' reports, based on conversations with officials in Kazakhstan.

25.   "Akayev on `Realistic, Fruitful' Talks," *Beijing Xinhua*, 14 May 92, FBIS-CHI-92-095 15 May 92, 7.

26.   "Electric Power Line Begins Supplies to China," *Moscow ITAR-TASS*, 1 Oct 92, FBIS-SOV-92-193, 5 Oct 92, 51.

27.   "Premier Leaves for PRC For Border Issue Talks," Moscow Radio Rossii Network, 3 Aug 92, FBIS-SOV-92-153, 7 Aug 92, 74.

28.   "Premier Leaves for PRC For Border Issue Talks," Moscow Radio Rossii Network, 3 Aug 92, FBIS-SOV-92-153 7 Aug 92, 74.

29.   "Xinjiang, Kazakhstan Plan Border Water Project," *Beijing Xinhua*, 23 Jan 93, FBIS-CHI-93-015, 26 Jan 93, 9.

30.   "More on Talks between Wu Yi, Tajik Counterpart," *Beijing China Daily*, 19 Jun 93 2, FBIS-CHI-93-117, 21 Jun 93, 12.

31.   "Signs Cooperation Agreements," *Beijing China Daily*, 14 Mar 92, 1, FBIS-CHI-92-051, 16 Mar 1992, 5.

32.   "Project Signed With Japan, PRC for Gas Pipeline," *Moscow InterTass*, 13 Dec 92, FBIS-SOV-92-242, 16 Dec 92, 49.

33.   "China Opens Embassy in Tashkent," *Moscow InterTass*, 15 Oct 92, FBIS-SOV-92-201, 16 Oct 92, 53.

34.   See, for example, *Beijing Review*, Sep 14-20, 1992, "Northwest to Revive The Silk Road."

35.   Carl Goldstein. "Final Frontier," *Far Eastern Economic Review.* 10 Jun 1993, 54.

36.   Leszek Buszynski. "Russia and the Asia-Pacific Region," *Pacific Affairs* 65, no. 4 (Winter 1992-93).

37.   "Trade Agreement Signed With Uzbekistan," Delhi All India Radio Network 31 Jan 92, FBIS-NES-92-022, 3 Feb 92, 43.

38.   "$5 Million Credit, Medicines To Be Given," Delhi All India Radio Network, 15 Feb 93, FBIS-NES-93-029, 16 Feb 93, 58.

39.   "Indian Ties to Curb Pakistan, Influence Eyed," *Moscow Izvestiya*, 19 Mar 92. Morning Edition 4, FBIS-SOV-92-056, 23 Mar 92, 8.

The FORMER SOVIET SOUTH and the MUSLIM WORLD

Patrick Clawson

*F*oreign Affairs recently ran a debate on the topic, "Is Islam a Threat?" Against this background of concern about the relations between the West and Islam, it is not surprising that Western analysts have been scrambling to learn more about the six newly independent Muslim-majority states of the former Soviet Union (FSU). These states are referred to here as the former Soviet South, as the term Central Asian states includes at most five—Kyrgyzstan, Tadzhikistan, Uzbekistan, Turkmenistan, and maybe Kazakhstan (these are also called the Turkic states, the exception being Persian-speaking Tadzhikistan).

The purpose here is to examine what the impact will be of the Muslim world on the former Soviet South, especially the three major Muslim-majority states: Turkey, Iran, and Pakistan, which are the nearest Muslim neighbors (other than ravaged Afghanistan) and the most active in cultivating ties to the former Soviet South.[1] The essay will deal only tangentially with the potential impact of the former Soviet South on the Muslim world. The issue drawing perhaps the most attention in the West is which of these states will have the largest influence in the region: will the Turkish model win out over the Iranian? The main thesis is that the more important issue for the future of the former Soviet South is the relative weight of ties to the north (Russia) vs. the south (the Muslim world). To the extent that the former Soviet South becomes truly independent of

Patrick Clawson is a senior fellow at the Institute for National Strategic Studies and the senior editor of *Middle East Quarterly*. His most recent books are *How Has Saddam Hussein Survived? Economic Sanctions 1990-1993, Iran's Challenge to the West,* and *Cultivating Liberty, Uprooting Leninism.*

Russia, it will inevitably develop closer ties to the south, which is its only practical non-Russian avenue to the outside world.

Three major types of relations can be distinguished: cultural/religious ties; economic ties in transport, trade, and investment; and security/military ties. In practice, in none of these areas is the former Soviet South today independent of Russia. Despite the trappings of statehood, the new republics do not have the basic characteristics of de facto independence. In the area of security, they have but the loosest control over their borders, and the Russian army and secret police remain an important guarantor of public order in each (with the possible exception of Azerbaijan). In the domain of economics, each is at the mercy of the Russian central bank for credits to finance imports; transport through Russia remains the most heavily-used route by far; and trade within the Russian-dominated FSU is the lifeblood of the economy. In the cultural domain, Russian is the language used for diplomacy, for contact among the peoples of the region, and for commerce. The basic question about the future of these states is whether the de jure independence will develop into de facto independence. The answer is by no means obvious. The political elites, as well as many of the economic and cultural elites, came to power by knowing how to work with the Russian elite, balancing their interests with local concerns. They may be more comfortable relying on that relationship rather than attempting to develop truly autonomous constituencies.

EMERGING RELIGIOUS AND CULTURAL ACTIVITIES

In 1990, Turkey and Iran each had great expectations about cultural ties with the former Soviet South, while Western observers were concerned about which direction the new states would take. These expectations and concerns have been tempered by time, as outsiders realized that Central Asia and the Transcaucasus were areas with peculiar and unique cultural and religious traditions and were not going to adopt wholesale the practices of another people.

To be sure, over the decades, the influence of the Soviet period will fade. The next generation of Central Asian and Transcaucasians will develop more cultural and religious exchanges with their southern neighbors. Not only will this process be slow, but furthermore the former Soviet states are as likely to change their neighbors' culture as the neighbors are likely to change theirs.

Religious Ties

The influence of Islam in the former Soviet South has been expanding at a rapid rate for more than a decade. Part of the explanation was the growing power of locals, as part of the "feudalization" of Soviet society under Brezhnev. Those local politicians could use their putative Islamic identification to win local support in the competition for influence with ethnic Russians. Indeed, local politicians throughout the Soviet period used Islam as one of their tools to resist Russification; the difference in the 1980s was that their efforts encountered less resistance from a Moscow prepared to turn a blind eye to the (mis)deeds of local satraps.

In addition, the decay of Soviet ideology left a vacuum in belief systems: what idealistic young person would be attracted in the mid-1980s to a Communist party that had increasingly become corrupt and soulless? Societies need an ideology to guide public morals and to set the tone for ethical discourse. Imperfect as it was, communism in its heyday provided such a framework. As belief in communism visibly decayed under Brezhnev, the search for alternatives became a mass phenomenon. Much as Christianity is mushrooming in Russia, so Islam can be expected to deepen in the FSU.

"Folk Islam" has strong roots in the former Soviet South. Soviet scholars estimated in the 1980s that 80 percent of the population of Muslim-origin performed some basic Muslim rites such as circumcision or religious marriage and burial.[2] These practices are deepening as the power of the traditional community reasserts itself. The most obvious example is in Uzbekistan, where the neighborhood organizations (mahallahs) are playing a more assertive role, such as providing more services and demanding more participation by the public in their activities. These organizations not only promote traditional practices consistent with Islam (such as modest dress for women), but they are also beginning to open mosques.

The increase in religious observance is impressive. It predates the end of the USSR. A May 1987 article in *Literaurnaia gazeta* estimated that Central Asia had 1,800 clandestine mosques in addition to the 365 officially registered—a phenomenon that did not exist ten years earlier.[3] A 1990 visitor to Kokand, a city of 150,000 in the Fergana Valley which is the center of Islamic revival, found 15 mosques compared to one in 1989.[4] That valley, which is largely in Uzbekistan but includes cities in Tadzhikistan and Kyrgyzstan, has been the home for a vigorous Islamic propagandist movement known by the same name as the puritanical movement that swept Saudi Arabia in the 18th century, namely, Wahabism. One prominent Wahabi leader, Mullah Abdullo Saidov, called for an Islamic state in Central Asia as early as 1986.[5] The influence of the Islamic extremists is growing in part because of the spread of inter-ethnic violence in the Fergana Valley in the last five years. Communities have been forced to arm themselves for protection, and the Islamic extremists are often the ones prepared to serve in local militias. Some of the armed groups in the Fergana Valley openly debate the desirability of armed struggle to establish a rigid Islamic state. A similar evolution—unrest and violence increasing the influence of radical Islamists—has been occurring during the Tadzhikistan civil war, as discussed below.

This growth in Islamic identification can only strengthen the impulse for more ties with the Muslim world. There should, however, be no mistake about the direction of causality: it is the home-grown revival of Islam that is driving better relations with the Muslim world.[6] It is an indigenous force and not primarily provoked by foreign propaganda designed to incite a Muslim revival. To be sure, there is foreign-financed propaganda such as the Saudi government's contribution of one million Korans. Some of that aid is blatantly political rather than religious, e.g., Iran's sudden enthusiasm for training Turkmen clergy at the Oare Bolagh theological school, its tame school for the nearly one million Sunni ethnic Turkmen in Iran.[7] But much of the propaganda is funded by the private-sector: believers take seriously the obligation to propagate the faith. Turkish fundamentalists are active in the region, e.g., at the university in Turkestan (Kazakhstan). The Pakistani missionary group *tablighi jama'at* is also well represented.[8]

The U.S. Government may not be pleased by these missionary efforts, especially those funded by Muslim governments, but Washington is in a poor position to complain. As any visitor to the former Soviet South can testify, the region is also alive with U.S.

national Christian missionaries, who are doing a good job of disturbing local sensibilities. Christianity and Islam are both proselytizing religions, and the faithful will do their best in the fertile soil created by the collapse of the Communist belief system.

To summarize: the Islamic revival in the former Soviet South is broad and deep—it involves millions of people, and its goal is the far-reaching Islamization of public life. But it is home-grown, not a foreign import. Our attitudes toward the phenomenon should mirror our approach to Islamic movements in general; we should not worry about Iranian propaganda as an instrument of incitement.

Cultural Ties

Even someone unknowledgeable about cultural matters should be profoundly skeptical of claims that strong ties will develop between the former Soviet South and Turkey (or for that matter Iran in the case of Persian-speaking Tadzhikistan), for the following reasons:

- Central Asia and the Transcaucasus are quite well developed culturally already. These regions are not wastelands in need of writers and educators, plus their literacy rates are higher than those in Turkey or Iran. Each of the peoples in the region has a strong sense of national pride. Furthermore, each has their own language, which is closely related to Turkish (or Persian), but it is distinctive (with the possible exception of Tadzhik). For instance, Uzbek and Azeri have lost the vowel harmony that is the distinctive feature of Anatolian Turkish. It is instructive to see representatives of the former Soviet South at meetings with Turkish officials—the language of communication is Russian (translated) or English, not some hybrid pan-Turkish.

- I have great faith in the ability of some Turks and Persians to offend with their sense of cultural superiority. That sense of Turkish and Persian chauvinism colors the policies of Ankara and Tehran. None of the peoples of the former Soviet South will take kindly to the idea that they are the "little brothers" of someone else. If there are to be closer cultural relations, there will have to be give and take on each side. Adding five letters to the alphabet for sounds in other Turkic languages, as was recently done in Turkey, is a good sign, but many more such steps will be needed. A point of history worth recalling: Istanbul never ruled Central Asia, but Central Asia ruled modern-day Turkey (under Tamerlane).[9]

- The former Soviet South has a tremendous amount of human capital invested in the Russian language and Russian society. Breaking those ties will be difficult. Consider the smallest of questions, the issue of replacing the modified Cyrillic alphabets (each republic has a slightly different alphabet)—so little has happened despite grand expectations.

- Experience in country after country has been that the culture most seductive is Hollywood. I do not believe for one minute that Turkish television will be any more successful in the former Soviet South than it is at home in competing against Hollywood productions. Music TV (MTV), not ersatz traditional Turkish music, is more likely to win the hearts and minds of the ex-Soviet Muslim youth.

The two cases in which cultural influence is likely to be most profound are Azerbaijan and Tadzhikistan, discussed in the next section.

SECURITY/MILITARY TIES

It is easy to romanticize the geopolitics of Central Asia: an area about which outsiders know little, a region with many neighbors from very different cultures, and of course an area replete with the history of the Great Game between Britain and Russia in the 1800s. But the reality is more prosaic: Central Asia is peripheral to the interests of most of the world's great powers, and it is far removed from most of Asia's conflicts. Consider for instance the Indian-Pakistani conflict: while it may be entertaining to fantasize about some grand Muslim encirclement of India, any such plan would be strategic nonsense—there is little if any prospect that Central Asia will have any impact on the Indian-Pakistani dispute.

But beyond the daydreaming over maps of Asia, there are some serious issues about security and military ties between the states of the former Soviet South and Turkey, Iran, and Pakistan. The main issues are nuclear weapons proliferation, the Tadzhik war, and the conflicts involving Azerbaijan.

Nuclear Proliferation
Western nations have been worried about nuclear proliferation originating from the Muslim states of the FSU. Many reports have appeared about "missing" nuclear weapons. In fact, so far as is now known, all the FSU's tactical nuclear warheads are in Russia;

the only nuclear warheads known to be in the former Soviet South are being removed from Kazakhstan, and these weapons are as much if not more under Russian control than under Kazakhistani control: it is the Russian Central Bank that provides the credits for the soldiers who guard the weapons, it is the Russian military (wearing its CIS hats) that commands the troops. If at any time there is reason to seriously worry that a nuclear weapon or enriched fuel has been transferred from the former Soviet South to another nation, then the world must hold Russia partly responsible. U.S. law has a concept useful for this situation, namely, the principle that two parties can be jointly and severally responsible for a wrong: each bears full responsibility, though each may have committed only part of the wrong. So, too, Russia will be jointly and severally responsible were some individual commander or some FSU government to transfer a nuclear warhead outside the FSU.

There have also been many reports that nuclear experts from the former Soviet South have gone to work in various suspected proliferating nations, such as Iran. Perhaps so: there are certainly thousands of unemployed people in the FSU who have skills that would be useful in a nuclear weapons program. From what little is known about such people and about Soviet training programs and an antisouthern bias at the better Moscow academies, it would seem that few are from the southern region and fewer still are ethnic Muslims. It would seem that Moscow is the right address for concerns about former Soviet nuclear experts. Also, it should be borne in mind that no matter how well-supplied with expertise, a proliferator who wants to develop a weapon has to build an enrichment facility. Those facilities are by their nature large and should be relatively easy to detect, especially with the lessons learned from the Iraqi case. So at least there would be prior warning about a proliferation attempt underway.

Quite separate from the issue of nuclear proliferation outside of the FSU is the question of nuclear weapons in Kazakhstan. After some initial waffling,[10] the Kazakhstan Government agreed to sign the Non-Proliferation Treaty (NPT) as a non-nuclear state. However, Kazakhstan President Nazarbayev has repeatedly stated that his country reserves the right to retain nuclear arms on its soil, consistent with the NPT and START, as part of a bilateral agreement with Russia similar to that between the U.S. and Germany.[11] Based on NATO precedents, Kazakhstan could fulfill its obligations under arms control treaties while nevertheless controlling nuclear weapons delivery systems, so long as the warheads are under Russian control. Two kinds of delivery system have been deployed on Kazakhistani soil: bombers at the Semipalatinsk base and SS-18 missiles. Under the START-2 treaty, signed in January 1993, the SS-18s are to be destroyed. It seems unlikely, for financial reasons if nothing else, that Russia would move other missiles to Kazakhstan, but it could very well transfer the bombers at Semipalatinsk to the Kazakhstan Air Force. Whatever policy followed by Kazakhstan in this regard, the effects on the Muslim world would be slight.

The Tadzhik War and Potential Spillovers

The continuing Tadzhikistan civil war threatens to bring Iran and Pakistan into conflict with Uzbekistan and the "communist" camp in Tadzhikistan—precisely the development that the Uzbekistan government has been eager to prevent.

The politics of independent Tadzhikistan have been tumultuous.[12] The November 1991 presidential election was won by Rakhmon Nabiev, who had been a Communist party leader during the Brezhnev years. Opposition forces, including some 50 private militias, rebelled against him in March 1992, primarily with demonstrations in the capital but also with some fighting. After 51 days of demonstrations, Nabiev brokered a compromise, but fighting spread during the summer. In September, Nabiev was forced to resign at gunpoint; Supreme Soviet Chairman Akbarsho Iskandarov became President. Supporters of the old guard stepped up their campaign during the fall, firmly assuming control by the end of 1992. The campaign against the reformist opposition was vicious, with the brutal slaughter of civilians and prisoners; Amnesty International estimates 20,000 people died, many from torture. Several hundred thousand refugees fled into Afghanistan.

The warring parties are often labeled the "Communist" forces and the "Islamist" forces. To be sure, the reform coalition included the Islamic Renaissance Party whose aim was an Islamic state, but the policies it actually implemented (and the policies to which the communist forces most violently objected) were the nationalist aims of the Democratic Party and the Rastokhez party—especially the promotion of Tadzhik language, the use of Persian script, and good relations with Iran. Furthermore, the main difference between the two camps was not ideological but sectional. The Communist camp came from the regions favored under Soviet rule, which were the northern Khudzhand region in the Fergana

Valley and the southwestern Kurgan-Tyube region. The Islamist camp came from the areas ignored under Soviet rule (though the most isolated and mountainous region in the east contributed little to the Islamist cause). The civil war was then a conjunction of factors: a regional dispute, a fight between an old elite and an aspiring new elite, and a confrontation between nationalists/Islamists and communists.

Uzbekistan actively intervened in the war from mid-1992 on. The 40 buses that carried the communist forces into the capital of Dushanbe in October 1992 all bore license plates from Uzbekistan. On the same day, Uzbek helicopters and armored vehicles invaded a stronghold of the reform government. During the peak of fighting in November and December, the Uzbek Air Force flew combat support missions. Uzbek forces, together with the Russian 201st Division, destroyed an opposition stronghold in December. In early 1993, an official of the Uzbekistan Defense Ministry, Alexsandr Shishlyannikov, was named Tadzhikistani Defense Minister. Also in 1993, the Uzbek Air Force is said to have bombed the remaining reform holdout cities in eastern Tadzhikistan.

Uzbekistan President Karimov justified his intervention in Tadzhikistan as necessary to protect his republic (with a 20 percent ethnic Tadzhik minority) against a spillover of violence, as well as to respond to the thousands of ethnic Uzbeks (who are 25 percent of Tadzhikistan's population, mostly in the pro-Communist north) who gathered on the border hoping to take refuge in Uzbekistan. He argued that Iran was supporting the Islamist opposition, an argument for which there is little evidence. Indeed, Tehran did little to help the reform forces, and it has been willing to continue relations with the new government despite the overtly anti-Iranian and anti-Islamic propaganda pouring forth from the Tadzhikistan capital of Dushanbe.

Uzbekistani officials are on more solid ground when they accuse Afghan rebels led by Gulbuddin Hekmatyar of aiding the Islamists; numerous Russian, Tadzhik, and Western sources testify to this aid. Since Hekmatyar was strongly supported by the Pakistani government for a long time, it is no surprise that Uzbekistan President Karimov also accuses Pakistan of aiding the Islamists; though to be sure, Pakistani relations with Hekmatyar have cooled since early 1992. Hekmatyar, in turn, accuses Uzbekistan of aiding the ethnic Uzbek Afghan general Rashid Dostam, Hekmatyar's sworn enemy who he succeeded in having expelled from Kabul, only to have Dostam threaten to set up an independent republic in northern Afghanistan in the region he controls along the border with Uzbekistan.

The result of the actions by Afghan politicians and the Uzbekistan government has been to convert a civil war in Tadzhikistan into an open sore among the countries of the region. It is almost inevitable that the conflict will continue for years, flaring up periodically. Given the vicious persecution under the current Dushanbe government, the Tadzhik reform movement is likely to be radicalized, meaning it will turn more toward a radical Islamic orientation. That particular radical Islamic opposition will look for aid from Afghanistan, Pakistan, and Iran—which will feel domestic pressure to provide the aid because of the anti-Islamic propaganda from Uzbekistan and because of the atrocities by the Dushanbe authorities. Plus, the Islamist movement in Uzbekistan—both among ethnic Tadzhiks and in the Fergana Valley among ethnic Uzbeks—is likely to draw from the fighting the lesson that they need to prepare for a violent crackdown by the Uzbekistan government, which will lead them to seek the international support that Tashkent so fears. In short, Uzbekistan has launched itself on a path of confrontation with its neighbors which seems likely to draw those neighbors into a supporting opposition movement.

Azerbaijan's Security Situation

Much as the Tadzhik civil war is a quicksand patch drawing in the neighbors, so too is the situation in the Azerbaijan Republic. Turkey feels closer to Baku than to any of the Central Asian states for the obvious reason of geography—the Azerbaijan Republic is the only one of the Muslim FSU states that Turkey borders. The relationship has become quite tight. When (then) Azerbaijani President Elchibey visited Ankara in November 1992, Turkish President Ozal assured him: "Turkey is your second country, and Azerbaijan is our second motherland." Elchibey responded by assuring him that all Turks are brothers, and Azerbaijanis are Turks.[13] More concretely, Ankara is said to provide support for the Azerbaijani Republic's armed forces, including military advisers.[14]

At the same time, Iranians feel worried about the Azerbaijan Republic. The territory of that republic was ruled by Iran for centuries until 1828. South of the republic are the three Iranian provinces of Azerbaijan, with a population of about eight million.[15]

146

The 1986 census showed that four million people in these provinces speak principally Azeri, and another three million claim to be bilingual in Azeri and Persian. The cultural influence of Baku is obvious in Tabriz, the largest city of Iranian Azerbaijan: many listen to Radio Baku or watch Baku TV. Indeed, Iranian officials regularly complain about the decadent Western influences coming into Iran from Baku. There are signs that Iranian Azerbaijan is astir. For instance, in East Azerbaijan Province, instruction in the Azeri language was authorized for 1992/93, ending 60 years of rigorous Persianization, and textbooks in Azeri were promised for 1993/94.[16] Certainly President Elchibey in Baku did his best to stir up trouble attempting to provoke Azeri separatism. He regularly complained about Iranian mistreatment of its Azeri population, and he referred to Iranian leaders as fascists lacking in true religion who should be overthrown.[17] Still, that is more temperate than his earlier remarks: he used to refer to himself regularly as the president of *northern* Azerbaijan, echoing the Soviet-era claim for unification of the country—a unification that Moscow claimed was voluntarily achieved in 1946 when it refused to withdraw the Red Army from Iranian Azerbaijan, which it had occupied for 5 years during and after the war.

Meanwhile, Baku has reason to be concerned about Tehran. Iranian ethnic Azeri businessmen are active in the republic, and that has provided Iran with an avenue of influence for a *de facto* reunification under Iranian influence. In addition, Iran has actively courted Gaider Aliyev, at one time the number three official in the Soviet Communist Party who returned to his native Azerbaijan. Aliyev had ruled in the 300,000-population enclave of Nakichevan, a part of the Azerbaijan Republic separated from the rest of the country by Armenia, which blockades it. Nakichevan's other neighbors are Turkey, which has only a 5-mile common border with one small road, and Iran, which is now supplying it with most of its needs—after that quintessential chameleon Aliyev made a pilgrimage to holy sites in Iran and called for more mullahs to be sent to Nakichevan from Iran. Aliyev was in open conflict with Elchibey, who sent troops to Nakichevan in October 1992 in an unsuccessful bid to sideline or replace Aliyev.[18]

To summarize: Turkey provides close support for the Azerbaijan Republic. That republic worries Tehran because it may provoke separatist sentiment among its large ethnic Azeri population. Meanwhile, Baku has reason to fear Iranian meddling.   This is a scenario ripe for conflict, especially since the issue at stake for Iran—territorial integrity—is its most vital national interest. Iran seems to have decided to act assertively to defend its interests. Turkish officials cite ample evidence of Iranian support for Turkish Workers' Party (PKK) Kurdish terrorists in Turkey, support which began in 1991.[19] Iran is also providing training for assassins, who Turkey's Interior Minister Ismet Szegin said were responsible for the murder of two journalists and a failed ambush on a prominent Turkish Jewish industrialist; he also said Iran may well have been responsible for the assassination of the well-known journalist Ugur Mumcu.[20] The 300,000 people who marched at Mumcu's January 1993 funeral chanted, "Mullahs to Iran; Turkey will never be Iran."

The repercussions from the independence of the Azerbaijan Republic are just beginning to reverberate throughout the region. It seems all too possible that Turkey and Iran will be caught in a downward spiral of violence over influence in the region, each seeking to forestall separatist movements among large minorities which it blames the other of sponsoring. The situation is not made easier by the clash in ideologies between Turkish secularism, a firm principle of the army since Ataturk's days, and Iranian radical Islamism. Each side has ample opportunities for meddling behind the scenes, and we can expect more such events. One obvious theater is the war between Azerbaijan and ethnic Armenians (the Republic of Armenia insists that international observers have verified its forces are not involved). Iran has followed a pro-Armenian policy for 50 years in reaction to the irredentist claims of Soviet (now independent) Azerbaijan. That policy has been tempered by Iranian sympathy for Muslim Azerbaijan, but Tehran goes no further than to admonish Armenia not to conquer territory in Azerbaijan.

Were Iran and Turkey to get caught in a spiral of escalating violence, the West would face a dilemma. Turkey is a NATO member, but the threat from Iran is likely to be too ambiguous —too small, too peripheral to NATO's central states, too plausibly Ankara's fault, too deniable by Iran—for some members to feel that NATO support is justifiable. On the other hand, other NATO members may feel that Iran poses a broad threat to Western interests, ranging from the Arab-Israeli peace process to proliferation and the security of the Gulf, in which case those members may welcome an opportunity to show Western solidarity with Tehran's opponents.

ECONOMIC TIES

The former Soviet South remains heavily dependent on Russia economically. If it is going to reduce its economic dependence on Russia, establishing relations with the Muslim world seems to be an obvious alternative. Let us examine the prospects for closer economic relations in three domains: trade, investment, and transport.

However, first a word about economic "models." In the early days of the dissolution of the FSU, some Turkish leaders had high hopes that Turkey could provide a model to the former Soviet South. They reasoned that Turks could speak the local languages more or less and that Turkey had much to offer in the way of expertise on running businesses and managing a market economy. The reality has been quite different. Turkey is not seen in the former Soviet South as an example of what they would like to be. Turkey is, after all, a country with an *etatist* tradition, and it has been repeatedly criticized for its heavy-handed state interference in industry (be it state-owned or nominally private). Turkey is a nation that has had difficulties containing inflation at below 50 percent per annum and is not a natural source of technical assistance on how to run either industry or the macroeconomy. The "Turkish model" looks rather uninviting to those who see Turkey as at best a second-class economy with profound structural problems—a foreign debt that has had to be rescheduled several times in recent decades, a growth record well below that in East Asia, and continuing macroeconomic imbalances (budget deficits and inflation), etc.

For all its weaknesses, the Turkish model is strong enough to at least be a contender in the former Soviet South. That cannot be said about the Iranian or Pakistani model, which hold no attraction for Central Asia and Azerbaijan. The former Soviet states are unlikely to see much to emulate in the policies of Pakistan, given the substantial differences in economic circumstances (Pakistan having a much lower literacy rate, many fewer industries, much more aid from foreign governments, and much more income from expatriate workers). Few would want to duplicate the record of the Islamic Republic of Iran, in which per capita income fell by half in the first 13 years after the revolution.

More important than the Turkish model are the East Asian model or the advanced Western model because the former Soviet South would much rather become like East Asia or the advanced West than like Turkey. The Central Asians want the fast growth that has or is transforming Korea and China, and they want the high technology and ample consumer goods of Europe, North America and Japan.

Trade

The trade pattern of the Central Asian states while part of the Soviet Union is shown in tables 1 and 2: 1 shows trade within the FSU, while 2 shows trade outside the FSU. The data are, of course, at the prices then prevailing, which means that (in general) agricultural products and raw materials like energy are valued at well below world market prices, while industrial goods, especially machinery, are valued at well above world market prices.

The largest categories of Central Asian exports to the rest of the FSU were light industrial products (7.4 billion rubles out of the total of 24.2 billion rubles) and energy (3.2 billion rubles). Exports to the rest of the world were primarily fuels, minerals and raw metals (1.2 billion devisa rubles out of 2.6 billion devisa rubles total; each *devisa* ruble being worth about US $1.25 then) and raw materials (0.9 billion devisa rubles). These are not products that would make much sense to export to the Muslim south, with the exception of oil and gas destined for world markets—a special case analyzed in the transport section below. For the other products, none of the key Muslim actors—neither Turkey, Iran, nor Pakistan—is an obvious market. Consider, for instance, light industrial products. These are precisely the products that the leaders of the former Soviet South are eager to produce more of; they complain that under Soviet rule too little of their raw materials were transformed in the region. The Uzbekistan authorities are particularly bitter that only 12 percent of that nation's cotton was processed in country.[21] It is difficult to see how Uzbekistan will be content over the long run to see its cotton crop exported to Turkey or Pakistan for processing into the vigorous textile industries there; nor is there much prospect that those two countries will be a good market for Uzbek cloth, given that each exports large quantities of exactly the kinds of cotton cloth that Uzbekistan could produce. To be sure, Iran is an importer of cloth, including cotton cloth, but the Iranian authorities have high hopes of reversing this situation and so are unlikely to be enthusiastic about a trade which they may see as undercutting a local industry. There is room for some business and perhaps some

Table 1. *Interrepublican Trade of Central Asia, 1988 (in millions of rubles)*

	Balance	Total	Kazak.	Kyrgyz.	Tajik.	Turkmn.	Uzbek.
Exports		**24,245**	**8,337**	**2,537**	**2,025**	**2,389**	**8,957**
Energy		3,227	1,405	111	88	809	814
Metallurgy		2,372	1,345	137	303	8	579
Worked metal		3,169	776	939	207	44	1,203
Chemicals		2,050	966	25	95	150	814
Food industry		2,306	632	521	225	95	833
Light industry		7,421	1,402	651	973	1,116	3,279
Agriculture	1,955	2,659	1,516	108	80	137	818
Other	1,962	1,041	295	45	54	30	617
Imports		**32,792**	**13,687**	**2,972**	**3,023**	**2,486**	**10,624**
Energy	673	3,900	1,844	365	368	116	1,207
Metallurgy	706	3,078	1,352	275	318	116	1,017
Worked metal	7,287	10,456	4,646	949	783	926	3,152
Chemicals	1,248	3,298	1,462	339	321	200	976
Food industry	1,654	3,960	1,377	264	403	434	1,482
Light industry	3,028	4,393	1,540	471	494	395	1,493
Agriculture		704	160	65	102	28	349
Other		3,003	1,306	244	234	271	948
Trade Deficit	**8,547**	**8,547**	**5,350**	**435**	**998**	**97**	**1,667**

Notes: "Regional Balance" is the region's total exports less imports (or, if shown in the import rows as is the case for most products, imports less exports). Source: Vestnik statistiki, March 1990, from RFE/RL Research Bulletin, April 2, 1993.

Table 2. *Central Asian Trade Outside the USSR, 1990*
(in millions of devisa rubles, worth about $1.25)

	Total	Kazakh.	Kyrgyz.	Tajik.	Turkm.	Uzbek.
EXPORTS	**2,607**	**1,112**	**67**	**413**	**140**	**875**
Fuels, minerals, metals	1,171	790	34	318	29	
Raw materials	880	111	9	78	95	586
Other	556	211	24	17	15	289
IMPORTS	**6,670**	**2,433**	**870**	**750**	**566**	**2,051**
Machinery	2,460	1,192	209	278	187	595
Food products	1,667	268	479	90	113	718
Consumer goods	1,171	243	78	113	204	533
Other	1,372	730	104	270	62	205
TRADE DEFICIT	**4,063**	**1,321**	**803**	**337**	**426**	**1,176**

Source: Vneshnyaya torgovlya suverennykh respublik i Pribaltiskikh v 1990 godu, as printed in RFE/RL Research Bulletin April 2, 1993.

large deals like the proposed Pakistani import of electricity,[22] but the problems predominate over the possibilities.

On the import side, the picture is a bit more hopeful: there are some prospects (limited to be sure) for active imports into Central Asia from the Muslim south nations. Almost a third of the Central Asian imports from the rest of the FSU was machinery (10.5 billion rubles out of a total of 32.8 billion rubles), while machinery was about 40 percent of imports from the rest of the world (2.5 billion devisa rubles out of a total of 6.7 billion devisa rubles). There are but few machinery exports from Turkey, Iran, or Pakistan. And to the extent that the Central Asian states are able to secure Western financing for development projects, this category of imports is likely to grow. On the other hand, the Central Asian states imported substantial amounts of consumer goods, including light industrial products and processed foods. These are products with which all three nations of the Muslim south can compete. They will surely face vigorous competition from the world's low-cost producers of basic consumer goods, namely the East Asians, but the advantages of lower transport costs and better knowledge of local tastes may provide Turkish, Iranian, and Pakistani producers with an edge.

The trends identified above are hardly surprising given the basic economic geography and the elementary principles of international trade theory, which say that trade is particularly advantageous between countries with different proportions of the factors of production (e.g., a capital-rich country trades with a labor-rich country). The former Soviet South looks economically quite similar to Iran or Turkey: some states have the mineral wealth of the former, others have the light industrial and agricultural base of the latter. We should therefore expect that, on average, the former Soviet South will be competitors with their important Muslim neighbors at least as much as they will be trade partners.

The fragmentary data on trade in 1992 suggest that the former Soviet South is indeed expanding its trade with the advanced industrial nations and the newly industrializing countries of East Asia, not with the Muslim world. Turkey reports that its total trade—imports and exports combined—with Central Asia was less than $300 million in 1992.[23] Interfax reported that the main customers outside the FSU for Kazakhstan products in 1992 were the US, UK, Sweden, Finland, the Netherlands, Austria, and Italy; the developed countries as a group took 60 percent of exports.[24]

Uzbekistan reported that, of its $1.1 billion in 1992 exports, 27 percent went to China and Korea while Switzerland, Belgium and the U.K. took another 30 percent. This trade with the West and East Asia is something new: in 1990, the main trading partners outside the FSU were East bloc states and Germany (on both the import and export side).

Investment

The former Soviet South presents some attractive investment opportunities, especially for exploiting raw materials such as oil, gas, and gold. However, it is difficult to see how the Muslim south could be in a position to be major actors here for at least three reasons. First and most important, Turkey, Iran, and Pakistan all have large foreign debts on their own; they are not well-placed to extend credit to other nations. Indeed, Iran has borrowed about $25 billion in the last 3 years, a debt that it cannot service: the result has been the accumulation of arrears that the president of the World Bank estimates at $3 to $5 billion.

Second, it is unlikely that international financiers will lend funds to Muslim states for the purpose of those states investing that money in turn in the former Soviet South. Turkish leaders had hoped that they could mobilize additional financing for such purposes, either from aid donors or from businesses and banks that saw the Turks as being well positioned to intervene financially in the former Soviet South. The economic realities, however, are against such a Turkish role as intermediary. The most attractive projects in the former Soviet South are gigantic mineral and fuel projects, which are by their very nature risky; no one can be sure until many millions (or billions!) have been spent whether world market conditions will keep prices high enough to make the investment worthwhile, plus there can always be surprises about the technical characteristics of the field (e.g., the crude oil turns out to be of a different quality than expected). In short, these investments are highly risky, which means they will most likely be done by multinationals who can afford to fail in one place because they operate on such a large scale that failures on one project can be counterbalanced with unexpected good fortune elsewhere.

Third, major investments are generally made by firms that can provide technical expertise as well as cash. In this regard, Iran is better placed than Turkey or Pakistan because Iran has a wealth of expertise in the oil and gas industries. Iran has been producing oil for 70 years and has a strong core of local engineers trained in difficult oil fields that share some characteristics with the Central Asian fields. Nevertheless, the Iranian oil industry is distinctly second-class compared to that of the United States or other major Western nations, and therefore it would not be the partner of choice in Central Asia even were Iran able to finance the development of oil fields, which it is not. Iran may play some role in the region's oil industry—more so if Iran insists on a *quid pro quo* for transporting oil and gas through Iran or selling it on Iranian markets—but this will be politically driven, not market-based.

As an example of how to combine technical assistance with investment to further a political agenda, consider the Israeli involvement in Central Asian agriculture. Lubricated with aid funds (including $5 million from the U.S. for the Israeli actions), financed by Israel's most powerful businessman (Shoul Eisenberg), and carefully chosen to provide Central Asia with a product that can make a quick profit (drip irrigation that cuts water use 66 percent and raises cotton yields 40 percent), the arrangement has been a plus all around.[25]

Transport

The one economic area in which the Muslim world is likely to become central to the future of the former Soviet South is in transport. At the moment, the new republics are heavily dependent on a transport network that goes via Russia. That puts them at the end of long transport routes, as well as making them hostage to the chaos in Russia—erratic and high taxation, periodic breakdowns at key points, and a host of intermediaries (some official, some private) demanding fees.

For the Central Asian states, the best alternative to the Russian routes is to the south. The reason is geography. To reach the ocean from Tashkent, one can go south via Iran or Pakistan to the Persian Gulf/Sea of Oman (1,400 miles), west via Russia to the Black Sea (2,000 miles), or east via China to the China Sea (3,000 miles).

On the shortest route—to the south—the best developed infrastructure is via Iran. Central Asia's most densely settled regions, Tashkent and the valleys along the Syr and Amu Darya rivers, are 1,400 to 1,500 miles from Iran's large modern ports at Bandar Abbas, near the mouth of the Persian Gulf. The two ports at Bandar Abbas handled 9.5 million tons incoming in 1990/91, and they have the capacity to handle quite a bit more with existing facilities.[26] Iran could shift towards more use of its other ports further up the Persian Gulf, which are coming back on line after being damaged during the war with Iraq.[27] A word of caution is in order, however. In order to get goods to these ports, Central Asians should not count on the much-discussed rail link between the excellent Central Asian rail net and the Iranian net. Iran has taken more than 10 years to build the only new rail line under construction (450 miles from Bandar Abbas to Bafq), and there is little reason to believe that the current forecast of a 1994 opening will be any more accurate than similar forecasts for each year since 1984. Furthermore, the guidelines for Iran's 1994-1998 Plan state flatly, "emphasis will be on upkeep, improvement, and reconstruction of existing (transport) facilities (and) completion of projects under way" rather than any new projects. Even if a connection were made to Iran's railroads, that system is not up to FSU standards[28] and would require an extra 500 miles to reach the sea compared to using the roads. But the roads are in good shape nearly the whole way from Tashkent to Bandar Abbas, with only a short stretch unpaved; the route is relatively flat, crossing only some gentle slopes.

Of course, the main problem with an Iranian route is political. Partly that means Iranian inexperience with international transit traffic, which has to be managed in a way that holds paperwork to a minimum while ensuring that the goods transiting the country are actually in transit rather than being smuggled in (transit goods do not pay customs duties in the country through which they are transiting, which means truckers have an incentive to falsely claim their shipment is in transit). Iran has begun to tackle this problem, with the customs director promising new rules to facilitate transit and a protocol to be signed with Kazakhstan on the subject.[29] More importantly, shipments to and from Iran may get caught up in the various restrictions on trade with Iran (the U.S. import ban on Iranian goods or the restrictions of many nations on exporting high-technology and dual-use goods to Iran) because of a fear they may be diverted to Iranian users or due to the general unwillingness of Western firms to deal via Iran.

Another technically good route from Central Asia to the sea is via Pakistan. The Pakistan route requires the crossing of Afghanistan—which means in practice crossing western Afghanistan, given that the route to Kabul is through the Sarang

Tunnel, which is already heavily stressed. The route via Herat in western Afghanistan and on to western Pakistan is technically a good route, but Afghan instability has been so frequent (in recent decades and recent centuries) that investors may be hard to persuade. Such a route would fit Pakistan's interests well, given its long-standing interest in the development of its southwest and in the construction of a new port to relieve Karachi (and to provide a port further removed from the Indian border). Pakistan has been soliciting investors prepared to build and operate a port in the southwest, but the project would not seem likely to proceed on a large scale in the near future.

Turkey had hoped to play an important role as a transport conduit for the former Soviet South, but it has found itself frustrated. The problem is apparent from studying a map: Turkey has no direct land route to any of the states of the former Soviet South, with the exception of a three-mile border with the Nakichevan enclave of Azerbaijan, isolated from the rest of Azerbaijan by Armenia and Iran. The problems are worse for reaching Central Asia, which requires either crossing Russia or using mixed modes with a sea link across the Caspian. And in any case, the Bosphorus and the Dardenelles are getting saturated with sea traffic as traffic on the Danube rises (and is expected to rise more now that the canal to the Rhine is complete); the development of Russian trade opening to more of the outside world will only exacerbate the situation. But Turkey has some advantages for transport from the former Soviet South, not the least of which are its truckers, who are famous for their familiarity with how to get from difficult areas into Europe. Unfortunately, the truck route has been affected by the strife in the former Yugoslavia, stretching the average time for a trip from Tehran to Frankfurt to 25 days by truck.[30]

Perhaps the most important transport issue is how to export oil and gas from the region. The former Soviet South is already a major exporter of oil and gas to the rest of the FSU. By the middle of the next decade, the region could well export the energy equivalent of one billion barrels of oil per year, with the largest shares from Kazakhstan and Turkmenistan, some from Azerbaijan, and possibly a lesser amount from Uzbekistan. These oil exports could earn the region $15 billion a year at present prices, or $250 per person per year.

Were politics not a factor, the solution to the oil and gas transport problem would be to use the existing pipeline network through Russia to the maximum and then build new pipelines into northern Iran. Iran uses about 700,000 barrels of oil a day in its north, where most of the population is located (in the western area around Tabriz, near the Azeri oil fields; in the center in Tehran; and in Mashhad in the east, not far from the Turkmen gas and oil fields). Iran could import oil from the former Soviet South for its needs in the north, a move which would then save Iran the cost of pumping the oil from its fields hundreds of miles away on the Persian Gulf coast, and then be able to export more oil from its Persian Gulf fields, which are proximate to world shipping routes.

But the decisions are clearly not going to be made solely on economic grounds. The oil companies are justifiably concerned that the political atmosphere is not right for a major Western investment in Iran. As one Western adviser told the *Washington Post*, "The U.S. government at the highest levels made sure that ("there's been a decision against any Iranian deal"). That was no accident."[31]

The oil companies are therefore considering two sets of second-best alternatives. One would be a convoluted pipeline via Turkey to Turkey's Mediterranean shore. The problem with any such scheme is that this route must pass through at least one country other than Turkey or the states of the former Soviet South. The best route would be to go across the shallow waters at the narrow belt of the Caspian Sea and then go up the Atras River Valley through Azerbaijan to hook up with the now-unused pipeline from Iraq; but this route requires the crossing of a 35-mile stretch in which the north bank of the Atras is in Armenia and the south bank is in Iran, neither of which states are eager to assist in such a scheme. The much-trumpeted Turkish-Azerbaijani March 1993 agreement for a $1.4 billion pipeline to carry 800,000 barrels/day to the Mediterranean sidestepped this, the major obstacle: it assumed that Iran could be induced to permit the pipeline to cross its territory (rather than Iran insisting on a pipeline that fed its own oil needs) and that Western financiers would be willing to lend capital for a pipeline crossing Iran. The alternative route to avoid Russia would have to go from Azerbaijan through Georgia and then across into Turkey, a route that is 200 miles longer.

Besides the Turkish option, the other way to avoid Iran is the Russian route. That seems the most likely in the short run: limited pipelines are already in place, and Russia is a major player in the world oil markets, which the multinational oil firms do not wish to annoy. This route is especially attractive to the region's largest oil field, the Tengiz field in Kazakhstan, which is within 50 miles of the Russian border; Chevron, Russia, and Kazakhstan have agreed to transport this oil via Russia.[32] Some of the problems with a Russian route are economic: the existing pipelines may not be able to handle much more throughput (especially in Turkmenistan),[33] and the route terminates on the Black Sea, where Russia has no port capable of handling the traffic and which is anyway quite far from the main potential markets for the crude oil. However, the main difficulties are political: How dependent do the new republics wish to be on Moscow? How tough will Moscow (and the local authorities and mafia) be in demanding high fees and bribes? How nasty will Turkey be in limiting traffic through the Dardenelles and the Bosphorus in order to discourage use of the Russian route? On the last point: Turkey has asserted its right under the 1936 Montreux Convention governing passage through the Straits to limit shipping for reasons of safety and the environment. While Turkey has a point about the dangers posed by many additional oil tankers, "some rivals see Turkey's environmental objections as a smokescreen for its drive to secure huge royalties that would flow from a pipeline across its territory."[34]

FINAL COMMENTS

Khalid Duran made a sober assessment of the Muslim world's chances for influence in the former Soviet South:[35]

> The Islamists will gain some ground . . . but the proximity of Iran's dismal example will be more of a deterrent than an inspiration. As usual, the Saudis will spend heavily but make more enemies than friends because of the anti-culture and anti-intellect element in their rigid interpretation of Islam. Egyptian paupers will be welcome to teach Arabic, but soon lose out to British Council, Goethe-Institut, and Alliance Francaise. After initial successes, Pakistani businessmen and technicians will have a hard time holding their own against Chinese and Japanese. Turkey, too, will have to overstretch herself and find it difficult to match the high expectations of the impoverished cousins in (Central Asia).

For two fundamental reasons, it is inappropriate to think about the former Soviet South's future in terms of a Turkish model, an

Iranian model, or a Pakistani model. First, the Muslim-majority former Soviet republics are as developed—culturally, socially, and economically—as these proposed models. If anyone is going to offer university scholarships in technical areas, it should be the former Soviet republics educating the Turks, Iranians, and Pakistanis. As far as economics is concerned, the newly independent republics have more to gain from trade, investment, and technical advice from the industrialized nations of the West than from their underdeveloped Muslim neighbors. Those neighbors do matter for the economic future of the former Soviet South, but as transport routes and potential trading partners (among equals), not as mentors.

Second, the basic issue for the region is the relative influence of Russia compared to all other states. The ties to Russia are deep and broad—so much so that true independence can only be laboriously built up, not declared overnight. The poorer the area while under Russian rule and the smaller the ethnic Russian population, the fewer are such ties and therefore the easier to break the bonds. On these grounds, Turkmenistan and Tadzhikistan seem the most likely to work free. The realities of geography in the one case and culture in the other make an important Iranian role likely in these two states.

The West must decide whether its interests are best served by the growing estrangement of Russia and the former Soviet South. One view is to promote decolonialization, with all its attendant costs for the former colonial power,[36] at least in part to check Russian power. The opposite view could come from those who worry about an Islamic threat, expect a Russian-Western alliance, or feel that depriving Moscow of a pre-eminent role in its "near abroad" will provoke Russian chauvinism. The choice is not easy. One can defend a Western interest in Russia's pre-eminence in the FSU's Muslim republics without going to the extreme of William Lind's thesis that Russia is Christiandom's left flank against the southern hordes.

NOTES

1.   This paper was written and originally presented in May 1993 and therefore is based on developments through June 1993, i.e., before the summer 1993 replacement of the Elchibey government in Azerbaijan and before the escalation in fighting on the Tadzhik-Pakistan border.

2.   Marie Broxup, "The crescent and the red star," *The Independent*, January 18, 1990.

3.   Sylvie Kaufman, "L'Ouzbékistan en retard d'une 'perestroïka'," *Le Monde*, January 1, 1988.

4.   Michael Dobbs, "New Soviet Freedoms Lead to Surge of Islam," *Washington Post*, October 24, 1990.

5.   On the history of these groups, see Allen Hetmanek, "The Mullahs vs. Moscow," *Washington Post*, September 25, 1988.

6.   Interview with head of al-Bukhan mosque in Samarkand, October 1992.

7.   *Keyhan Havayi*, August 6, 1992.

8.   Khalid Durán, "Rivalries Over the New Muslim Countries," *Aussenpolitik*, IV:1992, 379.

9.   A point taken from Daniel Pipes, "What Leverage in Central Asia?" *Christian Science Monitor*, April 8, 1993.

10.   In April 1992, President Nazarbayev's spokesman announced that Kazakhstan wanted to sign the NPT as a nuclear weapons state on the grounds that weapons had been developed and tested in Kazakhstan before 1967, the criteria for being a nuclear weapon state under the Treaty. See John Lepingwell, "Kazakhstan and Nuclear Weapons," *RFE/RL Research Report*, February 19, 1993, 59.

11.   During his May 1992 visit to Washington, Nazarbayev said, "The question of the continued presence of nuclear arms on Kazakhstan's territory after the terms of the START treaty have been met and will be dealt with by agreement between Russia and Kazakhstan." He repeated this formulation at an October 1992 press conference at the U.N. (John Lepingwell, *op. cit.*, 60).

12.   The information in this paper on events in Tadzhikistan comes from RFE/RL. See especially Christopher Panico, "Uzbekistan's Southern Diplomacy," and Bess Brown, "Tajik Opposition to Be Banned," both in *RFE/RL Research Report*, on March 26, 1993, and April 2, 199,3 respectively.

13.   Ankara Radio as transcribed in FBIS, November 3 and 5, 1992.

14.   *New York Times*, June 26, 1992, quotes "a senior (Turkish) Foreign Ministry official" as explaining that "diplomatic definitions get 'blurred,' indicating that (Turkish military attaches in Azerbaijan) acted as 'advisers' to the Azeri forces."

15.   The CIA's *World Factbook 1992* states that the Azeris make up 25 percent of Iran's population, or 14 million. That would seem to include many assimilated Azeri-origin residents of Tehran and other Iranian cities.

16.   *Iran Times*, July 24, 1992.

17.   For instance, FBIS NES, July 10, 1992; *Iran Times*, July 10 and 17, 1992, and January 8, 1993.

18.   Elizabeth Fuller, "Azerbaijan: Geidar Aliyev's Political Comeback," *RFE/RL Report*, January 29, 1993. After the cut-off date for this paper, Aliyev displaced Elchibey as President of Azerbaijan.

19.   FBIS Europe printed reports on January 9, 1992, of 43 PKK members killed after infiltrating from Iran.   On September 18, 1992, Prime Minister Demirel complained that 300 PKK members attacked a police station after crossing from Iran, killing 15 soldiers. On December 8, 1992, Turkey brought forward Iraqi Kurdish leaders who testified to Iran's support for the PKK. On October 25, 1992, the *New York Times* cited other Iraqi Kurdish leaders to the same effect.

20.   *Mideast Mirror*, January 27 and February 3, 1993.

21.   Sheila Marnie and Erik Whitlock, "Central Asia and Economic Integration," *RFE/RL Research Bulletin*, April 2, 1993.

22.   Farhan Bokari, "Power for the people," *Financial Times*, September 18, 1992.

23.   John Murray Brown, "Euphoria has evaporated," *Financial Times*, May 7, 1993.

24.   These data, and those on Uzbekistan, are as cited in Marnie and Whitlock, *op. cit.*, 43.

25.   On U.S. financing, see *Mideast Mirror*, July 29, 1992. On Eisenberg's activities, see *Jerusalem Post International Edition*, September 5, 1992.

26.   *Keyhan Havayi*, August 29, 1991.

27.   Bandar Khomeini was back in late 1990/91 to 6 million tons per year on an annual basis. Iran's imports in the peak year of 1991/92 were 18 million tons, of which 12 million arrived by sea (cf. *Middle East Economic Digest*, September 19, 1992).

28.   Though Iran Rail did increase its cargo carriage from 6 million tons in 1979/80 to 17 million tons in 1991/92 (Radio Tehran as transcribed in *Akhbaar*, April 11, 1992).

29.   *Iran Times*, March 19, 1993; Radio Tehran as transcribed in *Akhbaar*, December 29, 1992.

30.   *Middle East Economic Digest*, September 18, 1992.

31.   Steve Coll, "Central Asia's High Stakes Oil Game," *Washington Post*, May 9, 1993.

32.   *New York Times*, April 6, 1993.

33.   According to *Middle East* magazine (March 1993), Western oil firms in Turkmenistan have decided that the existing pipeline network in that republic cannot handle much if any additional flow.

34.   Coll, *op. cit.*

35.   Khalid Durán, "Rivalries Over the New Muslim Countries," *Aussenpolitik*, IV: 1992, 380.

36.   As a leading advocate of this perspective, Martha Olcott wrote, "If the region is decolonizing, then there are winners and there are losers, and colonial settlers are classically losers." ("The Decolonization of the USSR," Meeting Report from the Kennan Institute for Advanced Russian Studies IX, no. 10).

DISCUSSION

Ambassador Howard W. Walker
Vice President, National Defense University

Nothing symbolizes changes in international relations and its structures and components more than the emergence of the republics of Central Asia as players on the world scene.

Within the context of the papers today, we will discuss the implications of changes in this region and within these states themselves. They must come to grips with and begin to manage some of the diverse identities and interests within their borders, which were managed in other ways before. This also includes the relationships between these new states and the former members of the Soviet Union, including Russia, and other established states in the region, such as China.

Some of the central issues in these relationships include: ethnic ties; Islamic fundamentalism; economics; energy and regional power balances; influences from Turkey to Pakistan and other countries more closely located; and aspects of the "Great Game" in Eurasia and the U.S. as it relates to the former republics of the Soviet Union.

We are fortunate and honored to have attracted the participants and audience members here. We are particularly grateful to have with us this morning Ambassador Otunbayeva representing Kyrgyzstan, the Charge d'Affaires of Pakistan, and the U.S. Ambassador to Kazakhstan, William Courtney.

I. THE STRUGGLE FOR IDENTITY

●Author: Dr. Shirin Akiner, University of London
●Commentator: Dr. James Critchlow, Harvard University
●Moderator: Ambassador Roza Otunbayeva, Ambassador of Kyrgystan

PRESENTATION BY DR. SHIRIN AKINER
"Emerging National Identities and Domestic Stability"
My paper addresses the identities of Central Asian peoples during the pre-Soviet period. As Shakespeare noted—"past as prologue"—in order to understand the situation today, you must look to the past. Too often, people overlook the very strong sense of common identity that existed in the pre-Soviet period. These identities were developed and manipulated during this period, so they have a strong historical basis.

Identities were not constructed, but the histories of these peoples were considerably distorted. It was the Former Soviet Union's (FSU's) political, not historical task to construct and consolidate these as part of an over-arching Soviet identity. The Soviet regime was able to coopt local elites into the Soviet system. These populations were largely illiterate, so these local elites had an inordinately powerful influence. This was why the Soviet system could be rapidly grafted onto existing systems.

One peculiarity of the Central Asian region was its ability to adapt and to preserve an underlying continuity, particularly in personal relationships, power networks, and clan networks. The existence of these two networks, the public (pro-Soviet) and private (traditional identity) faces, far from causing tensions, led to a high degree of flexibility that helped the new system become grafted onto and co-exist with the old one.

The collapse of the Soviet Union put into question the issue of national identity (as part of an over-reaching Soviet identity). It is important to note that in Central Asia, there were neither liberation struggles nor even independence movements prior to December 1991. Therefore, independence came as a shock, causing a psychological and spiritual trauma that has necessitated redefining identities. Several strands of identities emerged:

Because of the nonattribution policy in effect during the conference, some participants making comments on the papers will not be identified.

- *A Return to Pre-Soviet Identities.* Clan, tribal and regional networks have assumed greater importance, and are more visible now.
- *A More Pronounced Split Between Urban and Rural Communities.* Urban communities are more cosmopolitan as a result of Soviet influence. Some rural communities have become more enamored with Islam which creates local, communal solidarity, and grants its adherents access to a broader international community. This has created problems in understanding the rural community which, by its very nature, is more conservative than urban ones.
- *Growing Generational Splits.* The younger generation wants more change, and of course, prosperity.
- *An Embryonic Form of Nationalism.* This region is so fragmented that "nationalism" may not be a good term. Nevertheless, a "group identity" is emerging, particularly in confrontation with other ethnic groups. Current ethnic problems were an inevitable consequence of the Soviet nationality policy, that defined nationality along ethnic lines, as opposed to modern, national citizenship that has to be non-ethnically based and non-discriminatory.

The main ethnic groups feel that they should have special rights within their "own" republics, leading to uncertainty, especially among non-indigenous groups. This in turn has led to migrations of various scales. On this point, a (two-fold) distinction has to be made between non-Turkic, non-Muslim origin immigrants and the rest:

- *Non-Muslim Immigrants.* So far, there has been no physical aggression against Slav immigrants, but there are fears among them in the new republics, especially as a result of new language laws. This is symptomatic of what they feel is a loss of civil rights. If they felt certain about the future of their civil rights, (Slavic) immigration would slow-down or cease.
- *Muslim Immigrants.* The muslim immigrants, on the other hand, are seen as direct competitors by the indigenous population in cultural, economic and political terms, and there has been physical aggression against them. For example, the Uzbeks and Kazakhs are conflicting with local immigrants.

Republican governments must address the core questions of citizenship and rights. Kazakhstan is different from the rest, inasmuch as everywhere else, the immigrants form a minority, whereas in Kazakhstan, the Slavs and the Kazakhs are roughly equally balanced. The Slavs feel particularly secure because they have a majority in parliament. However, the danger is that sooner or later, the Slavs may demand partition in order to pursue independence or unification with Russia. Kazakhs are therefore becoming more aggressive.

In none of these republics do we find strong opposition movements. There are several reasons for this:

• There is no tradition of formal opposition to the leadership. There is a tremendous respect for authority. This makes it difficult for people to indulge in criticisms of rulers.

• There is also great suspicion of political parties, given the legacy of the communist party. As a result, parties are small, weak, and centered on individuals. They cannot be considered to be significant opposition. They are not part of the debate. Nevertheless, the fact that they exist at all is interesting and to be welcomed.

In the West *and* in Russia, one of the key factors related to regional stability is Islamic fundamentalism. Yet, it is far from a monolithic phenomenon that is in fact fragmented in all possible directions. There are emerging (Islamic) national identities, individuals (new leaders who use Islam), and manipulation from abroad. This isn't coming so much from Iran—because Iranians are Shia not Sunni (which is predominant in Central Asia)—as from Saudi Arabia, followed closely by Pakistan. This is not an exhaustive list of outside countries influencing the region, and they often balance with and compete against each other.

Nevertheless, there is a revival of the practice of Islam. This practice was severely undermined during the Soviet period. The people are literally re-learning the basics of Islam. It is a link with the past, and it is beginning to be seen as the voice of protest as a result of past disappointments. Colonialism, Marxism/Leninism, and democracy have all appeared to be tools of Western imperialism. Even in Kazakhstan, these views are being expressed, particularly in the Ferghana Valley. But even here this is not yet a serious "Islamic fundamentalist" threat, and it has not expanded far outside of the Valley.

The real reasons for instability in Central Asia include: unemployment; impoverishment; and a sense of frustration and alienation. These societies are highly literate. People therefore have aspirations that cannot be satisfied.

To sum-up, the leadership in Central Asia is fairly secure. It is supported not only by a strong clan system, but also by all of the organs of state control. It will be difficult to shift them. However, their presence is also a guarantee of a certain stability. There will undoubtedly be sporadic outbreaks of low-intensity conflict. For this to coalesce into a larger opposition is not impossible. But as the Algerian case demonstrates, it is very difficult to dislodge these kinds of regimes.

In looking at the future of domestic stability in Central Asia, one cannot exclude the influence of outside forces, including, of course Russia, but also China, Turkey, and Iran. Russia and China are of major importance. So far, Russians have demonstrated surprisingly little knowledge of Central Asia because this region was considered to be of secondary importance. Russians have emotional reactions to developments in the region.

One further note on domestic stability that does not relate to the above is drugs. There has been a huge explosion of the drug culture over the past several years in a way that is astonishing and terrifying. This is not only smuggling but also cultivation and abuse. Drugs and related factors such as money and weapons will be important contributing (but not deciding) factors in determining stability in the area.

COMMENTARY BY MR. JAMES CRITCHLOW

I agree with most of Dr. Akiner's assessments. Some of the most positive aspects of this paper are as follows:

- She brings the five Central Asian republics to life as living breathing entities, and not just as some political science construct.
- She also stresses the idea of modernization and secularization. This is important, especially with regards to the elites that are typically the leaders in these republics. They are not a typical part of the Third World, and this is important to bear in mind.

Russia may at some point try to reassert some control over the region—something that has been dismissed, unfortunately, by some other observers. But she does downplay the fear of "Islamic fundamentalism"—I use this term in quotes because this is the term used by others, even though it is not that descriptively accurate. But the fear in the region is that there is a serious threat from the South, especially for the elites, who are afraid of Islam being imported from Afghanistan or Iran.

If Russia does get involved more heavily in the region, it may be a result of its own fears of fundamentalism, not just from the standpoint of security on its own borders, but from the standpoint of concerns Russians have with such Muslim minorities as Tartars and Chechens. Another factor that might provoke Russian involvement is the belief on the part of Central Asian elites that the Russians are less of a threat than the Ayatollahs in Iran, for example. This might account for the Central Asian leaders' ready acceptance that we see of the 201st Russian motorized rifle division on their territory (Tajikistan), or by the fact that over 80 percent of the officer corps in the Uzbek Army is Slavic-speaking.

The second subject is China. By implication, China would come to the aid of the Kazakhs, on behalf of the existing government. This gives rise to two questions. First, are the Chinese capable of such intervention? Second, are the Chinese ready to risk their somewhat improved relations with the Russians? If China were to intervene, it might be the result of a deal between China and Russia to keep the region's Muslims in check.

Specific comments on the paper follow:

- In the text of the paper, there is a reference to the nationalities deported to Central Asia during World War II: Koreans, Germans, Greeks, and Ukrainian Tartars. The Koreans actually were deported from the Eastern Soviet Union before World War II during 1937. Also, I was not aware that the Greeks were victims of sudden deportations of this kind.

- There is a reference to the shares of the indigenous populations as a percentage of the overall populations in the republics. In fact, the Turkmen's percentages are higher as referenced in Appendix II, despite statements to the contrary in the text.

- There is a reference that there was no serious resistance to the Russian invasion of the last century. I think that this is a myth of Russian and Soviet historiography. Since *Glasnost*, Central Asian historians have looked back to the past to restore a more truthful version of history. Take the invasion of Tashkent by the Russian Army around 1865, for example. The Russian commander was concerned because he did not have authorization to invade, so he filed a report that the region had fallen into his hands—at the invitation of the people. In fact the siege was brutal, and they only gave up when they ran out of water. Similar battles have been down-played in Soviet historiography.

- There is a reference to 19th century German romanticism—the idea being that there is some relationship between Russian intellectuals' readings of romanticism and their ideas. In fact, the mechanism was Marxist ideology.

• The discussion of the anti-corruption campaign may make too much of Russian papers' accounts of corruption in Central Asia. In fact, numerous arrests were made by an infamous Tellman Pullyan—an investigator sent to Central Asia by Moscow. He used 1937-style brutal tactics to extract confessions from people. Since independence, many of these former prisoners have been released. There is considerable evidence of exaggeration of these corruption charges.

- The paper states that Islam had become for the Central Asians little more than a "cultural affiliation." I wonder if this doesn't overlook the central role of certain life-cycle rituals that were in use even at the height of Stalinism.

• In the paper, the question of the extent of popular support for the two major Uzbek political groupings is addressed. The statement that they garner very little support is too sweeping because they were not really allowed to develop their support without constraint from the punitive organs in Uzbekistan.

• The paper states that as of 1991, not even the most radical activist had contemplated independence for Central Asia. It's hard to square this with Uzbekistan's 1990 declaration of political sovereignty.

It is true that Central Asians were astonished with the rapid movement toward independence, but I observed satisfaction (among Central Asians) with independence after the putsch. This seemed related to the onerous economic burden that Russian political control placed on Central Asian resources.

• The point is made that the Central Asian republics all have central banks that are independent institutions. But in fact, they are still under the thumb of Mr. Gerashchenko, the head of the Central Bank in Moscow that controls the issuance of currency.

- The paper lists 1989 data on Russian out-migration and argues that out-migration is much more limited from Uzbekistan, Turkmenistan, and Kyrgyzstan than from Tadzhikstan. That may still be true, but when I was in Uzbekistan, I talked to Russians who were desperate to get out for fear of their lives.

- The paper states that the Central Asians had previously preferred to emphasize their common Soviet culture. In my experience, this shared feeling was more one of a common enemy than a common culture. The Soviets placed political straightjackets on them.

- In the oral presentation, drugs were mentioned. It is important to note that drugs have always been on the scene in Central Asia.

DISCUSSION SESSION
Moderator: Ambassador Roza Otunbayeva
Commentator: James Critchlow
The key problem in Kazakhstan is that the northern oblats are dominated by majorities of Russians. To add to this, there are Kazakhs who are trying to stir-up anti-Russian feeling. The saving grace is that many Russians in Kazakhstan feel that they are better off living there now rather than in Russia. Also, Kazakhstan's President Nazarbayev is now brokering the situation as well as possible. Few of my friends are optimistic about the long-term survival of the Republic, though.

Question:
You used the term "welcome" and "watch" with respect to political party development in Central Asia. Those are rather passive words. Do these parties deserve to be encouraged, nurtured and worked with? And can you comment on the development of the electoral process in Kazakhstan and Kyrgyzstan? Is this something that should be encouraged actively, or should we be leery of the possibility that democracy will be viewed as another form of Western imperialism?

Answer:
Outsiders cannot do much to encourage democracy. If there is no culture of opposition, outside acts will be seen as manipulation. Parties created from the outside are likely to be seen as puppet parties. Election laws are fine. But the paper that they are printed on does not substitute for the reality in which they exist, in which they can be subverted. For example, the Kazakh opposition candidate could not obtain paper upon which to print his manifesto. On the positive side, education from the outside can contribute to the culture of democratic society, such as free and secret ballots, but one must be very careful not to allow the perception to arise that this is outside interference.

Question:
I accept the vast majority of comments made about Central Asian society. But I think that life is changing very rapidly. There is less certainty. This generation is very significant. They almost look like they never grew up under communism at all. This openness is likely to effect the political situation quickly, and challenge the authoritarian nature of regimes. It does take a long time to implant true democracy. But it is still possible to express grave dissatisfaction with existing circumstances, even if there is not a direct transition to democracy.

This aside, my question to any or all the panelists: What is the potential for unification? There has been talk of common Turkic alphabets, and common economic institutions. What are the prospects of a Turkistan confederation, for example, in the next few years, especially if the CIS military and economic structures should fail even more drastically. How much do you feel the authoritarian regimes will encourage or discourage this notion of unification?

Answer:
I would say regional cooperation "yes," but unification "no." A Turkic entity would be difficult to achieve because of a lack of trust. For example, the Uzbeks would dominate by means of their numbers, yet the Kazakhs do not trust them. Short of a cataclysmic event combined with the emergence of a charismatic leader, this is highly unlikely. It would be good to try to have limited cooperation, however, especially in the area of water resources.

Comment:
I agree entirely. A certain degree of cooperation is possible, but as we see with the EC (European Community), it is evident that an incredible degree of political maturity is required to achieve any form of significant cooperation. On the question of change, it is important to note that there is a hemorrhage of bright young people to the private sector. If there is stability, reasonable prosperity is possible. This economic stability is required if democracy is ever to come. This is perhaps too gloomy an outlook. The conservatism in society will help prevent too rapid a change as well.

171

Comment:
We need some cooperation, especially in the area of water rights and land issues. But we have never had common languages or interests. All of our problems were resolved in Moscow through structures in the Soviet Union. Now we need to resolve problems regionally. We must learn to speak with each other in a civilized form. Even though in my and in other regions, some people have European attitudes towards these things, this does not mean that this is a common form of communication.

Question:
Two questions and comments. What about problems between Uzbeks and Tadzhiks? It is so difficult to distinguish between the two. First, take the classical cities of Persian cultures. Some cities are the centers of Tadzhik culture, but are run by Uzbeks. If things continue to fall apart, and you look at an area between central Uzbekistan and Tadzhikstan, it seems that maybe there is not a question of forced unity, but that these people could resolve their problems through a communal entity.

Answer:
As for the question on Uzbek-Kazakh rapprochement— in the ideal world, this would be desirable. But positions have become polarized. The Kazakhs are fearful of the Tadzhik "sea" around them. Here, Tadzhiks can be the big fish in a small sea. If there was any unification with the Uzbeks, it would be on the Uzbeks' terms, and they would dominate. It is a matter of concern that some look to the Malaysian model. This situation is characterized by the indigenous people dominating all others. If there was a larger Uzbekistan, the Uzbeks would be sure to hold all positions of power and put the Tadzhiks in a somewhat subordinate position.

Comment:
The historiography of Central Asia must be examined and rewritten. The roots of these problems go back to the 19th and 18th centuries. Western archives have been used for histories, but Central Asian and Ottoman archives have to be examined. What the Russians have contributed to these areas in positive and negatives senses must be examined.

In addition, the Chinese perspective is important. They are so eager to gather information on Central Asian politics and political alliances, at the moment. I am not underestimating the Chinese position, but still, I think that before we talk about the "Chinese danger," we have to discuss the basic problem of how to bring the Central Asians into the civilized world, including raising the standard of living and improving human rights, etc. I hope that these issues will be raised, because, in addition to asking the "why's" about these people, let us do something useful that will be useful for their lives. They deserve it because they have suffered considerably.

Question:
Dr. Akiner talked of the search for indigenous traditions that could supplant the series of western borrowings. To a historian like myself, the only indigenous tradition is Genghis Khan. While I am not suggesting that we return to an era of Mongol hordes, there has been discussion of a role for the descendants of royalty in Europe. What about this possibility in Central Asia?

Answer:
Presidents in this region do, in fact, act in this style. But this can only go so far. No one has a hankering to bring back Bukharin. There is a notable difference, however, between settled people and their relationship to the past, and everyone else.

II. ISLAM AND THE FUNDAMENTALIST REVIVAL IN CENTRAL ASIA

- Author: Dr. Mehmet Saray, Turkish International Cooperation Agency (TICA)
- Commentator: Dr. Paul Goble, Carnegie Endowment for International Peace
- Moderator: Dr. Graham Fuller, Rand Corporation

Graham Fuller
The topic of "Islam and the Fundamentalist Revival" generates much excitement in the post-Cold War world. An almost visceral fear of Islam is arising around the world, and Central Asia is frequently viewed as an opportunity for the expansion of fundamental Islam. It is important to come fully to grips with all the basic internal and external roots and sources of Islam in Central Asia and to address the traditions which would either foster or hinder the establishment of fundamentalism in the region.

PRESENTATION BY DR. MEHMET SARAY
'The Root of Islam in Central Asia: A Brief Primer"

In order to fully appreciate the importance of historical antecedents in Central Asia, one must discuss the historical interaction between Turks and Islam. Turks first encountered Islam in A.D. 751 when Arab armies reached Talas. Widespread conversion to Islam began swiftly, aided by the similarities between Islam and the traditional Turkish religion of Goktengri. The first Muslim Turkish state, Karakhanates, emerged in A.D. 932. The interchange between Islam and Turkdom quickly began to flow in both directions, with Turkish philosophers and scholars such as Ahmet Yesevi and Imam-i Buhari influencing the development of Islam beyond Central Asia. The influence of Turkish scholars persisted well into the second half of the 19th century. Thus, when Russia expanded into the region, it encountered a highly developed and flourishing Islamic culture.

Historical Russian knowledge of Islam dates to the 16th and 17th centuries and coincides with the rise of the Ottoman Empire to prominence and leadership in the Islamic world. Peter the Great ordered the translation of the Qur'an into Russian and founded the Academy of Oriental Studies with the mission to study issues pertaining to Islam. Russian study of the Qur'an and Islam primarily served negative purposes. In particular, Russian scholars of Islam characterized it as a faith of the uncultured. More importantly, Islam was perceived as a threat to power and authority of the Russian Orthodox Church and the unity of the tsarist Russian Empire. The intertwined strength and legitimacy of both institutions promoted a cooperative effort to contain and discredit Islam. The Russian government embarked upon aggressive programs of russification and christianization of Turkish and other muslims. Children in Central Asia were given Christian and Russian schooling; local Turkic dialects were used to undermine the trend toward a common Turkic language.

Soviet relations with Islam and Muslim populations did not offer an improvement over the Tsar's government. Dr. Saray remarked that while the tsarist government had focused primarily on cultural aspects of Islam, such as education, the Soviet government launched their attack at the institutions which supported the Islamic culture. In particular, the Soviet government destroyed the economic power of the Islamic clergy and supplanted both

Islamic customary law (the "adat") and formal Quranic law (the Shari'at). The Soviet government also abolished Islamic education and religious practices; Mosques and Madrashas were closed and the publication of religious books outlawed. The spiritual community of Islam was attacked by arresting, and in many cases, executing prominent leadership figures. As one might expect, the campaigns waged against Islam by the Soviet government forced the development of an illegal and underground community. While Islam did not vanish from the cultural life of Soviet Turks, its formal and prominent role in society was destroyed. While Islam did not vanish from the cultural life of Soviet Turks, religious education and practice became very informal and dependent on an oral tradition passed from generation to generation.

Islam clearly did not fare well in its contact with first the Russian Empire and then the Soviet Union. Over the span of 200 years, the central spiritual and cultural institutions of Islam suffered from almost continuous attack.

Changes in Soviet policies towards Islam emerged gradually during the Gorbachev regime. *Glasnost* and *perestroika* created opportunities for missionaries from Christian and Muslim countries to operate in the Soviet Union. In addition, foreign radio broadcasts with religious and spiritual messages began to reach segments of the Soviet population after the government ceased jamming operations. While Christian organizations made great initial headway, international Islamic organizations rapidly moved in the same direction and a new rivalry between Islam and Christianity arose from the wreckage of the Soviet Union.

Islamic missionary efforts in the Soviet Union are concentrated heavily in the Caucasus and Central Asia. Iran and Saudi Arabia have emerged as the most active and aggressive proponents of Islamic missionary work in the region. Although the Iranian and Saudi missionaries promote different philosophies with respect to Islam, their apparent long-term objectives are quite similar. Both nations have committed substantial financial resources to support their missionary efforts, and both states are attempting to recreate Islamic societies consistent with their own societal model. Dr. Saray expressed doubt as to the likelihood that either Iran or Saudi Arabia would succeed in converting the states of Central Asia and the Caucasus into Islamic states of either the Iranian or Saudi model. Most likely, Saudi Arabia and Iran will continue to gain and exert influence over a variety of issues in the region. The future of official alphabets constitutes another battlefield in the competition between elements of the Islamic world. Evidently, the Saudi Arabian government has launched a campaign urging the states of Central Asia and the Caucuses to abandon the Cyrillic alphabet in favor of the Arab alphabet. However, Saudi efforts along this line seem to have little likelihood of success. A 1993 conference concluded with an agreement between official representatives of Kazakhstan, Turkmenistan, Kyrygyzstan, Uzbekistan, Azerbaijan and Turkey to adopt a common alphabet of 34 letters.

It is thought that the efforts of Iranian Shiite missionaries will meet with little more success than the efforts of the Sunni missionaries from Saudi Arabia. First, and most importantly, the Muslim population of Central Asia remains predominantly Sunni and continues to harbor a strong historical sense of distrust and dislike for Shiite Persians. Iran has, however, committed substantial resources to the propagation of religious governments in the newly independent states of Central Asia. Five percent of Iran's oil revenues are obligated to this objective.

Soviet foreign policy with respect to Islam differed rather dramatically from their oppressive domestic policy. The Soviet Union pursued a "pro-Islam policy and propaganda" with respect to the Muslim world beyond Soviet borders. This policy has been attributed to the "faults of the European countries and the United States in their policies towards Muslim countries."

COMMENTARY BY DR. PAUL GOBLE

This discussion illustrates the fundamental problem of distinguishing between the truly known aspects of Central Asian identity sources from the unknown aspects of Central Asian identity sources. What is known and what is unknown is a fundamental question of politics.

The difficulty of separating truth from conjecture faces all outside actors in Central Asia and is frequently compounded by their importation of ignorant and inaccurate assumptions. The unintended consequences resulting from these fallacies and assumptions reverberate even more strongly in the post-Cold War era.

First, what role and influence do external players have within Central Asia? Second, how will Islam, as both a known and unknown quantity play a role in establishing a Central Asian identity of the future. Third, and finally, how will the competition between Turkey and Iran effect the development of this future Central Asian identity.

Throughout the past several hundred years, the assumptions, usually based on ignorance or on calculation, have had real consequences on the people of this region. They have been divided up according to designs of people who did not understand what was going on. And this problem of not understanding this region and bringing in assumptions from the outside continues right through this day.

The collapse of the Soviet Union opened Central Asia to nations which, previously, had not played prominent roles in the region. Much like the reactions of individuals to rapid change, the nations of the West have proceeded through several stages in their understanding of Central Asia. The first stage is denial; the governments of Western nations wistfully hoped that some form of centralized government and control would persist in the relationship between Moscow and Central Asia. The U.S. government seems to be largely stuck in this phase.

The second phase consists of applying analogies to situations of rapid change. With respect to Central Asia, the most dangerous analogy involves the idea that this region is once again part of the "Great Game". While there will be competition among external powers for influence in Central Asia, the application of the "Great Game" to the region trivializes the peoples of Central Asia and denies their importance as actors in their own homelands. Governments, social movements, Islam in various forms, and various political parties are real actors. The fact that most of these actors can be bought off with enough dollars only serves to reinforce the truth that external actors must, in one fashion or another, deal with local actors.

Next, we look at the role of Islam in identity-building in Central Asia. The Soviet structure and incentives supplanted Islam's contribution to identity building. The particular consequences of the Soviet incentive structure include the delegitimization of Turkdom and Islam. The Soviet system created no forum or structure for Turkdom in the lives of Central Asians, while Islam was even more fundamentally rejected than Turkdom.

The consequences of recognizing the region as a series of distinct actors, as opposed to something that can be simply exploited by outsiders, are fundamental. External actors must now seriously consider the local actors' search for a redefinition of their identity. For the first time in several hundred years, the people are going to define themselves, rather than be defined by outsiders. The complexity of the Soviet and Russian legacy in Central Asia must be overcome. How the people of Central Asia overcome this historical legacy and redefine their identity constitutes the fundamental question with respect to the region.

With the construction of this initial platform, the role of Islam as a focus for redefining identity in Central Asia surfaces. The newly independent states of Central Asia differ dramatically from most other states in that their previous structures and incentives for defining identity were imposed by an external power, the Soviet Union. The Soviet governments created structures and incentives that rewarded those who defined their identity in a fashion consistent with Soviet identity and punished those who defined their identity outside of this narrow range. The Soviet structured identity required the delegitimatizition of the two alternative identity builders, Turkdom and Islam. The Soviet system possessed no forum for the articulation of either Turkdom or Islam.

Following the collapse of the Soviet government, popular interest in both Islam and Turkdom grew out of the general backlash against the ideals and norms of Soviet political and social culture.

The resurgence of Islam in Central Asia does not inherently constitute an unwelcome challenge to the region. First, outsiders know very little of the meaning of Islam for the people of Central Asia. Indeed, the diversity of the people of Central Asia indicates that there may be little or no common understood meaning. There is no particular reason to believe that the re-emergence of Islam as a central component of identity in the region will be inimical to the interests of the United States and other Western nations.

Any concerns emanate from the possibility that political oppression will result in the politization of Islam. Many of the current regimes in Central Asia are engaged in crackdowns against their political opposition. However, none of the regimes are threatening the Mosques. As all other avenues of political expression are shut off, Islam becomes the one remaining channel for political opposition and will, by definition, become fundamentalist. On the other hand, the return of Islam should be viewed as a natural part of the identity recovery process, just as the strengthening of orthodox Judaism followed the creation of Israel. The return of Islam is an inherent outgrowth of recuperating from Soviet and Russian rule.

Competition between Turkey and Iran over influence in the region, or more generally, the nature of all external involvement in Central Asia is a key issue for examination. The United States has misunderstood the current situation in Central Asia to a degree unparalleled by any other nation. By perceiving the Turkish-Iranian competition in a strictly win-lose fashion, the United States ignores the complexity of the problems and the possibility of multiple outcomes across the region.

Foreign influences on Islam in Central Asia must be differentiated along the lines of their distinct advantages and disadvantages. Turkey offers the ties of a common history and culture. Turkey, as a nation accepted by Europe and the West, presents opportunities to cement concrete economic and political relations with advanced industrial nations. Turkey also possesses a standard of living attractively higher than other nations in the region. Iran, on the other hand, offers access to cheap and efficient lines of communication and transport that will facilitate exports. The nations of Central Asia cannot export through Turkey without first passing through a third country. Geographic continuity ensures that Iran will play a role in the region, irrespective of the desires of any other nation. Iran's advantage is, conversely, Turkey's primary disadvantage. The lack of geographic continuity creates distinct economic disadvantages that constrain Turkey's influence. Fortunately, for those of us who are not terribly thrilled with all aspects of the Iranian government, Iran has a number of huge disadvantages: Shia, not Sunni; a cultural arrogance that rivals that of any nation on the face of the earth. Iranian cultural arrogance has not played well in Central Asia. The possibility of multiple outcomes implies that Iran and Turkey will most likely gain and lose influence in different areas. Inevitably, both Turkey and Iran will exert influence in Central Asia.

The attempts by Saudi Arabia to persuade the Turkic peoples of Central Asia to adopt the Arabic alphabet opened the doors for Iran to exert additional spiritual and cultural influence in the region. Similarly, Turkey's efforts to promote a common Turkic alphabet will most likely backfire and diminish Turkish influence.

REMARKS BY GRAHAM FULLER

The issue of internal forces on Islam in Central Asia and their effect on the influence of external actors is an important subject. While recognizing that not all participants would agree, I would argue that Iran has been on fairly good behavior in Central Asia compared to its behavior in other areas of the world. Iran appreciates the necessity for different tactics in Central Asia than those applied to Lebanon and with respect to the Palestinian issue. There has been little propagandizing in the Iranian press with respect to Central Asia and destabilizing behavior has been at a minimum.

Four factors will exert the most influence over Islam in Central Asia. The Turkic identity is somewhat fractured and cannot play as strong of a unifying role as had been predicted. On the other hand, Islam continues to represent the single factor that unites all the people in Central Asia.

• The identity question will continue to be very important, in particular vis-a-vis Russia. The quest to define an identity separate from the previous Soviet identity will almost certainly draw upon both pan-Turkic and Islamic elements.

• Islam will also play an important role in defining the legitimacy of governments in the newly independent nations of Central Asia. Ex-Communists hold power in all nations of Central Asia, with the notable exception of Kyrgyzstan. Political opposition and the struggle against illegitimate governments that have not been elected and do not represent the desires of their populations will gravitate toward either Islam or nationalism. Islam could become the sole vehicle for political opposition. This is especially worrisome as the ex-Communists in the various governments co-opt nationalism for their own purposes.

• The economic problems common to Central Asia may also serve to strengthen Islam, as the governments and opposition parties search for alternatives to existing policies. Islam offers the image of an ideal panacea.

• Finally, there is a distinction between "established" Islam and "new" Islam and the effects that each may have in Central Asia. "Established" Islam has long been identified with the communist government of the Soviet Union. Many of the important players in "established" Islam are now cooperating very closely with the new governments of Central Asian states. These ties to the previous and existing governments discredit the existing

Islamic structure. On the other hand, Islamism or political Islam is characterized by its status as an opposition group and does not suffer the ill-affects of these past associations. The only way that "established" Islam will compete successfully with Islamism is by joining in the opposition to the existing governments and their policies.

DISCUSSION SESSION

Question:
Has Dr. Saray encountered any concern over Turkey's growing role in Central Asia among Russian colleagues? In particular, is there any concern in Russia over the possibility that Turkey could move into a "protectorate" role with respect to the Turkic states of Central Asia?

Answer:
In order for Turkey to assume such a role, Turkey and Russia clearly would have to cooperate a great deal. Thus far, Russia and Turkey have demonstrated favorable and positive formal cooperation in support of the Turkish goal of moving the Central Asian Turkic peoples forward into modernity. Cooperation between Russia and Turkey in expanding Turkey's influence in the region will promote stability and peaceful change.

Question:
Could Dr. Goble and Mr. Fuller discuss the instrumentalities inherent in their respective views on the role and growth of Islamic fundamentalism in the region?

Answer:
The most important instrumentality hinges upon the status of Islam as the sole viable channel of political opposition. If the current government crackdown on all other forms of political expression and opposition continues, then Islam can hardly not become a focal point for political activity in opposition to the government. On the other hand, if the current governments permit political opposition and expression outside of the Mosque, then Islam should develop with less politicization and should be a healthful and stabilizing influence on the social growth of the region.

Comment:
Central Asia should not differ dramatically from other Islamic states with similar situations, such as Algeria. The role of Islam in a nation's society depends strongly on the availability of other avenues of political expression and the overall health of the nation's economic, political, and social institutions.

Question:
What should the role of language and alphabet be with respect to Tajikistan. In particular, should Tajikistan be considered separately from the Turkic states of Central Asia?

Answer:
Language will not predetermine the outcome of social growth and change in Central Asia. Certainly, language may favor some outcomes and impact upon the course of events. In Central Asia, the Turkic heritage and affinity for Turkic languages will constrain and undermine Iranian influence in the region. One must not view Central Asia as a monolithic set of people sharing one language and one culture.

Comment:
The different language families found in Central Asia are not all that widely split. With respect to the separation of Tajikistan from the other Turkic peoples, the Tadzhik people could integrate with the other Turkic people without much difficulty. If the Tadzhiks are given a set of alternatives with respect to language, then they will choose the most appropriate ones, i.e. the Turkish language and a latin alphabet.

Question:
Recalling events in Iran during the late 1970's, will Islam in Central Asia react against increasing Western corporate presence, including capital investment?

Answer:
Increasing Western investment and presence will result in increased resentment among the population and further increases in the politicization of Islam. The visible relationship between foreign investment and the secular governments of Central Asian states will contribute to the radicalization of Islam.

However, there are many historical and empirical models of Islam's reaction to increases in foreign presence and investment. The multiplicity of models indicates that the reaction could differ markedly from experiences in Iran and Algeria.

Question:
Will the transition from the secular societies imposed by the Soviet Union to an Islamic society greatly effect the status and treatment of women? Under Soviet rule, women in Central Asia enjoyed a certain amount of liberation.

Answer:
Not one of the speakers had predicted the complete replacement of the existing society with an Islamic society similar to those found in either Iran or Saudi Arabia. In the context of Central Asia, Soviet rule was highly liberating for women. However, gradual changes have occurred elsewhere in the Islamic world that have resulted in some degree of liberation for women. Modernization and urbanization have forced changes upon much of the Islamic world and will effect the status of women in Central Asia as Islam's influence grows.

Comment:
The Soviet Union did not contribute greatly to the liberalization of women in Central Asia. Whatever liberalization occurred was from "one cell to another" with respect to the overall human rights picture. Widespread discrimination against women persisted throughout the period of Soviet rule, albeit in different fashions from the oppression associated with Islam. The varieties within Islam permit a wide range of liberalization for women. In Kazakhstan, women have never worn veils and have participated in many areas of society.

Comment:
The speaker disagreed strongly with the concept that actors will either win or lose in Central Asia. The notion of competition between Iran and Turkey fails to reflect the truly important issues at stake for these newly independent nations and the other nations of the region. The interests of all actors, local or otherwise, would be best served by regional cooperation with due respect to the independence and sovereignty of the Central Asian states.

Attention should be focused on economic development and cooperation rather than on matters pertaining to language and alphabets. Pakistan serves as an effective example of a nation without a truly indigenous culture or language that has succeeded in addressing important issues of political and economic development. While Islam is an important component of life, it must be contained from radicalization that threatens political and economic development.

Question:
Regarding the issue of the evolving relationship between Afghanistan and the states of Central Asia, each panelist was asked to comment on the future impact of Afghanistan on the region.

Answer:
Tajikistan's location between Turkic nations prompts them to look at Afghanistan, with its large ethnic Tadzhik population, as a natural counterbalance and ally. The current situation involving Uzbekistan, Tajikistan, and Afghanistan will most likely deteriorate, forcing the Tadzhiks to aggressively seek assistance from their ethnic compatriots to the south.

Comment:
Afghanistan tends to focus on an alternate identity to a greater extent than most of the states of Central Asia. Islam constitutes the most prominent element of identity in Afghanistan, especially in the wake of the extended civil war and Soviet occupation. Islam as a source of identity offers the Tadzhiks an avenue to counter Turkic nationalism and to increase ties with potential allies such as Afghanistan and, possibly, Iran.

Comment:
If one reads the Qur'an and compares it to the Bible, you realize that Islam is a religion, not a complete and total universe. Islam permits the successful co-existence of a deeply religious culture and a state characterized by secular institutions. Turkey offers the states of Central Asia a thriving model of such a relationship. The model's appeal in Central Asia is evidenced by the secular leanings of the Central Asian governments. While these new governments must display proper deference for popular Islam, the

thrust of the policy continues to be secular in nature. Moreover, the attitude of the people toward Islam remains somewhat apathetic. Although a large proportion of the population subscribes to the new Islam rather than established Islam, attendance at the mosque persists essentially as a social function similar to attendance at Church on Sunday in the United States.

Question:
Many Turks feel distinctly uneasy with Islamic fundamentalism. While fundamentalism has gained influence throughout the Islamic world, including Turkey, the Turkish government continues to embrace its status as a secular state. How can a secular Turkey comfortably embrace policies toward Central Asia that promote religious governments? The governments and people of Central Asia remain somewhat leery of Turkey and harbor a sense that they were abandoned by Turkey during the 1920s and 1930s.

Answer:
The government of Turkey is implementing a variety of assistance programs in Central Asia, encompassing both secular and religious efforts. In addition, many Turkish private organizations participate in assistance programs independent of the Turkish government. These private programs include secular education and culture, religious education and culture, economic and business assistance and other issues related to development. The ability for both public and private assistance programs to co-exist overcomes any potential contradiction between the secular government and policy of Turkey and the development of Islamic culture in Central Asia.

Comment:
Outside actors place a great deal of emphasis on religious education, given their perceptions of profound and widespread religious ignorance in Central Asia.

III. MOSCOW'S SECURITY PERSPECTIVE, THE COMMONWEALTH, AND INTER-STATE RELATIONS

- Author: Dr. Eugene Rumer, Rand Corporation
- Author: Dr. Bess Brown, RFE/RL

- Author: Dr. Maxim Shashenkov, Oxford University
- Commentator: Dr. Stephen Sestanovich,Carnegie Endowment for Internation Peace
- Commentator: Ambassador William Courtney, U.S. Ambassador to Kazakhstan
- Moderator: Mr. Jed Snyder, Institute for National Security Studies

PRESENTATION BY DR. EUGENE RUMER
"Russia and Central Asia After the Soviet Breakup"

Russia does not have a clear view of its interests in the region, so its policy is not clear. There is no strategy. This feeling is not quite mutual on the part of Central Asian states, but there is a strikingly similar lack of coherence coming from the Central Asian side. However, there is a strong desire on the part of Central Asian elites to preserve links with Russia.

How did we get here? History must be reviewed. The Central Asian republics, of all the republics, were least prepared to embrace full sovereignty. Throughout the final year of the Soviet regime, the five Central Asian states comprised the key pro-centrist forces in the "nine-plus-one" negotiations aimed at renegotiating the inter-union federal treaty. They were a counterweight that Gorbachev could bank on when dealing with centrifugally-oriented forces like Russia and Ukraine.

After August 1991, the centrifugal forces gained new momentum. It became clear that Central Asia would pursue some form of independence. Throughout the final stages of the union through the fall of 1991, Central Asian leaders still held onto a mirage of the Soviet Union. All of this was shattered by the centrifugally-oriented republics in December 1991.

The Russian perspective of that time was that Central Asia was a burden. Russia had lost a war in Afghanistan and withdrawn. Central Asia was a security and economic burden on Russia. This was articulated by Gorbachev democrats and hardline "little Russia" proponents who wanted to "go home." In this view, Russia had shared too much, and had been the worst victim of its own policies. The huge socio-economic and environmental problems in Central Asia fueled this feeling.

The feeling was quite the reverse on the Central Asian side, especially among Central Asian leaders. In their view, the federal distributive function would continue to provide them with resources and markets. The break-up of the Union, and the political and ideological victory of the little Russia coalition dashed these leaders' hopes, and Central Asia entered into a brief period of post-independence euphoria. Central Asia was now free to pursue its own external and internal relations. But these hopes on both the Russian and Central Asian sides were quickly dashed.

Evidence of Russians' and Central Asians' reawakening to each other emerged in the spring of 1992. The author travelled there after the Bishkek summit, before the Tashkent summit of May 1992. It seemed in Russia and Central Asia that the Commonwealth was on its last legs. What changed the views of most Central Asian leaders on this link were the developments in Afghanistan, and the realization or perception that Russia was needed by Central Asia as a stabilizer. None of the outside powers (e.g., Pakistan, Turkey) could play this external stabilizing role.

These were the views of the elite, and were not shared widely by the masses. What emerged in the Tashkent summit in the spring of 1992 was in effect a security treaty between four out of five Central Asian republics—Kyrgyzstan was the one notable exception—and Russia.

The treaty recreated a commonwealth security organization and committed Central Asia to close cooperation with Russia. On the part of Russia, there was a commitment to the internal as well as the external borders of the Central Asian region.

However, this development was not the result of the coming together of Russian and Central Asian ruling establishments with common strategic or national interest views. Rather, it was the indication of a common political and ideological trend. This coincided in Russia with the emergence of the first opposition to the Gaidar plan in the spring of 1992, and the re-initiation of internal discussions of Russia's national interests.

This also coincided with the emergence of the Civic Union and the old defense industrial lobby, and with the reemergence of Russian democrats who were preoccupied with Russia's national interest. The break-up of inter-union economic links clearly threatened the Civic Union. Also, people like Sergei Stankevich played an important role in the break-up of the union, and had to disassociate themselves from this. They did this by looking for a new mobilizing platform that focussed on Russian power, and the protection of ethnic Russians abroad. Overall this is a fairly chauvinist perspective that has increasingly become the beginning of a consensus in Russian foreign policy vis-a-vis the far abroad (West) and the near abroad (the former republics, including Central Asia).

The emergence of the Committee for Defense and Foreign Policy on the one year anniversary of the coup has lacked any clear tangible expression of the national interest or economic interest in Central Asia. Russian interest in the region is generally to preserve security and stability, and to avoid intervention. There is a general recognition that Islamic fundamentalism is not a great threat—most Central Asian Muslims are Sunni, not Shia.

Perhaps the cotton mills in Vinovona are an important enough motivating interest for the Russians. The one Central Asian state that is of great importance to Russia is Kazakhstan. It is not even traditionally considered to be part of Central Asia. It is almost a barrier state between Russia and Central Asia. Russia would be most hurt by instability here. Let us not forget that there are still some nuclear weapons deployed here, and that Russia has an interest in the Balkonur space center.

But still what is missing in understanding Russia's growing security interests in the region is a sign of a clear and present security threat to Russia. Therefore, Russian policy has been held hostage to internal political events in the region, as well as to internal political discussions in Russia. There have been no incidents of persecution of ethnic Russians in the region, and, as a result, this has *not* become a political or security concern for Russia.

Tajikistan and Uzbekistan have become the principle consumers of Russian security in the region. Russian policy has evolved from a muddling through on the basis of the agreement made in Tashkent in May of 1992. Russian troops have attempted to pacify the borders not necessarily successfully. Russia has tried to look the other way and not say anything about Uzbekistan's military intervention in the war in Tajikistan. And Russians have reacted with little concern (veiled relief) about the fortunes of Muslim democratic forces. The alternative would have been de-stabilization in the region—something Russia wants to avoid.

Russia's interests are not limited geographically. Russia has a large Muslim population—eight percent or fourteen million persons. Islam will grow as an issue because of the centrifugal forces in Russia itself. Otherwise, Russian policy will continue to be laissez-faire, perhaps barring some major de-stabilization in the region. If that were to happen, Russia's commitments would exceed by far Russia's capabilities to intervene.

MR. SNYDER, MODERATOR
We will next hear from Bess Brown. I hope during the discussion that we can come back to two themes. The first is the question of whether or not there has been an evolution in Russia's interest in the region over the past two years. And second: Will the Russians look at the region as only a threat, or will they see it as a strategic opportunity as well?

PRESENTATION BY BESS BROWN
"Security Concerns of the Central Asian States"
Central Asian security concerns affect how Russia perceives the Central Asian region and how Central Asia perceives its place in the world.

First of all, the dissolution of the Soviet Union came as a huge surprise. Although in the previous year there had been indications that independence might be coming and the Central Asians were complaining bitterly about the terms of the relationship they had had with Moscow over the past 60-70 years, they did not believe that Russia would "let them go," to borrow the expression the Baltic states used.

Suddenly, there was the impression that Moscow was irrelevant. They did not know what to do. However, the Central Asians did not cooperate with the other (non-Russian) states—namely the Baltic states—to (mutually) place strictures on the terms under which they would join the Commonwealth. Instead, they were the ones who placed conditions on joining the union, insisting on being treated as equal founding members. Already their self-respect had developed to the point that they wanted to be treated as equals.

Once the Commonwealth existed, the Central Asians saw the traditional concept of security concerns as secondary to the economic concerns that had been deteriorating over the past several years. The Central Asians believed that they were not what the Russians said they were—parasites feeding off of the system. They believed that they had made a contribution that was at least equal to the support that they had received from Russia. Now they were having to face this issue squarely. Was it true that their contribution had been reciprocal? Meanwhile, the economic ties with Russia were breaking.

The results are well-known. Kyrygystan's economic statistics are horrid. Where are they going to turn? To the outside world. Akayev, the Kyrgyz president, was in Moscow in the winter of 1993 telling Boris Yeltsin that he would agree to any sort of relationship with Russia (in return for Russian assistance and ties). It is not clear how this meeting went. But the fact that they have now agreed to adhere to IMF rules indicates that even turning to Russia did not reveal very satisfying results.

This is the reason why Kazakhstan under Nazarbayev has, since the creation of the CIS, argued that what is needed is some kind of coordinating structure that will replace these lost economic ties. This would not be dictated from a center in Moscow, or wherever this mechanism was erected. But it would oversee consensual agreements. It would assure that when relations are established between two countries, that their agreements will be carried out. This can prevent the kinds of crises like the one that arose between Ukraine and Turkmenistan in which Ukraine eventually cut-off Turkmenistan's ability to ship gas to the Ukraine.

This all demonstrates how there are objective reasons why political stability is so desperately important. It leads one to carefully consider the kinds of de-stabilization that democratic activities could generate. In the cities, democracy might be possible, but in the country side, it is inconceivable. Given the importance of economic factors, if one was to ask Central Asians what their primary concern was, their answer would be economic factors. To be sure, security concerns exist, and are part of state sovereignty.

But Central Asians prefer to leave them to the Commonwealth and to the Russian government. Four out of five republics have developed something of their own military establishments. Kyrgyzstan is the only exception. In April 1993, when President Akayev was in Japan, he boasted of this. There are ideological reasons for this, perhaps, because he wants to see his country become the Switzerland of Central Asian. But there are other considerations as well. They simply do not have the money. Armed neutrality is effectively making a virtue out of necessity.

Turkmenistan will not sign anything. They will remain members of the Commonwealth, but they refused to sign the Tashkent agreement. And in April 1993 they refused to sign another agreement. They want everything on a bilateral basis. They have worked with the Russian military structure to create a common army. They have not received a formal agreement on this. Turkmenistan also has been the least concerned about the situation in Tajikistan.

The civil war in Tajikistan has had an immense effect on Uzbek leaders' perception of their position within the Commonwealth and with Russia. Last year, there were fairly high frictions between these leaders and Russia over the issue of the price of cotton—again we are back to the importance of economic considerations.

This year, the question of the Uzbeks turning to Russia for military assistance and support to limit the conflict within Tadzhikstan and to limit the repercussions of the conflict on other regions has had an important effect on these two countries (Russia and Uzbekistan). The question that arises: How genuine is the fear that has been most articulated by Uzbekistan's President that fundamentalists must be dealt with? To what extent is he consciously or unconsciously using this to deal with his own opposition with which he has always been uncomfortable?

In repressing political opposition (as does the Tadzhik leadership), are not the Central Asian leaders creating the very same threat to their own security that they profess to fear? We are likely to find this out in the very near future. Meanwhile, it is transforming the question of the security role that these countries play in the Commonwealth. It has taken on an entirely different meaning than it did when first contemplated.

PRESENTATION BY MR. MAXIM SHASHENKOV
"Central Asia: Emerging Military-Strategic Issues"
Two facts are crucial to understanding the military transition in the region. The first one is that we are dealing with a very transitional, fluid period. Military issues are part of the wholesale change in the region, and are intimately related to political and economic developments. Second, we are in a very embryonic stage of military development. Despite the fact that many documents on security and military issues have been signed, most of them remain valid only on paper. There is still very little rapprochement between the parties. Attitudes and realities are valid, not the words printed on documents that poorly reflect the situation on the ground.

To understand the position of Central Asians in military affairs during the Soviet period, it is important to reference the elites. The process of de-colonization, when independence was thrust upon Central Asia, led to the continued power of pro-Russian elites combined with the weakness of anti-Russian forces. This phenomenon of elites seeking the continued assistance of Russia creates the foundation for understanding the entire military situation in the region. These elites want to rely on Russian security assurances in order to stay in power.

It was obvious that the Central Asian region would be marginalized in CIS security debates. In CIS talks, regional leaders expressed a desire for joint forces. But for their insistence on rights of draftees, they have not asked for or received anything substantive in the policy area. However, they have asked that, since they were the recipient of Russian assistance, that they not contribute anything to the joint forces.

This was the situation up until 1992 when the emerging regional and national dynamics created a slightly different situation in Central Asia. Then, the two biggest states—Uzbekistan and Kazakhstan—realized that in addition to the Commonwealth, they needed to be more (militarily) self-sufficient. They therefore created their own military institutions and armies.

Kazakhstan became the first to adopt a post-Soviet army (the 40th Army) under its wing, and Uzbekistan became the first to remove its forces from the Soviet Army. The other republics were very reticent on defense issues.

This created an ambiguous situation. By the time of the Tashkent collective security treaty in March 1992, there was extreme ambiguity on the question of where Russian troops were actually to be stationed. Turkmenistan preferred to participate in a joint army with Russia. Tajikistan wanted a close alliance with Russia. Kurdistan articulated its desires for neutrality. The Tashkent agreements underscored a great change in the perspectives of all parties.

Russia realized two things. First, Afghanistan and Tadzhikstan demonstrated that a deterioration of the security situation would be detrimental to Russia's own national interest. They began to think about how to stabilize the situation. Second, with troubles in other parts of the former Soviet Union, Russian elites started thinking about how to save what could be saved: namely Central Asia.

The Tashkent agreement served to legitimize Russian military involvement and commitment to the Central Asian region. This general umbrella (the agreement) gave Russia the right to negotiate bilateral relations and cooperation with each of the Central Asian republics. It is interesting to note that Kyrgyzstan signed onto this agreement, despite its aspiration to neutrality.

Turkmenistan, as we have heard from earlier speakers, did not sign the Tashkent agreement. Its leaders do not want to make excessive security commitments to the Commonwealth, and prefer to maintain cooperation at the economic level only. In fact when President Nyazov tried to set up a joint army, the officers who are 90 percent Slav wrote Yeltsin and told him that they would withdraw under these conditions, leaving Turkmenistan with no army at all. Thus the military status of Turkmenistan was created out of necessity.

Plans to create bilateral forces in Central Asia fall into three areas: nuclear, strategic border forces and peacekeeping. As far as joint armed forces are concerned, this idea was articulated by Central Asians, especially the President of Kazakhstan. These would be freely structured forces. However, only Kazakhstan has contributed to such a force, while others continue to debate the question of how these forces are to be structured. Problems remain on how to finance such a force and where to deploy troops. So, we are speaking of intentions, so far, not of actions.

Under all this, a high command was created under the leadership of Marshall Shaposhnikov. The people in this command developed their own vision of Russian security which often conflicted with Defense Minister Grachev's view and the Russian Defense Ministry. Apart from these joint armed forces, and multilateral structures, the real cooperation and progress has been made in bilateral relations. Many people in Russia believe that bilateral cooperation is much more beneficial and much more profitable for Russia.

These agreements between Moscow and the republics or so-called "mutual friendship" treaties that have been signed with Turkmenistan, Kazakhstan, Uzbekistan, and Kyrgyzstan allow these states to use common military installations and create a common defense "space," and in a sense legitimizing Russia's military-strategic alliances with each of these states separately. Routine business is conducted on the basis of these bilateral agreements.

There are two problems with these bilateral relations. First, they underpin Russia's central role in the emerging military-strategic situation in Eurasia. Russia's defense ministry prefers to promote these relations, whereas Shaposhnikov tries to create more diverse CIS structures. The debate now is: what is the best way for Russia and the Commonwealth? A Warsaw Pact system, or a NATO-type system?

While Russia and Uzbekistan prefer the Warsaw Pact model for emerging joint armed forces, Kazakhstan, Kyrgyzstan, Armenia, and Uzbekistan have spoken of the necessity of creating a NATO-type alliance. This issue is not settled. Russia does not want to be trapped in a position where it cannot control when (and whether or not) to send troops, which troops to send, and at what cost. At the same time, Central Asians do not want to return to the situation where these decisions are determined solely by Moscow.

Returning to bilateral relations, the most intensive cooperation was between Russia and Kazakhstan. Numerous documents were signed in the end of May and presumably in early June. A comprehensive Russian-Kazakh military agreement will soon be signed creating joint training, the creation of joint regiments, the sharing of military installations, attempts to create high-tech weaponry, etc.

If we turn to another field—so-called "peacekeeping" troops—there are a lot of problems and issues to be discussed. The original problem was determining where these troops were to be stationed and deployed. But the conflict in Tadzhikstan has highlighted the problems that could emerge if the Commonwealth really decided to send its troops into volatile areas.

There would be fewer problems if there were equal concentrations of Russians and Central Asians in an area. But the problem is that many Central Asian borders are entirely artificial creations with corresponding ethnic groups in these (adjacent) countries.

For example, if you send troops of Russian and Uzbeki origin into Tadzhiksitan where there are 300,000 Russians and a substantial Tadzhik minority, the question is, how will these ethnic minorities react to the presence of these ethnic troops? There were certain Uzbek-Tadzhik frictions as a result of the deployment of Uzbeks as well as Russians in Tajikistan. In fact, the Tadzhik leadership wanted Kazakhstan and Kyrgyzstan to send troops instead, for this reason. But this option was rejected by respective national parliaments. This is a key issue for the future, because many republics would not consider participating in peacekeeping actions for this reason.

The entire coherence of Russian-Central Asian peacekeeping relations is at risk as a result of these difficulties. In addition, there are internal Russian disagreements as to the appropriate use of Russian troops. For example, despite pleas by CIS Commander in Chief Shaposhnikov, the 201st Division was not used for peacekeeping purposes.

The more fundamental question though is: Are these forces really peacekeeping forces? Some want to deploy troops along the Afghanistan-Tajikistan border. However, this fulfills the second function of joint forces; the *prevention* of conflict along national frontiers.

To sum up this set of issues: first, Russia is emerging as a major partner with the Central Asian republics. Despite the fact that Central Asians have been active in developing their political positions, little has been done in the military sphere. Realistically speaking, the possibility of Central Asia being militarily self-sufficient in the short-term is quite small. For the time being, especially if current leaders stay in power, Central Asians are likely to turn to Moscow as their major strategic ally.

In all republics, the issue of independent armies is crucial, especially because they suffer the same problems as the Russian army, namely budget deficits, low morale, low discipline, drugs, etc. There is total disarray. For this reason, figures on current strengths are deceiving. For example, the International Institute for Strategic Studies (IISS) figures are stated with great confidence, but when I was in Central Asia, the official figures were one thing, and the reality was another. Often, numbers will indicate large forces where in fact, only one motorized regiment is capable of fighting. In Kazakhstan, officials say there are five divisions, when in fact there are only two covering the border with China.

Central Asians need time to create their own armies, strengthen civil-military relations, train their own officers, produce their own spare parts, etc. The question for Russians is: how to use the (now necessary) linkage with Central Asia to their benefit.

The issue of the army is most urgent in Kazakhstan and Uzbekistan. In Kazakhstan, with the division within the population between Slav and indigenous peoples, the question surrounding the army is: should there be conflict, will the army remain separated from this conflict, or will it get involved? If it is involved, given the fact that more than 70 percent of the officers are Slavs, we can see what might happen. Another question on the agenda is, how will the Russians use their influence among the Slav-dominated officer corps to influence the political situation in Kazakhstan?

For the Kazakhs that I have spoken with, the most important issue is military professionalization. They are training as many officers as possible. They just reached an agreement with the Russians to train 450 officers there. In the meantime, they are trying to create their own military faculties.

The most important issue is the Russian-Central Asian military-strategic configurations, and the emerging debate surrounding this issue. Two things here are obvious. One, we are dealing with an emerging new structure. The question is: Will this structure be sustainable? In Russia, there are people who are very much in favor of this structure, seeing an opportunity to stabilize borders and create a potential counterbalance against Islamic forces and NATO, etc. These voices are strongest among the high command of the joint armed forces.

On the other side, you can find a high number of politicians and analysts who are very much opposed to these Russian-Central Asian military structures. It is not yet clear which side will take the upper hand. It is clear that political developments in Russia and Central Asia will continue to determine military questions.

Several things are important. First, even if created, could such an alliance really stabilize the area? Obviously, this could be a channel for Russia to maintain military strategic influence in Central Asia. At the same time, could it lead to inter-ethnic or inter-religious clashes? Second, if this alliance structure comes into being, will Russia be put in the awkward position of supporting pro-Russian elites who are in power?

Many Russians believe that such structures are a good idea because in five to seven years, Moscow will want to intervene on behalf of these elites as they become entangled in political, economic, military and ethnic difficulties. So in a sense, many politicians and analysts believe that we could return to the 19th century where there were strong divisions between the Russian war ministry and the Russian foreign ministry, with the former being pro-activist, and the latter being more cautious. We are likely to see strong conflicts within Russia over this issue.

Secondly, if a NATO-type structure is created towards Central Asia—something which I still think is very unlikely—Central Asians would have a strong say in Russian decision-making. It would be very difficult for Russians to avoid very strong impulses from various republics for radical change in foreign policy.

COMMENTARY BY STEPHAN SESTANOVICH
Beginning with Gene Rumer's paper, I strongly disagree with the "Civic Union" history of Russian foreign policy to-date. First, the initial moves of Russia on the international scene after the break-up of the Soviet Union supported the Euro-Atlantic initiatives of Kozyrev and Geidar. Second, it was impossible to hold to this strategy for a number of reasons, including the government's commitment to radical economic reform. Third, as a result, there has been a steady move away from the Euro-Atlantic policies towards one that treats the preservation of Russia's great power status as crucial. Fourth, Russia is involved in Central Asia because its withdrawal from this region would lead to a loss of its status.

This is the Civic Union history of the last two and a half years. It seems to take the criticisms of Yeltsin and Kozyrev at face value. It's the picture of Foreign Minister Kozyrev, Gene Rumer says, chatting with Parliamentary Foreign Affairs Chairman Ombartsumov. It's what you get by reading the Nyza Vyeetza Magazyetta not to mention Sovietska Seversya. It's a little skewed, not surprisingly. Many of these people are no longer analysts but are participating in the process. The reality is a little different than this Civic Union version.

To be sure, the critics of the Yeltsin-Kozyrev policy could have hoped that Russia could truly ignore Central Asia in some way that was harmful to Russia's interests, and that this would give them a political hand-hold in their attempt to mobilize opposition to the government. But they have had a hard time making Central Asia a central issue in Russian policy debates. After all, it is not clear why a Euro-Atlantic tilt is inconsistent with pursuing a prudent Russian policy in Central Asia. In fact, what is true of civic union policy is true of foreign policy too. There is not a well-founded alternative there once you scratch beneath the surface of the resentment of not being a superpower. In reality, I cannot think of a single major divisive policy in Russia today concerning Central Asia.

There has been more attention towards Central Asia than there originally was in December 1991 when Russia broke up. But one of the important reasons for this has been the difficulty of managing Russian relations with Ukraine. Russia has needed an alternative axis for the Commonwealth, so instead of Russia-Ukraine, you have had Russia-Kazakhstan. This is an inconvenient fact for the civic union view of the world, because according to the civic union, Ukraine really wants to be part of the Soviet Union, and of course, it does not.

There has been a stronger, declaratory, consensus for keeping Russia a great power. We should not emphasize the impact of this in the case of Central Asia to the extent that it foretells or conveys a great activism in this area. There are three reasons for this.

First of all, even in the Civic Union and certainly in the Russian government, there is a considerable reluctance to get bogged down in the internal, internecine problems of Central Asia. Yeltsin said, "Russia is prepared to take part in peacekeeping operations in Central Asia, but of course Russia cannot bear the cost of these operations, both moral and financial, single-handedly." The question is: Who is going to pay if Russia gets involved in Central Asia? Yeltsin also commented on the causes of conflicts in Central Asia. He said "you look into it, and you realize that the causes of these conflicts are always the same—violations of human rights." This reflects the common Russian view that Russia is a backwater of repression and that Russia will only get in trouble if it gets involved there.

This reluctance to get involved is reflected in Russia's reluctance to send peacekeeping troops to Tajikistan. This is an issue on which you find rare agreement between Ruslan Kasbulatov, Sergej Tupofind, the Chairman of the Defense Committee of the Parliament, and Andre Kozyrev. It is important to note, by the way, that the unit that was formed to go to Tajikistan was made up of volunteers. The idea was that nobody should be forced to go to Tajikistan.

The second reason to not overplay the importance of Central Asia in an assertive, national interest-based Russian policy is this. It's quite easy for Russia to maintain a minimal influence in Central Asia with more or less minimal effort. Russia's military assets in Central Asia are so huge that a Russian leader would have to be fanatically isolationist to not be involved. A Russian leader would have to make a major effort rejecting all Central Asian proposals for cooperation to do this. As Maxim Shashenkov has pointed out, a majority of the officer corps in these republics are Slav.

The relationship between Russia and this region, based upon Russian resources there, is highlighted in an interview with Kasimov, a 39 year-old Kazak general. In the interview given in Krasnaya Vezda, he talked about manpower problems that he delicately described as "mass desertion." He expressed great gratitude to the Russians for their understanding and help in "cadre policy." Unless Russia continues to train Central Asian armies, there will be no Central Asian armies.

The third reason not to overplay the impact of this consensus on the likelihood that Russia will be active in Central Asia is the consensus of the Central Asian states. Gene Rumer is right to speak of the interest and active cooperation of all of the republics, but it also has its limits, as has been pointed out.

For some critics of Yeltsin's foreign policy who felt that Russia was not paying enough attention to the former Soviet Union, there was the feeling that by cooperating with parts of the former Soviet Union, it would be possible to put a brake on reform because these states are more conservative. However, the link between Central Asia and Russian domestic politics has not played out the way that they envisioned.

Take a specific example. The communist restoration in Tajikistan has not been feared by Russian liberals. I have not heard any Russian liberal say that this is the prelude to the restoration of communism in Russia. Similarly, conservatives hardly see it as important to their domestic goals to help conservatives in Central Asia. They just do not see a pay-off there.

In some ways, the link between Russian domestic politics and Central Asia has been the opposite. Gene Rumer stated that the impact of the Russian economic crisis is that Central Asia became more important as the Russian economy got into trouble. This *may* be sequentially true. But in fact, the Russian deficit will make it more likely that Russia will cut credits to Central Asian governments, raise energy prices for them, and push these governments outside of the ruble zone. This—getting tough on Central Asia—is politically the path of least resistance, and can be done without much domestic criticism.

I have given some reasons not to treat Central Asia as an arena where Russian desires to make a mark for itself in the world will be played out. If the critics of Yeltsin want to successfully attack the pro-Western orientation of Russian foreign policy, they will have to find problems with that orientation itself. And as a matter of fact, the focus of their attack on Russian foreign policy is the START Treaties.

The fact that Central Asia has not been a major part of Russian policy to date does not mean that it will not play this role in the future. Gene Rumer suggested that the principal way this could happen is if the Kazakh situation took a central turn. By contrast, Tajikistan, which is now seen more in the news and is much more of a problem, is probably a decreasing problem over time for Russian policy. In fact, if present immigration patterns persist, there will be no more Russians in that Republic, except for a few. For example, according to some sources, 200,000 Russians have left Tajikistan out of a total of 400,000.

How are Russian-Central Asian relations being institutionalized? These institutional structures have not been very well developed. As Marshall Shaposhnikov has pointed out, "they are both hanging in mid-air." There is little prospect that this will change. In all of the former Soviet Union, the process of building institutions has been very slow, and I suspect that in a collaborative effort it will be even slower.

Instead, the dominant pattern will be bilateral relations worked out between Russia and the Central Asian states. Multilateral cooperation will be loose and ad hoc. There are substantial differences in interests, and independence gives the Central Asians a chance to defend their interests.

We can better understand what this means for Central Asia by putting it in some comparative perspective. How do the individual policies of the Central Asia states look when seen from Moscow? How do they compare to those of the Europeans, for example? If you ask the question this way, the differences between these states and Russia look more reconcilable. For example, there is nothing comparable in these cases to the final, irreconcilable break between Russia and the Balkan states. No one asks in the Baltic states: "Will you continue to train our soldiers in the future?" Also, it is instructive to compare the issue of dealing with nuclear weapons in Ukraine and in Kazakhstan. It's much easier in Kazakhstan.

Central Asia offers no case of all out war between former Soviet states of the kind you have between Armenia and Azerbaijan—nothing comparable to the spill-over into Russia of the violence in Abkhazia and Ossetia. Russia's borderlands with Central Asia are relatively quiet. The Russian reaction to the war in Tajikistan is a reminder of how much the Russian outlook has changed. Compare it, for example, to the feverish concerns in 1979 that led to the intervention in Afghanistan. Now there is comparative complacency in Russia about what is happening in Tajikistan. They send one battalion, and they are not very happy about that level of effort.

It seems like Central Asia almost offers Russia a respite from the short-run difficulties in the former Soviet Union. Consider, for example, Marshall Shaposhnikov on the question on how to structure the CIS forces—whether this should be on the Warsaw Pact or NATO model. Maxim Shashenkov's paper reports that Russia wants the Warsaw Pact model. Perhaps, but when the Marshall was asked, he said that the NATO model would be acceptable too. They are very relaxed about this.

I am not convinced that the bilateral relations already described constitute a "second-best" to the more tightly interwoven, multi-lateral institutional options often discussed and that some people in Moscow might prefer. I am hard pressed to identify the Russian interest that is compromised by bilateral relations. I have not seen that interest identified in any of the papers, except that the multilateral institutions might afford more control. That might be true if the purpose of the CIS was to restore the USSR or to reassert full control of Russia over the former Soviet Union in some other form. But I do not see much Russian appetite for that. Both sides see many more advantages in more flexible, bilateral relations.

Let me end with a comparison between Central Asia and the other parts of the former Soviet Union. For Russia, Central Asia presents a smaller problem now, but perhaps a larger one over the long-term. What Russia is trying to do now is to create a better framework for relations so that it is in a position to promote good outcomes in the future. Moscow's way of doing that involves a mix of arrangements and policies. This reflects the different range of problems it faces throughout the region and its substantially diminished interest in the region as a whole.

COMMENTARY BY AMBASSADOR WILLIAM COURTNEY

Maxim Shashenkov's comment on the importance of politics determining military policy is entirely true, and I would like to explore that a bit further. His paper describes at some length the measures and declarations for cooperation in the region that have been announced. And he and others add that, for a number of reasons, as under Gorbachev, these agreements have not yet been implemented. I do not want to say that the documents are not helpful, or that their purposes of multilateral collective security and bilateral cooperation are not important and should not, over time, be implemented.

The critical factor in the Central Asian security outlook from the U.S. Government's perspective will be the development of democracy. At present, Kyrgyzstan and Kazakhstan are making good progress towards democracy, and perhaps it is no accident that their bilateral relations are the best in Central Asia. Uzbekistan, Turkmenistan, and Tajikistan have made less progress towards democracy. In general, our observation is that non-democratic practices can increase political instability despite efforts to show superficial, short-term stability by, in some cases, determining who can participate in the political process and their form of participation.

Each country in Central Asia will enhance its own internal security, respect for human rights, and ethnic tolerance, by building democratic institutions. Especially important to that process will be free and fair elections. Each country in Central Asia can enhance its own security by promoting democracy in neighboring states. Border disputes, ethnic conflicts, tensions across borders, and perceptions of threats from neighbors will all be diminished to the extent that democracy develops in Central Asia. The Kazakhstan-Kyrgyzstan relationship is illustrative. Also of great importance in promoting security in the region is economic development, which means restored economic ties within the region and with Russia.

What political scientists call "relative deprivation"—the difference between people's economic expectations and reality—creates conditions of insecurity in the region. Most regional leaders are aware of this. Thus, they see as one of their main tasks legitimizing their regimes, ending the sharp economic slide by securing economic success. In Kyrgyzstan and Kazakhstan, public support for economic as well as political reform is high, and progress is being made in those countries' reforms. As we recently saw, Kyrgyzstan introduced its own monetary system, qualifying it for its first IMF "stand-by" agreement, the first such agreement in the region.

In these two countries, the center of gravity in the economic debate is moving each month in the direction of reform, although not necessarily shock therapy, per se. In these two countries, leaders are trying to keep a broader consensus behind reform than Yeltsin has been able to sustain in Russia. Kazakhstan has launched a new privatization initiative with World Bank support. This is going to be particularly important in the future in decentralizing economic activity. An earlier effort became controversial because it facilitated *nomenklatura* privatization. After several months, they caught their mistake and are now trying to reorient that program.

In Kazakhstan, ethnic relations, economics and politics are intertwined in a particularly interesting way. Maintaining the territorial integrity of Kazakhstan will require ethnic Russians living in the north of Kazakhstan to believe that they are living as well or better than the Russians to their north. Likewise, economics are vital to counter what many see as an increasingly prosperous China. President Nazarbeyev has probably been the most successful in the region in promoting economic ties. He has also been the most successful at promoting defense cooperation. He is doing this for internal as well as external political reasons.

There are two security questions, in addition to the broader economic and political reforms, that are particular to Kazakhstan. One is the question of Baikonur, the space center run by the Russian space agency that receives its launch vehicles from the Ukraine. The evolution of this relationship is very important. Another is that there are many military testing ranges in Kazakhstan. How those are used in a cooperative fashion is also extremely important in the region.

As for strategic forces, just after the failed coup in Moscow, Kazakhstan closed off nuclear testing at Semipalatinsk. It was the first state to ratify the START Treaty, several months before any other party did. It has agreed to join the NPT as a non-nuclear weapons state and has agreed to remove strategic weapons from Kazakhstan seven years after the enactment of the START Treaty. There is every reason to expect that Kazakhstan will carry out its agreements.

With regard to military construction, military leaders throughout the region are trying to figure out how to construct militaries that will enjoy public support. It is clear that Russia will be very helpful in the region in assisting countries to do what they could not do alone. There are some things though that Russia is not particularly good at, such as helping construct militaries that operate in democracies and report to democratically elected authorities.

Also, at least for Kazakhstan, the importance of promoting a small mobile army suitable to addressing security threats makes cooperation with Russia very important.

With regards to the questions of peacekeeping troops, the idea of peacekeeping forces is so controversial that they have had to create the illusion that the troops are for protecting borders in order to retain public support at home. The notion of sending troops to Tajikistan has not yet received broad mass support.

With regard to U.S. cooperation in the security area, we, along with other countries, are trying to develop International Military Education and Training (IMET) programs. We are cooperating and assisting Kazakhstan in the safety, security, and dismantlement area.

Has anything changed in the last year in Russia which has an impact on Central Asia? When Vice President Rutskoi raised a cry about protecting ethnic Russians in Central Asia, that caused less of a rustle in the region than it did in Russia. But since then, it has caused even less concern. Russia seems more absorbed in the integrity of Russia itself than it is about areas beyond its borders. Again, for the long term, democracy, economic reforms, economic cooperation—including the construction of Chevron oil facilities—and the construction of military structures that are suitable and appropriate to realistic security threats all go hand-in-hand to enhance the security situation in the region.

DISCUSSION SESSION
Dr. Rumer
I think that Steve Sestanovich and I are largely in agreement on most issues. Perhaps I should read my own paper to see where I over or understated things. I should say that I do not condone the views of the Civic Union.

Dr. Brown
One thing that has not been mentioned here much is the effect on Russian policy of the memory of the Afghan war. I wonder if this is not affecting Kazakhstan's reluctance to get involved there. Is this not partially a response to memories that this can be a no-win situation that becomes endless?

Dr. Shashenkov
I want only to emphasize two things. The first is that the military situation is the most stable as far as Central Asian relations are concerned. So far, I have not found any information to indicate that these states plan to train troops in Turkey or Iran or in any Muslim state, for example. There was a team of Kyrgyz officers who went to Turkey, but the rest went to the West. I must add that the Russians truly debated the merits of training others who could one day be fighting against them. But, I think that Russians realize that it is better to preserve this channel of influence.

Question:
There seems to be a slight disagreement between Bess Brown on the one hand, and Ambassador Courtney on the other. If I heard Dr. Brown correctly, she seemed to be saying that if you push too hard for democracy, that might lead to destabilization. Yet, I heard the Ambassador say that democratization is a major interest, and it does lead to long-term stability. In light of what we heard this morning about the possibility that repression could push people into the Islamic camp, I would like both of you to respond.

Answer:
There are objective reasons behind the arguments that Uzbek President Karimov offered Kazakh President Nazarbavev. Introducing what they see as democratization may be dangerous. The question is the different perceptions of Western observers, as opposed to the Central Asian elites themselves. Since these elites are not allowing this experimentation to take place, who can say, except by looking at someplace like Kyrgyzstan.

There, we do not have the element that Karimov cares about, that he calls "fundamentalist," but that it would be best to call "nationalist Islamic traditionalist types," who are not fundamentalist in the sense that they are pro-Iranian or necessarily want to establish an Islamic state tomorrow. Karimov and

Rakhmonov in Tajikistan are in danger of creating the situation that they profess to fear. But pressing for the Western concept of human rights from the outside is not going to help either. U.S.-Uzbekistan relations soured for a while because of this kind of pressure. This cut-off the possibility that Westerners could make their feelings known there.

Comment:
My perception is that in the region, there is a combination of educated people and people who are much more aware of what is going on in the outside world than just several years ago. That is quite an impressive group, and denying effective political participation to certain groups under these circumstances is the best way to promote ethnic or political extremism.

Comment:
Who are the Central Asians arming themselves against? There are four possibilities. The first is external threats. This is partially the case with Kazakhstan's cross-border problems. Or is it to prevent inter-republican fighting? This is potentially serious but there has not been any such fighting, at least not yet. Or is it internal peace-keeping within the Republic for which they are arming? Lastly, is it possible that this arming is for internal regime protection? I imagine that this last reason ranks quite highly for all the rulers, except Kyrgyzstan.

This gets us back to Russia. I agree that a lot of Russians do not want to get involved in these messes, and that Russian liberals are not that upset about it. Basically, Russia would be happy with the status quo, allowing a lot of authoritarian people to stay in power, as long as it does not get out of hand. My sense is that the more that these places democratize, the more that nationalist and potentially Islamic forces are going to strengthen. This would present Russia with a greater problem. If I were Yeltsin, I would just want to keep things cool in Central Asia, and not worry so much about democracy.

Comment:
I agree but I think that it is important to distinguish between what it means for Russia to see things go bad in the "real" Central Asia, and what it means for things to go bad in Kazakhstan.

Comment:

The Russian logic is that if Russia does not arm the Central Asians, someone else will. Also, Russians look upon military-strategic leverage as essential in Asia, and would like to preserve it. Furthermore, Russians are aware that they are capable of preserving control over Central Asians over the long-term, not only because of the dominance of the Slav officer corps, but because of spare parts, supplies, etc.

Concerning the point about Karimov and Nyazov, etc., in the early stage, there was an attempt to find an alternative leadership, even a democratic one. Stankevich even said at one point that Russia could find itself like the Americans in Iran, supporting a certain unpopular regime that then would be overturned. But pretty soon, Stankevich was told that there were no democratic institutions in Central Asia. So I think now they are looking for so-called "traditionalists." The Institute of Canada and the U.S.A., for example, is now seeking such leaders.

Question:

First, who do the Turkmen and Uzbeks and the rest see as their enemy? Why are they building armies with Russia? Second, are the Russians coming back to Central Asia, if not now, in the next decade or two? Third, in light of what Ambassador Courtney said, should democracy really be the top priority? Would the panel agree that this was a good ordering of priorities?

Answer:

On the first issue. It was first put by Nyazov last year that having a military establishment is a necessary part of state sovereignty. He has said this year that Turkmenistan has no external enemy. The only state to my knowledge that has suggested one is Kazakhstan, voicing concern about giving away nuclear weapons with two large nuclear-armed neighbors. The Chinese cannot be pleased that there are five independent states in Central Asia. It makes them hard pressed to dismiss claims for independence in parts of China.

Comment:

Part of the reason why they are building their armies is because they can. With respect to Russia's return as a sovereign, I disagree. It clearly has returned as a stabilizing force. Its involvement may be minimal, but we should not discount the potential for its return, especially if the Civic Union remains important in Russian politics. As long as we have two agendas in Central Asia—the elites and the masses—this will continue as long as the elites that are in place remain.

Question:
You seem fairly confident that the Kazakhs are going to live-up to their nuclear agreements. I have been talking with some Kazakhs who see something developing in Kazakhstan, albeit in different circumstances, that we also see in Ukraine. Namely, executive leaders are in favor of adherence to treaties, whereas parliaments are not. Are these situations, despite their political differences, similar when it comes to the nuclear agreements?

Answer:
Let me just say something about the Russians coming back first. I agree that it should not be ignored, so long as people in Russia are talking about it. The obstacles are very high. If the Central Asian states are a success, it will be very hard to establish control. If they are a failure, nobody in Russia will want to establish control. On the question of the Kazakhs living up to their commitments, the difference between the Kazakh and Ukrainian case is very much related to what we have been talking about here. That is, the nature of the cooperation between the republican and Russian military establishments is different. A lot of Ukrainians are prepared for the kind of break with Russia that not living up to that commitment would involve. For the Kazakhs, this is a much harder decision to make.

Comment:
With regard to questions about democracy. In Tajikistan, the outbreak of conflict is not the result of democracy, but of the lifting of communist repression. With regard to Russia returning as a sovereign, at least in Kazakhstan, the question on most people's lips is: "is Russia going to remain sovereign on its territory?" The question of whether or not Russia is going to move south is less pressing.

With regard to nuclear weapons, the parliament in Kazakhstan ˜ been much more pragmatic and reasonable. There are a ˜ of explanations for this. One that I find interesting is that

Ukraine felt a greater sense of personal humiliation with the fall of communism, whereas Kazakhstan always saw communism as a system that was imposed from the outside. As a result, the politics of anger that is more prominent in Russia and Ukraine is much less prominent in Kazakhstan.

The practical outcome of this, for example, is Kazakhstan's new constitution, which is very good. It is very good for a number of reasons, including the fact that they were willing to accept outside assistance, especially from the U.S. technical assistance program sponsored by the American Bar Association, and they also had advice from other jurists. This provides for fundamental freedom, and even national treatment for foreign investors, which would have made Soviet ideologist Michael Suslov turn over in his grave. This is not coincidental; the Kazakh parliament is very pragmatic and rational.

As for the nuclear issue, the Kazakh parliament and executive understand reasonably well that Kazakh security, in light of its position between two nuclear powers, lies in full integration into the international community. Economic, political, military and cultural ties will help.

Comment:
To introduce democratic institutions will take time. We cannot expect that they will become democrats in a year or two. When I said, "let us take them into the civilized world," I meant democracy and human rights. But I worry that if they open their doors to free countries, there might be a kind of confusion that frightens them. They first want security.

When I was in Central Asia in April 1993, I mentioned this to my Uzbek friends. I said that when they signed an agreement with the United Nations and other institutions, they became members with responsibilities for the conditions and principles of membership. Thus, you have to recognize the rights of the people to some extent. You do not have to recognize Mohammed Sarri as an opposition leader, but you do not have the right to put him into jail. This was a sharp criticism that they received from the Turkish delegation.

Question:
Ambassador Courtney, how do you come to the conclusion that the Kazakhs and Kyrgyz are more ready for democratic development than the Uzbeks or Tadzhiks or even Turkmen?

Ambassador Courtney:
I did not say that, nor did I offer that conclusion. I said that Kazakhstan and Kyrgyzstan have made considerable progress.

Comment:
I do not see how you come to that conclusion. I was astonished in Turkmenistan. They have a process whereby they ask questions of their leaders. These were very harsh questions that you would not see in parliaments. You did not say anything about these developments as they relate to democracy in Turkmentistan.

Ambassador Courtney:
The developments in Turkmenistan cannot be said to be indicating steady progress towards democracy. I did say that. Again, I would emphasize that there are a lot of highly educated people in some of these republics and in Russia, and that this is a powerful combination of factors for democracy and economic development oriented towards the outside world.

Question:
How are you going to develop democratic thinking and introduce these ideas to your area as a U.S. Ambassador?

Ambassador Courtney:
The Kazakhs are doing it themselves. We provided some technical assistance, and prepared tax and electoral laws for a constitution, and gave them advice as to how to run political campaigns, but the changes that have occurred have occurred because of the people themselves.

Comment:
I just wanted to pick-up, Ambassador Courtney, on your comments on Kazakhstan. I think its new constitution is a step forward, but it is not as good as you imply. Many Kazakhs are concerned about the broad-ranging powers that the Kazakh president has to dismiss officials—powers that if misused could certainly lead to the creation of a dictatorship. This is even more pronounced in Uzbekistan, which also passed a constitution, recently.

New laws are important, but so are mechanisms that can assure that these new laws are implemented. It is one thing to have, as in the former Soviet Union, good laws on paper, but it is another thing to have them carried out. So far as the democratization in Kazakhstan, I think that the political parties there are still extremely weak, not well-organized, and almost entirely ethnically based. So far as they proceed, they are most likely deepening the rifts that exist between Slavs and Kazakhs. I feel that democracy has a long way to go, and that the priority in all of these republics is stability. These governments are prepared to put up with very considerable repression. In all of these republics, there is a greater degree of repression today than there was in the last days of the Soviet Union.

Ambassador Courtney:
I agree with what you said, with the exception of the last point. With regard to the weakness of political parties, that does not take away from the enormous strides made towards democracy. With regards to the constitution, it is pretty good, given the circumstances. Perhaps more importantly, there is a political consensus behind implementing the constitution. From our

observation in Kyrgyzstan and Kazakhstan, there is a good political consensus to implement these agreements.

It is very useful that these states are coming of age just as communism, welfare states, import substitution and other models that were prominent have now lost their appeal. There is not much debate in these states as to whether or not to go forward. The only question is, how to proceed? So far so good in Kazakhstan and Kyrgyzstan.

Comment:
With respect to Kazakhstan, I would make one comment. The way back is not necessarily only towards communism, and the way forward is not only towards democracy. We do not have much information in Kazakhstan. Most information comes from Russian language newspapers. But I do not see the kind of enduring societal consensus in Kazakhstan that would provide the underlying foundations for this constitution to be durable.

Comment:
Stability, especially in Kazakhstan, Uzbekistan, and many other republics is based on a balance of fear. Russians fear that if they start fighting first, the Kazakhs will take the upper hand. Similarly, Kazakhs fear the same only opposite. In this climate, if you introduce Western-style democracy, you create a very deep political crisis. Kyrgyzstan is a perfect example of this.

IV. Security Implications of the Competition for Influence Among Neighboring States

- Author: Mr. H. Ross Munro, Foreign Policy Research Institute
- Author: Dr. Patrick Clawson, Institute for National Strategic Studies
- Commentator: Dr. Ellen Laipson, Central Intelligence Agency
- Commentator: Dr. John Garver, Georgia Institute of Technology
- Moderator: Hon. Paul D. Wolfowitz, National Defense Univeristy

PRESENTATION BY ROSS H. MUNRO
"China, India and Central Asia"
India's role in Central Asia is a relatively small and unimportant one that reflects India's situation today of overall political, economic, and strategic weakness. The collapse of the Soviet Union constitutes the most important contributor to India's current

relative weakness. India and the Soviet Union shared a special relationship which granted India access to all components of the former Soviet Union. While that relationship vanished in the debris of the failed communist regime, Pakistan realized exceptional opportunities with respect to establishing ties with the new states of Central Asia. Very quickly in India, fear was articulated that somehow, Pakistan would be able to create a bloc of nations sharing not only an Islamic character but an anti-India character as well. The response by India was a flurry of diplomacy. This diplomacy yielded very little in the way of tangible results. The Indian campaign to re-establish New Delhi's special relationship with the successors to the Soviet Union was hindered by India's overall position of weakness. In particular, India found itself facing a definite lack of resources which could be offered to the Central Asian republics. Diplomatic delegations and heads-of-state from Central Asia would receive grand welcomes to India, only to depart with extremely modest promises of assistance. While the Indian government clearly pursued a variety of objectives through these diplomatic efforts, their primary goal was to guarantee access to military supplies for their Soviet equipment.

India's inability to exert influence to any large degree in Central Asia results from several factors. First is the weak state of the Indian economy. India does not have the resources to offer the republics of Central Asia. Indeed, there have been substantial indications that the governments of Central Asia have been profoundly disappointed with the offers made by India. Above all, we are talking in international terms about a profoundly weak economy that is so non-competitive that it represents only one percent of world trade. India has been pushed out of the garment and textile industry by nations with more efficient production lines turning out less expensive and higher quality goods than those originating in India. In addition, India is physically isolated from the republics of Central Asia by Pakistan and the People's Republic of China. This isolation results in dramatically higher transportation costs on goods traded between India and Central Asia. In the past, these costs were absorbed by the special relationship between India and the Soviet Union.

As events played out following the collapse of the Soviet Union, India discovered that fears of an imminent realignment of nations in opposition to India were greatly overstated. The Central

Asian republics are far too occupied with domestic affairs to concentrate effort on foreign policy more extensive than the procurement of aid and assistance. Pakistan and other Islamic nations have additionally found the Central Asian republics to be less than enthusiastic about entering into either confrontational foreign policies or alliances based primarily on the security concerns of another nation. As a natural result of the decreasing degrees of anxiety, New Delhi gradually curbed its diplomatic efforts aimed at Central Asia.

In stark comparison to India, the People's Republic of China will emerge as a major actor on the stage of Central Asia, whether it so desires or not and without respect to the amount of effort deliberately exerted toward Central Asia. Alarm and caution marked the initial reaction of the PRC to the demise of the Soviet Union and the emergence of independent states in Central Asia. The demise of Soviet communism, when coupled with the events surrounding Tiananmen Square, posed a serious threat to perceptions of the legitimacy of the PRC's government.

The breakdown of the Soviet Union also jeopardized traditional Chinese interests in Central Asia. The communist government in Bejing and its predecessors historically viewed Central Asia as a source of instability and turmoil along China's western frontier; one that could generate unrest in Xinjiang province. Chinese policies that supported these interests are primarily defensive. Civil disturbances had plagued Xinjiang province from 1989 through 1991, with reports indicating actual insurrections among elements of the Turkic Muslim population, who now constitute 60 percent of the population. Independent Turkic republics in Central Asia naturally raised concerns in Bejing with respect to border security, internal unrest, pan-Turkic nationalism, and an Islamic revival. The media in Xinjiang province sounded the cry for greater vigilance from the local militia in guarding the borders and attacked "splittists" and other subversives in the Xinjiang Uighur Autonomous Region.

The spring of 1992 witnessed an attitude shift within the Chinese government. Analysts within the PRC determined that neither Islam nor pan-Turkism comprised serious threats. Only the short-term threat was dismissed by Bejing. The potential for threats to emerge from either quarter in the future was not dismissed. Long-term Chinese interests in the region are defined by promoting the stability of the five Central Asian republics in order to inhibit both pan-Turkic nationalism and Islam. In addition, China will pursue the complementary aim of increasing its influence over the Central Asian republics. Finally, the PRC views the Central Asian republics as an opportunity to establish a new series of transportation links to the West. This "New Silk Road" coincided with and supported the drive for economic reform surfacing in Chinese policy. A favorable economic policy posited on mutually beneficial trade would both promote stability and increase Chinese influence in the region. The Chinese policy toward economic relations, especially mutually beneficial trade, was well received by the new governments in Central Asia.

The true and tangible indicator of shifting Chinese concerns over the decline of the Soviet Union materialized during Deng Xiaoping's January, 1992 tour of the southern provinces. Deng pronounced that the Soviet collapse originated in its inability to provide an adequate standard of living for the Soviet people. Unless the communist government of China implemented market-oriented reforms, Deng judged that the People's Republic would shortly follow the skidmarks of the Soviet Union. Increased exports and foreign trade formed a strong component of the economic reforms. While the world's attention was naturally and rightfully focused on the effect of these reforms on Chinese coastal areas and southern China, there was an echo of the trade and export oriented policies for economic growth in the Chinese provinces bordering on Central Asia.

China's emerging, economics-based approach to Central Asia is best understood by first examining the dramatic developments in its relations with Kazakhstan since 1991. A sequence of statistics evidence the growth of Chinese-Kazakh economic relations over the past two years. The statistics are hard to confirm and are far from satisfactory. However, all indications are that Chinese-Kazakh trade exceeded $200 million in 1992, with the vast majority of the trade passing through Xinjiang province. This figure represents trade passing the border in both directions. Kazakhstan currently imports over 50 percent of its consumer goods from the PRC, while the PRC now imports large quantities of badly needed industrial commodities such as fertilizer, steel, and ores. The PRC has also been extensively involved in direct investment and joint ventures; some evidence exists of Hong Kong's involvement in these investment projects. The involvement of capital from Hong Kong demonstrates the ability of the People's Republic to call on the resources of "Greater China". Chinese experts have followed the flow of investment capital, providing technical skills and frequently replacing departing Russian advisors. All indications are that "China's two-way trade with Kazakhstan alone exceeded Turkey's trade with all five republics."

Demographic and ethnic policies between the two nations are resulting in dramatic changes along the frontier. The PRC is permitting extensive migration of ethnic Kazakhs from Xinjiang province to Kazakhstan. The migration has the benefit of increasing the proportion of Han Chinese in Xinjiang while simultaneously increasing the ratio of ethnic Kazakhs to non-Kazakhs in Kazakhstan. In addition to the migration of ethnic Kazakhs, a small but steady flow of ethnic Han Chinese have crossed over into Xinjiang in order to escape the population and birth control policies of the PRC. Economic relations between the PRC and the remaining four Central Asian republics are developing more slowly.

The obvious questions are whether growing Chinese influence is coming at the expense of Russia and what will the consequences be of such a power transition? Do overall and regional trends support the hypothesis that such a transition is indeed occurring in Central Asia? Russian decline certainly seems irreversible in the short term, while the PRC's economic growth appears similarly unstoppable. However, the period of power transition offers little likelihood of serious or violent conflict, although Moscow harbors some concern along these lines. The future of Chinese and Russian influence will be determined by two great events occurring in Eurasia, the breakup of the Soviet Union and the ascendancy of the People's Republic of China to true superpower status.

The current phenomenon goes beyond the extension of Chinese influence into the border regions in Central Asia. The "New Silk Road" is a dream appearing in the media in the PRC. I now feel that this reflects China's vision or part of China's vision of where it is going in the next century. All of this talk about road networks, railways, and pipelines from east to west indicates China's desire to construct a "transmission belt" that will convey Chinese influence and power westward while bringing wealth and economic growth eastward.

PRESENTATION BY DR. PATRICK CLAWSON
"The Former Soviet South and the Muslim World"

The ties built by the five republics of Central Asia to the Muslim world will determine, to a large extent, whether these newly created nation-states achieve true independence. True independence will elude the five Central Asian republics so long as the strength of their ties to Russia in the north outweigh the strength of their ties to the Muslim world to the south. To the extent that the Central Asian republics become independent, they must inevitably develop these relations with the Islamic nations to the south, as that is the only practical non-Russian avenue to the outside world.

While the Central Asian republics may have *de jure* independence, they do not have *de facto* independence. The Central Asian republics do not meet many of the simplest conditions that define an independent state. First, none of the republics are capable of effectively providing for either their own border control or their internal and external security. Second, these states lack even rudimentary control over their money supply and credit posture. Third, they have no effective control over their trade and lack the transport linkages and infrastructure to exert such control. In all three areas, the republics of Central Asia depend heavily on Russia. In the area of security, the Russian army and secret police remain an important guarantor of border control as well as internal and external security. Although this is changing, the ruble continues to serve as the primary currency, and the Central Asian republics are, therefore, dependent on Moscow's central bank for their money supply. Transport through Russia remains the most heavily-used route by far; and trade within the Russian-dominated FSU is the lifeblood of the economy. The extent and permanence of this dependence will serve as the primary anchor for true independence for the Central Asian republics.

Three major areas of relationships between Central Asia and its Muslim neighbors must be explored: cultural, military, and economic.

With respect to cultural issues in Central Asia, while this area has received the most attention, it will in the long run deliver the smallest impact on the region. Let me suggest a number of points. First, Central Asia is quite well developed culturally already; they are not wastelands in need of writers and educators. Second, cultural relations between Central Asia and other nations must demonstrate give and take on all sides; the people of Central Asia do not consider themselves the "little brother" of another, greater culture. Third, the amount of human capital invested in the Russian language and the Russian/Soviet imposed society will prove highly resistant when it comes to severing the old ties to Russia in favor of new cultural ties to the Islamic world. Finally, the cultural influence that has had the largest impact around the world will have a similarly large impact in Central Asia. Hollywood, with Rambo and MTV, will prove more successful in achieving change in Central Asia than Mohammed and the Qur'an.

The Central Asian identity has begun to incorporate Islamic influences that had disappeared under Soviet rule. However, "folk Islam" as opposed to formal Islam contributes the most to the new sense of Central Asian identity. The power of basic Muslim faith is deepening as the power of traditional Central Asian communities begins to reassert itself. Thus, the Islamic revival in Central Asia owes more to its domestic roots rather than any external influence. However, the growth of domestic "folk Islam" will inevitably lead to better relations with the Muslim world.

Far too much contemporary strategic thinking with respect to Central Asia results from daydreaming over maps and romanticizing the geopolitics of the region. Two main issues regarding military and security ties between the states of the former Soviet south and the Muslim neighbors need to be addressed: nuclear non-proliferation and the spill-over of the Tadzhik conflict.

The fears of nuclear proliferation articulated by Western nations will prove largely groundless. Previous reports of tactical nuclear weapons missing from Kazakhstan have proved false. All information indicates that all tactical nuclear weapons are currently in Russia. The only nuclear warheads of any type known to be in the former Soviet south are in Kazakhstan and are quite effectively under Russian control. In fact, if at any time there are substantial concerns about the transfer of nuclear weapons or fissile material to an outside nation, then the world must hold Russia at least partly responsible. The extent of Russian command and control over nuclear weapons would prevent such an occurrence without their knowledge and, at least, tacit approval. The legal principle of joint and separate responsibility should be applied to

Russia if either individuals or former Soviet republics transfer nuclear weapons or material outside of the former Soviet Union.

Additional concern has been voiced in the West over the fate of Soviet nuclear technicians and their possible recruitment by Muslim nations seeking to develop a nuclear capability. These concerns cannot be dismissed as quickly and easily as fears concerning actual nuclear weapons. There are certainly thousands of people in the former Soviet Union out of work who have skills that would be useful in a nuclear weapons program. However, from what little is known about such people, it would seem that few are from the region and fewer still are ethnic Muslims. It would seem that Moscow is the right address for concerns about the former Soviet nuclear experts. A nuclear weapons program requires extensive and hard-to-hide physical capital which should be easy to detect. In sum, the potential danger posed by mercenary nuclear scientists from Central Asia should not be overstated.

In relation to the ongoing civil war in Tajikistan, while the most visible opponents in the conflict are communists and Muslims, the true conflict is fought along ethnic and national lines. It is the ethnic and nationalistic nature of the conflict which originally drew Uzbekistan's and Russia's intervention; and now threatens to bring Iran and Pakistan into conflict with Uzbekistan.

Outside involvement in the Tadzhik conflict began with Uzbekistan's active intervention in late 1992. There is mounting evidence that Uzbek forces were key in installing the current government. Indeed, Uzbekistan President Karimov justified active intervention as necessary to protect against a spillover of violence from Tajikistan to Uzbekistan. In addition, Karimov claimed that the 20 percent ethnic Tadzhik minority in Uzbekistan and the 25 percent Uzbek population in northern Tajikistan required active protection from ethnically motivated violence. He also argued that Iran supported the Islamic opposition. There is little evidence to support the latter charge. On the other hand, there is considerable evidence that Afghan rebels led by Gulbuddin Hekmatyar were aiding Islamic opposition groups in the Tadzhik war. Hekmatyar has long received support from the government of Pakistan. It came as no surprise, therefore, when Karimov accused Pakistan of actively taking sides in Tajikistan. I surmise that the accusations against Pakistan are credible, in that Pakistan maintains considerable influence over Hekmatyar's activities and clearly realizes the extent of his involvement in Tajikistan. In the spirit of fair play, Hekmatyar has accused Uzbekistan of aiding ethnic Uzbek Afghan General Rashid Dostam to establish an independent republic in northern Afghanistan along the border with Uzbekistan in the region he controls. Dostam is, of course, the sworn enemy of Hekmatyar.

In sum, the conflict in Tajikistan that began as a two-sided civil war has expanded to a war involving Uzbekistan and Afghanistan and could easily drag in Pakistan, Iran, and other neighboring countries. Moreover, there is every sign that the conflict will drag on for years and consume a considerable portion of scare resources. The increasingly Islamic Tadzhik opposition groups and the viciousness with which the Dushanbe government is prosecuting the war against both combatants and civilians raises the likelihood of international support from Iran and Pakistan. Already, both governments are feeling domestic pressures to actively support the war against the "communist" government in Dushanbe.

Despite the great hopes of 1990 and 1991, the fact is that none of the nations we are discussing, Turkey, Iran, or Pakistan, are obvious markets for the products of Central Asia. The truth of the matter is that the economies of Central Asia are almost identical to the economies of Turkey and Iran. A comparison of imports and exports across both regions indicates similar sets of imports and exports. None of the nations produce very much that the other nations require. What few possibilities exist are overshadowed by the desire of Central Asian governments to move away from their traditional role as raw material suppliers. Thus, it is unlikely that Uzbekistan would remain content exporting cotton to Turkey or Pakistan for processing into the vigorous textile industries there. Likewise, it is unlikely that either Turkey or Pakistan will provide Uzbeki manufactured textiles and garments access to their markets.

Only one opportunity for investment is likely to attract outside capital, the exploitation of raw materials. I am skeptical that either Iran, Turkey, or Pakistan would emerge as a major actor in this area. First, the large foreign debt structures of all three nations limits their ability to extend credit to the Central Asian republics. Second, it is highly implausible that international financiers will lend funds to Iran, Turkey, or Pakistan for the purpose of in turn investing that money in the former Soviet south. Turkish experience along these lines certainly discourages any hopes along this avenue. Third, major investment in raw material exploitation usually encompasses technical expertise as well as investment capital. Iranian expertise in oil and gas industries will provide an inside track vis-a-vis other Muslim nations, but remains second-class in comparison to the technological capabilities of the U.S. and other Western industries.

Transportation is the one strong offering of the Muslim nations to the south of Central Asia. The existing transportation net leaves the Central Asian republics almost exclusively dependent on Russia. This net puts them at the end of extremely long transport routes, and makes them susceptible to the chaos in Russia. More precisely, the transportation linkages through Russia are characterized by poor maintenance and carrying capacity as well as periodic breakdowns in infrastructure. Transporting goods through Russia also involves high taxation and endemic graft and corruption.

Three options exist for reaching the ocean from Central Asia: south through Iran and Pakistan to the Persian Gulf and the Sea of Oman (1,400 miles), west via the Russian transport linkages discussed above to the Black Sea (2,000 miles), or east via the People's Republic of China to China Sea (3,000 miles). Geography dictates that the simplest alternate routes all head south to the Persian Gulf and the Gulf of Oman.

When choosing between the southen alternatives, it is important to note that Iran possesses not only the shortest route, but the best infrastructure. Transporting goods through Pakistan requires passage through Afghanistan. The route to Kabul through the Sarang Tunnel is already overstressed, dictating that traffic from Central Asia employ the route through Herat. While the Herat route is technically good, Afghani political instability continues to scare off potential investors and business partners. On the other hand, while Turkey boasts a favorable political and economic climate, access to the land transportation routes through Turkey is difficult at best.

Iran emerges as the obvious choice in developing transportation routes to the outside world. The large major ports in southern Iran can handle additional surface tonnage with the existing facilities, and the northern ports damaged and closed by the war with Iraq are beginning to return to operation. Although the rail net and road net both fall short of the standards found in the former Soviet Union, they provide relatively easy transportation over forgiving topography. However, that additional infrastructure will not emerge in Iran. The rail-link between the Iranian rail net and the Central Asian rail net remains more a topic of discussion than an active construction project. The Iranian government has, furthermore, declared in the 1994-1998 Plan that emphasis will be placed on maintaining and improving existing facilities and completing existing projects.

One frequently overlooked aspect of Central Asia's transportation requirements involves energy exports. By the middle of the decade, Central Asia could well export the equivalent of 900 million barrels of oil each year, largely in the form of processed petroleum products and natural gas. These energy exports could bring the region annual earnings of $12 billion in current dollars. If politics were not a concern, then Central Asia could rely on existing pipelines through Russia to the maximum while building new pipelines into northern Iran for access to the Persian Gulf.

The Turkish model looks rather uninviting to those who recognize Turkey as a second-class economy. Turkey has heavy foreign debt, a high rate of inflation, and social indicators such as literacy rate, life expectancy, and the like that are little, if any, better than those of Central Asia. With respect to technical skills, Turkey and Central Asia share the same shortages in expertise and technical knowledge. The new republics would much prefer to gain technical skills from recognized world leaders. In actuality, the more appropriate model might be South Korea.

Much of the discussion of Iran's involvement in Central Asia assumes that Iran is interested primarily in religious missionary work. Iran's true objectives in Central Asia blend Persian nationalism and Islamic fundamentalism. With regard to Central Asia, Iranian ambassadors are Persian nationalists. Great power politics is as much, if not more, of a consideration than Islam, as evidenced by Iranian support of christian Armenians in their conflict with Turkish supported muslim Azerbaijan. Moreover, Iran has not emphasized missionary work by Mullahs.

Finally, the United States has few interests at stake in Central Asia. With no truly strategic interests at immediate risk, two policy options exist. First, the United States can support the decolonization and true independence for the Central Asian republics. Such a course of action would, of course, deny Russia a preeminent role in the region. Second, the United States could support a continuing set of strong ties between Central Asia and Russia. This course of action would serve as a counterbalance to the dangers posed by radical Islam and would prove safer for all parties.

COMMENTARY BY DR. JOHN GARVER

I take issue with the central thesis of both the written paper and the presentation by Mr. Munro: that the People's Republic of China is likely to emerge as the dominant or even preeminent power in Central Asia sometime soon, possibly within the next decade. This conclusion involves an estimate of the intent and capability of the PRC. Implicitly, if not explicitly, the PRC intends on becoming the first non-European superpower and has the capability to become a massive economic power. While both of these estimates are essentially correct, they do not necessarily lead to the conclusion that such intent and capability will manifest itself in Central Asia.

Regarding intentions, several broad factors influence China's policy toward Central Asia. The centers of Chinese political and economic power are in the coastal regions of the country. The coastal regions have benefitted the most from the "Open Door" policy after 1978. The inequality between the coastal regions and China's interior are less likely to increase, rather than diminish. With respect to political power, most of China's leadership comes from the coastal regions. The majority of Politburo members have origins in the coastal regions. Very few individuals from the interior, let alone the far west, rise to significant positions in the leadership. The economic and political inequalities between the coastal regions and the interior and western regions may prompt the western provinces to increase trade with Central Asia in an attempt to redress these gaps. This particular phenomena occurs throughout China, with southwestern provinces expanding economic ties with Burma and other Southeast Asian states. Despite this new trend, it is unlikely that China's central leadership will decide to place a policy priority on international relations with Central Asia.

The People's Liberation Army (PLA) is an increasingly powerful force in Chinese politics and is likely to become even more powerful when Deng Xiaoping dies. All evidence indicates that the PLA is defining its roles and missions in a fashion that supports

223

their drive for high technology weapon systems and capabilities. The pursuit of advanced systems and capabilities results from the perceived threats, such as the United States. These threats dictate an emphasis on naval and aviation capabilities, rather than ground forces. As a result, the strategic direction followed by the PLA leads away from Central Asia and toward an increased presence and capability in the maritime regions.

A vision of the path to Chinese greatness constitutes the third factor which indicates that China's central leadership will not become overly involved in Central Asia. There is a historical legacy of maritime power as the path to national greatness and empire. This interpretation of history contends that China's great dynasties have been outward-looking and maritime dynasties. These are the dynasties that sent great fleets around the world and established strong commercial links throughout the Indian ocean. The current leadership of China clearly embraces the maritime interpretation, as evidenced by the growth in the naval budget and the merchant marine fleet.

If the coastal areas represent an avenue to expansion and empire, then Central Asia represents the barbarians on the edge of culture and civilization. The role of Central Asia in China's historical pattern of foreign relations provides the fourth factor limiting the importance of Central Asia in Chinese policy. Chinese involvement in Central Asia has always been infrequent and brief. Chinese armies ventured rarely into the region and then, only for very brief periods of time. In contrast, China's natural sphere of influence is in East Asia and Southeast Asia. In these areas, one finds civilizations, nations, and people that drew readily and for long periods of time from the font of Chinese civilization. China has an extensive history of sustained and active involvement throughout East and Southeast Asia.

Central Asia is likely to be an area of low priority for Chinese leadership. Indeed, of all the areas around China's peripheries, I think that Central Asia will be the area of lowest interest to China's central leadership. I must embrace the orthodoxy that Mr. Munro rejects, which argues that the policy of China's central leadership is essentially reactive and defensive. Basically their interests are to keep the neo-communists in power, and failing that, to keep the Islamic fundamentalists out of power. Concerning the relative capabilities of China and India with respect to Central Asia, I have an admittedly more optimistic perspective on India's future. India is unlikely to become the non-entity forecasted by Mr. Munro, although the bureaucratic control over the economy and inefficiency of the state sector does lead to a large degree of stagnation. However, the Indian government recognizes these problems and, since the mid-1980's, instituted reform programs to correct the deficiencies. India also boasts a great number of strengths, including a world-class intelligentsia and a large pool of skilled labor and individuals schooled overseas. Indeed, India could be on the verge of an economic take-off, as opposed to a collapse. The political system provides India's key strengths and contrasts sharply with the weaknesses found in China. Despite the problems of caste and regionalism in India, there remains a broad consensus in India across the Indian political spectrum regarding the importance and legitimacy of liberal democratic institutions.

In China, on the other hand, there is a deep crisis of legitimacy. Most Chinese do not believe in the current system and there is great doubt about the ability of the Leninist-Maoist system to continue after Deng Xiaoping's death. The Chinese are very uncertain as to the system which succeedsthe current regime and institutions. Fears of national fragmentation and ethnic conflict are currently very real among the Chinese.

The positive interpretation of India's economic and political strength implies that India can play a fairly significant role in Central Asia. Russia will also remain heavily involved. Most importantly, both Russia and India possess both the interests and the capabilities to project a significant presence into the region and will not be eclipsed by rising Chinese power.

If, however, Chinese influence in Central Asia increases, then India will respond by taking all possible measures. India views China as its nemesis, posing the most severe long-term threat to Indian national security. While Pakistan presents a more immediate danger, that danger is nonetheless manageable. If Mr. Munro's analysis is correct and China increases its influence through centrally driven policies, then India is likely to take countermeasures.

The scenario involving Chinese dominance of Central Asia overlooks the probable Central Asian reaction to the continued "Chinesization" of Xinjiang province. There is a deliberate policy of demographic transformation employed by the Chinese government to manufacture a majority population of Han Chinese in Xinjiang. I project that the Central Asian reaction will be one of fear and distrust, as already demonstrated by the Mongolian reaction to the demographic transformations enacted in that region of China. The Central Asian republics will most likely pursue other avenues rather than risk overly extensive entanglement with China.

All in all, the substantial interest and capabilities of other actors in the region will combine with minimal Chinese interests and capabilities to limit Chinese involvement in Central Asia.

COMMENTARY BY DR. ELLEN LAIPSON

I recognize Dr. Clawson's identification of the "sober realities" of Central Asian relations with neighboring countries as the paper's main strength. The economic aspects of Dr. Clawson's paper are particularly robust, although I am surprised that so little attention was paid to the Economic Cooperation Organization (ECO) involving Turkey, Iraq, and Pakistan. The current membership has invited the Central Asian republics to join this formal institution of economic cooperation. I will organize my remarks around the security issues drawn out in the paper.

First, however, the initial over-reaction to the collapse of the Soviet Union centered attention on a competition over influence in Central Asia between Turkey and Iran. That rivalry has not become as full-blown as many expected, and neither state may serve as a functionally attractive model to the Central Asian republics. It may be too early to pass final judgement on either Turkish or Iranian involvement in the region.

I agree that the Tadzhik war presents a significant challenge to the region. The real and immediate security threats posed by the war and its potential escalation shape the perceptions of Pakistan and Iran with respect to Central Asia.

Most importantly, Dr. Clawson correctly identified the true long-term aspirations of all three states. Iran, Pakistan and Turkey all view the emergence of an independent Central Asia as a potential economic windfall. Central Asia represents an adjacent market that shares a certain degree of cultural and political affinity. All three nations recognize that the economies of Central Asia are not flush with cash, and may prefer to enter into economic and trading relationships with world-class economic powers. However, if the world class players such as Japan and the United States find minimal interest in Central Asia, then the middle-class economies of Iran, Pakistan, and Turkey may offer the most attractive and convenient alternative.

Iran, Pakistan, and Turkey will find the ties between the Central Asian republics and Russia prove difficult to break. In addition, the governments and people of the Central Asian republics are not looking for yet another 'big brother' relationship with foreign powers.

I object to the cursory dismissal of cultural and religious influences on the future relationship between the Central Asian republics and other muslim nations. Cultural and religious influences may not materialize in the initial period of independence. The programs instituted by Iran, Pakistan, and Turkey focus on educating the next generation of Central Asians and will not bear fruit for some time. Cultural and religious influence will manifest itself over a period of decades, rather than a few brief years. The competition between Iran and Turkey will only serve to complicate any analysis of the impact made by religion and culture. Similarly, pan-Turkic nationalism should not be dismissed out of hand.

I am concerned over a possible contradiction within Dr. Clawson's paper. The argument that the republics of Central Asia do not exhibit all of the characteristics of sovereign states clashes sharply with the argument that these states possess societies strong and independent enough to resist external cultural and religious influences. Even though the Central Asian republics existed under foreign domination for many years, they may still possess the attributes, capacities, and capabilities to become independent states.

I consider that the central question raised by the paper is: how important will Central Asia be to the foreign policy of these three regional states and to what extent is security the variable that drives their respective policies? In the case of Turkey, Dr. Clawson understated the economic dynamism of the nation while simultaneously overstating the political weakness and probability of a military-led coup. Turkey is, in fact, doing much better than either Pakistan or Iran on both economic and political grounds.

The euphoria in Turkey which followed the independence of the Central Asian republics has faded, due in part to the death of Turkish President Turgut Ozal. Ozal can be credited with pushing Turkey further and faster toward rediscovering its Turkic heritage than many observers believed possible. The folkloric connection between the people of Turkey and their ethnic cousins to the east continues, with Turkish leaders donning historic costumes and participating in traditional ceremonies. The Turkish rediscovery of their ethnic Turkic roots represents a startling development and indicates that Turkey is experiencing a period of "post-Attaturk" revisionism. Long forbidden elements of history, such as the migratory origin of the Turkish people, are becoming important features of contemporary Turkish identity.

Turkey's interests during the 1990's do not lie heavily in Central Asia, but elsewhere. Central Asia will not constitute the primary focus of Turkish foreign policy during the next decade, and represents as much of a headache as an opportunity. Turkey will continue to vigorously pursue improved relations with Western nations and institutions. The instability and conflict on Turkey's immediate borders with the Balkans, the Middle East, and Armenia/Azerbajian will produce greater security concerns than distant conflicts involving their Turkic cousins.

Turning next to Iran, Persian nationalism currently dominates Islam as the theme of Iranian foreign policy. However, security concerns continue as the true driving force behind their immediate policy objectives. The conflicts in Azerbajian and Tajikistan both threaten to spill across the Iranian border, stimulating ethnic identity and unrest that pose long-term problems for Tehran. Short-term security concerns and the current dominance of Islam by Persian nationalism do not rule out the long-term possibility of an Islamic alliance emerging between Iran and the republics of Central Asia. Even if Iran does not view Islamic relations as "spreading the revolution," an Islamic alliance or association would portray solidarity among the participating states. In the end, Iranian interests lie outside of Central Asia; they lie in the Persian Gulf and in developing stronger economic relations with the West. Iran will view relations with Central Asia through the prism of managing relations with the West.

First and foremost, Pakistan's foreign policy is defined almost exclusively in terms of India. Central Asia, therefore, must be viewed in the world-view of Pakistan's competition with India. The Pakistani government also perceives a legitimate interest in the region and that, as Muslims, they hold a comparative advantage over India. An Islamic alliance or brotherhood makes a very solid long-term objective for relations with Central Asia. Short-term opportunities are limited by the conflict in Tajikistan and enduring instability in Afghanistan. Pakistan clearly understands that there will be no breakthrough in relations with Central Asia. Despite the opportunities presented by Central Asia, Pakistan finds itself occupied with other matters. The domestic political concerns and the task of breaking the isolation following the Cold War will divert Pakistan's major foreign policy efforts away from Central Asia. Medium level interests in Central Asia will not substitute for the vital interests of improving relations with wealthier industrial nations.

COMMENT BY H. ROSS MUNRO

Dr. Garver seriously misrepresented the position taken on China's role in Central Asia set forth in my paper and presentation. My purpose was to demonstrate that an economically dynamic China must be considered a player in the region and that other actors in the region must seriously regard China. Under no circumstances did I wish to convey the impression that China would become "the" preeminent or even dominant power in Central Asia. One thing I am guilty of is addressing this topic, for which I am very enthusiastic, in a very moderate tone.

The true definition of a superpower is a state that radiates influence over much of the globe. A superpower does not face an "either-or." If China becomes a superpower, then it cannot but influence events in nearby Central Asia and that influence should be significant, given the proximity. While China does focus its influence and capability on Southeast Asia and its coastal regions, China will become a major player in Central Asia almost by default. In other words, China's emergence as a significant maritime power in Asia in no way precludes their exercise of substantial power and influence in Central Asia.

COMMENT BY PATRICK CLAWSON

I agree with Dr. Laipson's argument that Central Asia is not vital to Iran, Pakistan, or Turkey. My primary thesis is that Iran, Pakistan, and Turkey are not vital to Central Asia. Based on conversations with officials in the Iranian government which characterized the Organization of Economic Cooperation as a "joke" that meets every year and passes the same resolutions, I refute Dr. Laipson's support of the ECO as a functional institution. Turkey also offers very little in the way of educational opportunities. The universities of Central Asia far outclass the universities of Turkey.

Returning to the argument pertaining to national models of development, Iran and Pakistan offer an even less attractive model than Turkey. Most importantly, Turkey offers a lesser model than the developed industrial nations. I was only suggesting that there is no reason to confine our viewpoints to just Turkey and Iran. In fact, the republics of Central Asia are much more interested in looking to the world-class economies and world-class powers. The primary question should not be which of the Islamic nations offers the best model and will wield the most influence, but which industrial nation will provide the model and how much influence will Russia continue to exert.

DISCUSSION SESSION
Comment by Paul D. Wolfowitz

The government of Pakistan had abandoned support for Hekmatyar in January, 1992. The government of Pakistan has no interest in becoming involved in the on-going conflict and only seeks friendly relations with all of the nations in the region.

There is wide-spread cooperation between the private sectors of all three members of the ECO. More importantly, the transportation routes dismissed by Dr. Clawson are indeed valid and attractive options to the states of Central Asia. Pakistan's route to the sea offers both stable politics and favorable geography.

The panelists overlooked important weaknesses of the Indian economy, which detract from the attractiveness of strong relations between the Central Asian republics and India. First, India's economy is heavily protected by a variety of barriers to trade. As a result, it is neither extremely competitive nor able to produce high quality goods.

Comment:

South Korea presents a highly seductive model. The South Korean economy is characterized by a reasonable degree of centralized governmental control that utilizes the economic engine to move forward and provide social welfare for the population. The discussion of influence within the region also seems fairly one-sided. If the republics of Central Asia succeed in establishing stable and working political and economic systems, these states will invariably have an impact on the other states of Central and Southwest Asia. In the near term, however, the impact of an independent Central Asia is likely to be increasing instability and conflict that threatens to spill across national boundaries into Turkey and Iran. The United States should concentrate its attention on this immediate concern.

Comment:
I object to the treatment of the People's Republic of China as a static force, not subject to domestic forces and change. Clearly, recent history indicates that even the most successful of the communist states are vulnerable to the dynamic forces of ethnic division and conflict. Why should China prove invulnerable to such forces? China's population contains a large number of ethnic groups boasting sizable populations. The long-standing ethnic conflict that Bejing strives to suppress could explode and dismember the PRC. If ethnic divisions forced the collapse of the PRC, then both India and Pakistan would be faced with extreme dilemmas. India would undoubtedly rejoice at the collapse of its mortal enemy, but would face the possibility of almost complete encirclement by independent Muslim nations. Pakistan, on the other hand, would lose one of its primary and most reliable patrons and trading partners and would potentially gain additional Islamic allies in close proximity to India. The geopolitical situation in Southwestern Asia would change dramatically if China began to unravel under the strain of domestic conflict. Of course, Russia cannot be displeased by a faltering and disintegrating China. Russia's influence over Central Asia can only increase if a collapsing China is forced to turn inward. A collapsing China and a somewhat resurgent Russia threatens a terrible conflict, with Central Asia sitting in the middle. The forces of democratization offer a possible peaceful solution. If Russia and India maintain their democratic systems and China's regime moves toward greater democracy, then some form of an inevitable grand crunch does not have to be in the cards. A democratic process will have quite a defining, limiting, and restraining influence on all of these three great nations.

Comment:
I question the effectiveness of Israeli involvement in the region. Israel and the Central Asian republics face similar challenges with respect to water access and agricultural development, and Israel has already sent technical assistance to the Central Asian republics to address this problem. The Israeli effort has met with some success. Israel has announced some joint-ventures in Central Asia and Kyrgyzstan announced that it will open an embassy in Jerusalem, becoming the first Muslim nation to do so. Will Israel continue to establish strong relations with the new republics?

Comment:
Turkey offers a valid model to the Central Asian republics. Turkey's transition from dictatorship to democracy and from a closed economy to an open, market economy parallels the challenges currently facing Central Asia. As noted by Dr. Laipson, it is far too early to write off Turkey as a productive and substantial influence on the region.

Comment:
The republics of Central Asia are indeed searching for a model which may guide their progress. However, a model oversimplifies the challenges facing Tajikistan and the other republics. Any path charted by Tajikistan must be a Tadzhik path, not an oversimplified set of solutions borrowed from another nation's model.

Tajikistan and Turkey have opened very friendly relations, with Turkey providing useful assistance shortly after Tajikistan's independence. Tajikistan seeks direct relations with the United States and other Western industrial nations. The PRC will, of course, be active in the region with both positive and negative consequences.

Comment:
Israel constitutes a successful role-model for the Central Asian republics. The concept of a new "Silk Road" certainly merits additional attention. Both issues bear further attention.

I doubt that the PRC would succumb to domestic pressures any time soon, if at all. Kazakhstan and the PRC have found additional common ground in their mistrust and dislike of the Uigher population that spans their borders. Uigher separatists exist on both sides of the Sino-Kazakh frontier and represent a threat to both nations.

Kazakhstan legitimately fears both Russia and the PRC as threats to their security. Kazakh security policy displays favor toward the PRC as an ally and possible guarantor rather than increasing ties with Russia.

Comment:

I agree with the assessment of Israel's success in Central Asia, and further achievements are clearly possible. However, if the political and social climates in the Central Asian republics were to shift toward Islamic fundamentalism, then the doors to better relations would close upon Israel.

Comment:

As regards the issue of national differences and Chinese internal security, clearly, the leadership of the PRC takes the issue of nationalism very seriously and is very concerned about the repercussions of events in the USSR. While it is true that 95 percent of China's population is ethnic Han, the remaining five percent control a large amount of the national territory. The Chinese are further concerned by the involvement of foreign powers, which continue to exacerbate the situation. The rebellion in Xinjiang in 1991 was significant. The Chinese reports involved organized resistance over several hours.

Comment:

Turkey truly does not constitute a valid model for the Central Asian republics. The governments of Central Asia continue to look to the advanced industrial nations for guidance as well as economic assistance.

Comment:

Israel is not a significant player in the region, even compared to India. Distance and other factors place severe constraints on the extent of Israeli involvement in Central Asia.

ABOUT the EDITOR

Jed C. Snyder is a Senior Fellow at the Institute for National Strategic Studies, National Defense University, where he leads the research and analysis program on the Middle East/Persian Gulf regions, the Mediterranean theater, South Asia, and the southern regions of the former Soviet Union. He is also directing a project on regional approaches to the proliferation of weapons of mass destruction.

A founder and former President of the Washington Strategy Seminar, Mr. Snyder served in the State Department in the first Reagan administration. At the end of the second Reagan administration he was appointed to Vice President Bush's Middle East Advisory Task Force. Mr. Snyder was also a consultant to the Office of the Secretary of Defense from 1988-1992.

Mr. Snyder has written extensively on international security and defense issues. He is the author of *Defending the Fringe: NATO, The Mediterranean, and the Persian Gulf* (Westview, 1987) and is co-editor and a contributor to *Limiting Nuclear Proliferation* (Ballinger, 1985). His publications have appeared in a number of leading journals including *National Interest, Washington Quarterly, Journal of Strategic Studies, Mediterranean Quarterly*, and *Jane's Intelligence Review*.

*U.S. G.P.O.:1995-387-330:20011